MONASTIC WISDOM SERIES: NUMBER SEVEN

Guy Oury, OSB

Dom Gabriel Sortais

An Amazing Abbot in Turbulent Times

I0809209

MONASTIC WISDOM SERIES

MW1 Cassian and the Fathers:
Initiation into the Monastic Tradition
Thomas Merton, OCSO

MW2 Secret of the Heart: Spiritual Being
Jean-Marie Howe, OCSO

MW3 Inside the Psalms: Reflections for Novices
Maureen F. McCabe, OCSO

MW4 Thomas Merton: Prophet of Renewal
John Eudes Bamberger, OCSO

MW5 Centered on Christ: A Guide to Monastic Profession
Augustine Roberts, OCSO

MW6 Passing from Self to God: A Cistercian Retreat
Robert Thomas, *OCSO*

MW7 Dom Gabriel Sortais:
An Amazing Abbot in Turbulent Times
Guy Oury, OSB

MONASTIC WISDOM SERIES: NUMBER SEVEN

Dom Gabriel Sortais

An Amazing Abbot in Turbulent Times

by

Guy Oury, OSB

Translated by

Brian Kerns, OCSO

Preface by

Emmanuel Coutant, OCSO

Afterword by

Laurence Bourget, OCSO

CISTERCIAN PUBLICATIONS
Kalamazoo, Michigan

Cistercian Publications
Editorial Offices
The Institute of Cistercian Studies
Western Michigan University
Kalamazoo, Michigan 49008-5415
cistpub@wmich.edu

The work of Cistercian Publications is made possible in part by support from Western Michigan University to The Institute of Cistercian Studies.

Library of Congress Cataloging-in-Publication Data

Oury, Guy Marie.
[Dom Gabriel Sortais, abbé général des Cisterciens réformés, 1902–1963. English]
Dom Gabriel Sortais, an amazing abbot in turbulent times / by Guy Oury.
p. cm. — (Monastic wisdom series ; no. 7)
Includes bibliographical references and index.
ISBN-13: 978-0-87907-007-6 (alk. paper)
ISBN-10: 0-87907-007-2 (alk. paper)
1. Sortais, Gabriel, d. 1964. 2. Trappists—Biography. I. Title. II. Series.

BX4705.S6833O8713 2005
271'.12502—dc22

2006000664

Printed in the United States of America

CONTENTS

TRANSLATOR'S NOTE

It is now forty years since the dramatic death of Dom Gabriel Sortais at Monte Cistello. Much has happened in the meantime, both within the Order and without. History has yet to assess his role completely. One thing is certain. He stamped the Trappist Order in a highly personal way. The form he gave it is still with us today, despite all our efforts to modernize. Dom Guy Oury has told the story of Dom Gabriel with a view to historical accuracy, as far as it is obtainable from primary sources: witnesses and documents. Yet, as with many other famous personages, one always has the sense that the whole story has not been told. As Dom Emmanuel Coutant indicated in his preface, perhaps it is not yet time to do so. Meanwhile, this is the most comprehensive life of Dom Gabriel Sortais available to us.

Dom Guy Oury himself went to the Lord on Sunday, November 12, 2000, at the age of 71. It is a pity he could not have seen the publication of this English translation. He was conversant in English and spent many years in the States. He kindly looked over the manuscript and pointed out the exact sense of certain French phrases which I had missed. I cannot do justice to Dom Guy in this short preface. His literary output alone was impressive. He is perhaps best known for his work on Blessed Marie of the Incarnation, foundress of the Ursulines and on the Desert Fathers. He is responsible for numerous other biographies and studies. There are over 80 books and 300 articles, according to the article on him published in the *Lettre aux amis de Solesmes,* a quarterly review published by the Abbey of Solesmes in France, Dom Guy's own monastery. His last book was the fruit of his last researches, *Dom Guéranger, moine au coeur de l'Église.* He had been named the postulator of his cause. The fact that he had also been named novice master nine months previously indicates the truth of the phrase in the same article, that he was an indefatigable worker.

This translation has also benefited from the helpful criticism of several who read the manuscript at various stages. Among them the foremost is Fr. Laurence Bourget, who knew Dom Gabriel intimately, and who has kindly consented to write an afterword which throws light on many aspects of the story. Fr. Anton Rusnak of Gethsemani also read over the manuscript and suggested numerous improvements, as did several others. If the book is still imperfect, it is because I have not always followed their suggestions.

Br. Brian Kerns, ocso
Abbey of the Genesee
Piffard, New York, U.S.A.

PREFACE

The following pages were written on first-hand testimony, and they represent reasonably well the memories that Dom Gabriel Sortais, abbot of Bellefontaine, later Father General, of the order, has left us. There is no reason to add to them or to summarize them here.

Was it necessary that these pages be written? Dom Gabriel had thought of what should be done with his body, if he were to die away from home (he had enjoined his secretary, "Bury me wherever I fall"), but he had certainly not thought about what should be done with his life. Would he have forbidden us to have it written? He had a lively awareness that the graces he had received came from the divine mercy. The tribute to be given God, the consolation it would be to those who had experienced difficulties or even weaknesses similar to his own: Such thoughts might have deterred him from leaving such a prohibition among his last wishes. The simple fact is that none of this ever entered his mind. He was so humble that he no longer had to concern himself even with self-effacement. This leaves us free, whatever the paradox may be.

This absence of a prohibition, however, would not of itself have made us decide to publish these memoirs. The profit derived by those who read *Les Choses qui plaisent à Dieu,* a collection of excerpts from his circular letters and conferences, was a more positive sign. If the counsels or instructions of the late abbot general found an echo in a certain number of readers, both men and women, of every age and every walk of life, it was certainly because the man who gave them had, in his person no less than in his words, something more to tell them. Therefore, this effort to make him known better is worth making.

In these years of uneasiness and contention he gives testimony of his self-assurance and freedom, and he tells us what they cost. This man knew where he was going himself, and he knew where he was leading others. Without ever recoiling before sacrifice and suffering, although he admitted he was afraid of them "like everybody else," he obeyed God as completely as can be imagined: this obedience was not servility but love—and passionate love. A longstanding fidelity, including profound detachment from self, made him sure of God and free about all the rest.

Detached from self and therefore open to others as well as to God, he drew from God that interior dynamism that led him to give himself. He was a man "for others," having an acute awareness of the "body" to which he belonged: his community, his order, his church, his native land, and finally he discovered that he belonged to the body of humanity, in the course of endless journeys in every latitude and longitude. He was eager to render service by risking his own skin, by spending himself, by giving up self, even as a hostage to the enemy, during the period of occupation. And throughout so many steps, letters, conversations, and meetings, he was constantly ready for prayer and fascinated by the presence of God.

We had to try to bring all that back to life, and much more besides, but it was hardly fitting that someone close to him should be given the responsibility; a certain distance seemed preferable. We are deeply grateful to Dom Guy Oury for having agreed to write this biography. Foregoing a detailed and exhaustive history of events—the time has not come to speak of some of them anyway—he has paid particular attention to the personal story of the man. We have certainly discovered his face in it ourselves, and we believe the others who knew him will also discover it, especially the monks whom he "shepherded with an upright heart" (Ps 77:72).

Dom Emmanuel Coutant, OCSO
Abbey of Bellefontaine, France

FOREWORD

When the abbot of Bellefontaine asked me to work on the composition of a biography of Dom Sortais, manifesting great confidence in me, Father Émile Dixneuf had already spent more than ten years gathering and classifying the existing archives relative to the former abbot general. All I had to do was freely draw upon this treasure, except that I completed the documentation by consulting the archives of the Generalate, to which I had free access, thanks to the kind authorization of the Most Rev. Dom Ambrose Southey, abbot general of the Reformed Cistercians. Father Clément de Bourmont, secretary of Dom Sortais during his term as Abbot General, has also been so kind as to furnish me with all the written and spoken clarifications that I could wish. These are the individuals I wish to thank first of all. Besides that I was allowed to interview the monks of Bellefontaine and the nuns of Les Gardes individually. Dom Sortais had been abbot of the former and Father Immediate of the latter. I wish to thank all of them, nuns as well as monks, for their testimony.

The book has also benefited from many suggestions and clarifications made by the Most Rev. Dom Ignace Gillet, who succeeded Dom Sortais as head of the order and is now retired at the Abbey of Les Dombes, and the Right Rev. Dom Emmanuel Coutant. I wish to thank them both for their willingness to read my manuscript. A special word of thanks is also due to Dom Vincent Hermans, definitor for the Dutch and German languages, who welcomed me to the Generalate with much kindness, and to Dom André Fracheboud, former definitor for the French language. I hope that the Right Rev. Dom Emmanuel Coutant and his community will be so good as to accept my dedication of this work to them.

Chapter 1

AT STANISLAS SCHOOL

It is related of St. Ignatius Loyola in *The Story of the Pilgrim* that he rode a mule to the Abbey of Montserrat[1] to place his sword at our Lady's feet. He met a Moor, and they began a conversation on the virginity of Mary; the knight did not succeed in making the Muslim admit that Mary remained a virgin in giving birth to her child. Thereupon the Moor broke off the discussion and moved on. "Ignatius was indignant at the Moor, and he felt he himself had done ill in allowing him to hold such opinions about Our Lady. He believed it was his duty to avenge her honor, and he wanted to overtake the Moor and give him a few good blows with his fist for what he had said."[2]

One day Sergeant André Sortais heard an unseemly joke about St. Joseph and the Virgin Mary in the non-commissioned officers' mess. He jumped on his fellow soldier, grabbed him by the collar of his coat, made him sink to his knees, then brandishing an empty bottle over his head, called on him to take it back. This happened just before he entered Bellefontaine.[3]

[1] Montserrat is a mountain near Barcelona in N.E. Spain, which reaches a height of 4,054 ft. and rises abruptly from the Llobregat Valley. The celebrated Benedictine monastery is on a terrace at an altitude of 2,400 ft. *Columbia Lippincott Gazetteer of the World,* ed. Leon E. Seltzer (New York: Columbia University Press, 1962).

[2] *Le Récit du Pélerin, Autobiographie de Saint Ignace de Loyola,* éd. A. Thiry (Bruges: Desclée de Brouwer, 1956) 58–59 (n. 15).

[3] Letter to a monk, August 12, 1933. Bellefontaine is a Trappist-Cistercian Abbey located in the diocese of Angers, near the city of Cholet in France. *Dictionnaire d'Histoire et de Geographie Ecclesiastique,* ed. R. Aubert (Paris: Letouzey et Ané, 1934) t. 7, col. 843.

"At the moment I thought I was doing the right thing," he would later declare, "and if the joker had not said out loud that he was sorry, I am quite sure I would have killed him."

Although they are three centuries apart, there is a similarity between the two episodes. In both there is the same knightly anger, the same impulsive and as yet uncontrolled generosity, and the same intransigence for Our Lady's honor. If guided by a better understanding of the gospel and disciplined by a rule, it is to be supposed that this generosity would go without hesitation to the very limit of God's demands, even to the complete gift of self.

André Sortais was born not long after the beginning of the century; the date was September 22, 1902, a Monday. Vacation was over. Foreseeing the imminent birth, the family had rented a villa for the summer that year, on the lovely wooded hillside of Bellevue, between Meudon and Sevres, preferring to remain near the capital.[4] It was at that time almost a country district near the big city. After his day's work M. Louis Sortais would rejoin his family there. It was a most quiet place.

Louis Sortais was then about 42. At 30, in 1888, he had won the second Grand Prix of Rome in the division of architecture. It had been a most disastrous epoch for teaching, "which hovered in inaccessible regions and immersed itself in dreams, while the projects presented to the faculty included immense rooms which it was impossible to light or ventilate, colossal porches which absorbed two thirds of the space on the plans . . . and supports 20 times heavier than necessary."[5]

It was during this period that the Villa Medici[6] opened its doors for four years to this student of architecture. The enchantment of Rome was poor compensation for a study that was rather routine and academic; none of the contemporary board-

[4] "Bellevue . . . . Capital." All these places are located at the confluence of the Oise and the Seine, near Versailles. *Grand Larousse Encyclopédique* (Strasbourg, France: Larousse, 1960) t. 2, 49.

[5] H. Chaine, "Concours pour le Grand Prix de Rome de 1889," in the *Encyclopédie d'Architecture,* eds. A. de Baudot, H. Chaine and P. Gout (Paris, 1888–89) ser. 4, vol. 1, 7.

[6] The Villa Medici is on the east side of the city, opposite the Porta Pisciana and the Aurelian wall. *Larousse,* op. cit., t. 9, 362.

ers left a name to posterity. Among those of the Villa Farnese,[7] on the other hand, we might mention, besides Monsignor Duchesne, Charles Diehl, C. Enlart, R. de Lasteyrie, excellent historians or archaeologists, and such literary men as Pierre de Nolhac and Georges Goyau. The various members of the French colony were united by frequent communication with one another. Louis Sortais collaborated in the excavation and restoration of the Villa Adriana, near Tivoli.[8] Afterwards he wanted to complete his artistic formation with a year in Greece; then he would settle down in Paris and begin practicing as an architect. His academic titles would make him acceptable as an architect of public buildings and national palaces. Thus he was led to collaborate with Charles Girault, creator of the impressive Petit-Palais,[9] in 1900; its neoclassical lines have becomingly enough spanned a century. Rodin asked him to set up his studio at Val-Fleury and make it a branch of the museum in the Hotel Biron.[10] In gratitude the great sculptor made him a gift of some pieces which later adorned the Sortais apartment.

Louis Sortais was 36 years old when he married Georgianne Burguerie, a girl seven years younger than himself, on December 7, 1896. She came from an old family of ship owners in Nantes,[11] one of whose ancestors had been a privateer. The marriage was celebrated at La Possonnière in Anjou,[12] on the banks of the Loire, not far from the little shrine of Our Lady of

[7] The Villa Farnese or Farnesina is located along the Tiber, flanked by three palaces. Ibid.

[8] Tivoli is northeast of Rome. Ibid.

[9] The Petit Palais was a monument created for the World's Fair in 1900. It occupied the place of the former Palais d'Industrie and displayed collections from the Museum of fine Arts of the City of Paris. Ibid., t. 8, 95.

[10] Rodin donated his works to the government and thus made the creation of his museum at the Hotel Biron possible. Ibid., t. 3, 18.

[11] Nantes is a manufacturing and commercial city of northwestern France on the Loire River, 107 miles west of Tours, connected by ship canal to St.-Nazaire on the coast. *Webster's New Geographical Dictionary* (Springfield, MA: Merriam Webster, 1972) 412–13, 808.

[12] Anjou is the historical region now divided into the departments of Maine-et-Loire and parts of Indre-et-Loire, Mayenne, and Sarthe. These departments are all adjacent to one another and located in western France. Angevin is a possessive adjective denoting what belongs to this region, especially the inhabitants thereof. See *Larousse,* op. cit., t. 1, 421 and 404.

Béhuard.[13] There the Burgueries owned La Chauminette, a kind of little chateau rebuilt in 1847 and set up between two windmills on the hillside that looks towards the *Mauges* region. The Burguerie family spent a long vacation there each year.

The young couple went to Paris to set up housekeeping at 62 Rue de Rennes; four children were born in close succession: Marcelle in 1897, Jean in 1899, Marie in 1901, then André, the baby, last of all. He was baptized privately the day after his birth in his parents' home and received the names of André, Marie and Johanny. The ceremonies were not completed until much later, on May 8, 1904, at St.-Germain-des-Prés.

André Sortais did not remember his first home on Rue de Rennes very distinctly. It was in 1905, when André was only four, that Louis Sortais found another lodging in the parish of Notre-Dame des Champs at 80 Rue d'Assas. The Luxembourg Gardens could be viewed from the window; this street-level apartment proved to be more practical for little Marcelle, for a hip ailment caused by an accident had confined her to a bed on wheels.

Louis Sortais was a quiet man with an attentive heart. He surrounded his sick little daughter with special affection. His wife, on the other hand, was lively, spontaneous, quick and enthusiastic, with a love for laughter and jokes. There was breadth of life and tender love, and the family circle was made up of those for whom children's development was managed without problems.

André had received his share of bubbling, demonstrative and noisy vitality; he was very obstinate, combative and affectionate, and he showed a predilection for tin soldiers. His memory was uninhibited, and his gift for acting had already declared itself. When he was a child, anyone would be glad to hear him recite by heart the passages concerning the death of the Pretextatus from Augustin Thierry's *Récits des Temps Mérovingiens*. He put a lot of conviction into it. Shortly before his election as abbot general of the Cistercians, Dom Sortais, journeying to Burgos, would make a bet that he could recite verses from *The Cid* for a

[13] The chapel of Our Lady faces the village from an island on the Loire. It owes its existence to the future Louis XI who made a vow when he escaped from a whirlpool while sailing on the Charente near Ruffec. The vow concerned the restoration of the chapel of Our Lady of Béhuard, patroness of shipwrecked sailors. *Catholicisme* (Paris: Letouzey et Ané, 1954) col. 1378, t. 1.

quarter of an hour in front of Chimène's tomb and would have no trouble winning it.

The parents were very strict, allowing no caprice, even of the little invalid, to pass. They had some trouble with André, who was subject to violent anger when anyone thwarted him. But after the crisis was past, he knew how to "come around," and he found a thousand acts of kindness to win pardon for himself. Lying was not tolerated. Monsieur and Madame Sortais watched over the honesty and loyalty of their children. Vacation time came around each year. It was spent either at La Chauminette in the peaceful countryside of Anjou, in the valley of the Loire with its slightly suffocating heat, or perhaps at the isle of Noirmoutiers,[14] where they had cousins at La Blanche. La Blanche was an old Cistercian abbey that had been first founded in the islet of Pilier, beaten by wind and waves; it was transferred to the larger island about 1205. It was a fitting rival of the monastery on the Isle of Ré,[15] where Isaac of Stella is said to have been lost with his companions at the end of the 12th century "in the vast ocean, on the most remote piece of land, shipwrecked, practically exiles from the universe."[16] La Blanche preserved some of its ancient monastic buildings, in which the Sortais had their quarters marked out, there near the sea. Monastic reminiscences could not help being engraved on the restless and impressionable mind of the child.

It seemed as though the years would continue to pass unimpeded, filled with the tranquil and unperceived happiness of family life, when an event occurred that upset the established order. Louis Sortais died on April 20, 1911, from the effects of a serious attack of influenza contracted while visiting the building site of a young colleague. He was only 51 years of age. His

[14] Noirmoutiers is an island in the Bay of Biscay, about 20 miles south of the seaport of St.-Nazaire, along the western coast of France; it is about 12 miles long and 4 miles wide, and it belongs to the Vendée. It holds the ruins of an ancient monastery. *Webster's New Geographical Dictionary,* op. cit., 412–13, 851.

[15] The Isle of Ré is further south in the bay of Biscay, about 10 miles out from La Rochelle on the coast and 30 miles northwest of Rochefort. Ibid., 412–13, 1003.

[16] Isaac of Stella, Sermon 27, *Patrologia Latina* (PL), ed. Jacques-Paul Migne, 194, col. 1778A, and Sermon 19, 1756B. New ed. Sources Chrétiennes (Paris: Cerf, 1974) 207:40, 140.

eldest daughter, Marcelle, the little invalid, was 13, while André was a little more than eight.

The latter would have found the absence of his father painful: with his impetuous, independent, strongly assertive, yet very affectionate nature, he would have needed, besides a mother's love to understand and comfort him, the calm mastery of his father to channel the disorderly and riotous energy that his adolescence would awaken. Madame Sortais was going to be obliged to confine herself too absolutely to the role of head of the household and to exert authority. Owing to this, André found his exuberant affection somewhat curtailed by the necessary role Madame Sortais had to assume. Instead of finding in her the natural confidante of his little trials as a child and adolescent, he saw only the force destined to restrain his violence and errors. His tenderness tended, then, to turn back sadly on itself, for, although Madame Sortais sometimes found her feelings asserting themselves, she showed much firmness. Secretly André would have desired to show her how much he loved her. In any case he was to virtually adore her all his life.

When he was six and a half, André was sent to Collège Stanislas for the first time. It was quite close to his parents' home, located at 22 Rue Notre-Dame des Champs. He entered the first grade on January 8, 1909. He walked the short distance from the Rue d'Assas to this school, which he hardly liked, four times a day until 1920.

On Sundays and feast days the pupils of Stanislas were dressed up like little police constables. On other days imagination in the matter of dress was tolerated, but the discipline remained military, "carefully enforced by the prefects of discipline and controlled by a kind of chief of police whose strong build and loud voice commanded universal respect. His name was M. Bonhomme . . . Beneath a surly and authoritarian discipline, he hid a compassionate heart whose goodness I often experienced," wrote one of his former pupils.[17] The house enjoyed a reputation for extreme severity. No one joked there on the subject of discipline: infractions were rigorously punished.

[17] Letter of R.P.P., October 11, 1966.

André was not attached to his school. His intelligence was lively and his memory sure. That dispensed him from intense labor. He passed from one grade to another without serious impediment, as well as without notice of distinction, lost in the crowd of mediocre pupils. He would willingly have made his own the reasoning of Justin McCarthy, staged by Philippe Aubert de Gaspé:

> Only fools waste their time studying. Either the teacher will ask me for the lesson, or he will not; if he asks me and calls on me second, I will always know enough of it to escape a beating, and if he calls on me third or fourth, I will know it just as well as all the imbeciles who studied it; if, on the other hand, he does not ask me for the lesson, it would be completely wasted effort to have studied.[18]

The teachers and supervisors found André distant and distrustful, "not concealing his desire to be free of every restraint."[19] Returning home where he felt self-assured, he unwound himself and played all kinds of devilish tricks, so much so that his mother threatened to send him away to boarding school at least twice. André was saved from justice by Marie's tears, when she pleaded with Madame Sortais not to do such a thing. Happily for the boy! As a boarder he would no longer have had the leisure to unbend himself and recover his equilibrium in the midst of his brother and sisters, who loved him for his heart of gold. Too tall for his age, poorly adapted to the milieu of his school, in dead revolt against the restraints imposed on him from the outside, he did not succeed in becoming an integral member of the class. He had only one real friend at Stanislas, François Brière. Among his relatives, though, it was another story: He got along admirably with his cousins, both boys and girls, whose games he noisily directed. André showed himself at vacation time, but only at this time, an excellent pupil, well-endowed for the theater.

Beginning in 1914, wartime Paris was not exactly an environment conducive to study. How could anyone work when the great personalities were talking about the events of the day,

[18] Philippe Aubert de Gaspé, *Mémoires* (Montreal: Fides, 1971) 228.
[19] Letter of Canon P., August 13, 1968.

when all energies were being spent in the common effort, and when the older boys thought of nothing but leaving in their turn? André was 12 years old when the war began; his whole adolescence was marked by it. In his childhood he had thought only of tin soldiers, but in his adolescence it was the innumerable soldiers of France that occupied his imagination. That is where the easily-offended nationalism was forged, of which he would later give evidence, as well as his almost unlimited love for his country. Was there any time or desire left to think about studies?

René Heron of Villefosse has recalled in a few pages his teenage memories of wartime Paris:

> The East railway station, August 3, 1914, the enthusiastic and surging crowd searching for spies, looting the Maggi shops, sandbags piled up to the top of public monuments, the first air-raids, German prisoners, dimmed lighting and the wounded in the streets. Weapons were frequently distributed at the Hotel des Invalides,[20] and the trophies of war were displayed just as frequently. You could see the uniforms of the Allies in the streets, and multicolor flags were the permanent decoration of certain balconies.[21]

The Zeppelins[22] appeared at night in 1915 and 1916, but beginning on January 30, 1918, Parisian life became dangerous because of regular Gotha bombardments.[23]

> On March 15 we were at our studies like good pupils just before the 2:00 P.M. class, even though it was a lovely afternoon. Suddenly a fearful explosion opened the windows so

[20] The Hotel des Invalides of Paris on the Avenue de Breteuil is flanked by the École Militaire on the west and the Hotel Biron on the east; to the north are the Esplanade des Invalides and the Gare des Invalides. This building program for the Invalides was inaugurated by Louis XIV to care for soldiers wounded in war. The Esplanade des Invalides is 532 1/2 yards long by 300 2/3 yards wide. *Larousse,* op. cit., t. 6, 204 and t. 8, 176.

[21] R. Heron de Villefosse, *Histoire de Paris* (Paris: Editions de Paris, 1944) 385.

[22] Zeppelins were dirigible airships named after a German general: Count von Zeppelin who designed them around 1900. *Webster's Dictionary of the English Language, Unabridged Encyclopedic Edition* (Hoboken, NJ: 1977) 2124.

[23] Gothas were German guns with a range of over 60 miles, also called *Friedrichschafens,* used at the end of the First World War, especially in 1918, against Paris. *Larousse,* op. cit., t. 5, 543.

> abruptly, that we all thought an aerial torpedo had exploded near the building. All Paris had heard the same explosion and felt the same power. Thousands of house windows and sheets of glass littered the sidewalks. Millions of grenades had exploded along the Courneuve.[24]

After that Big Bertha's shells exploded at regular intervals. Even so, other boys continued their study in the same conditions. André Sortais did not. He had, as a matter of fact, too much to suffer at Stanislas, especially at the ages of 15 and 16.

Was he imprudent? Was his intense lively affection noticed? The fact is that some teachers (and certain parents followed their example) warned the other children not to associate with him. The suspicion was unjust; it shocked and wounded him profoundly, as he later confided to one of his monks. This sadness, together with many others, made the school definitely distasteful to him. He lived in his own corner, relating only with some comrades by whom he was better accepted.

Among all the subjects that he barely passed, literature had an attraction for André. It was more suited to him, and he had the benefit of an admirable teacher in the person of Msgr. Calvet. He was attracted by the romantics, as are almost all teenagers. Poetry found an echo in his intensely alive sensibility and in his indomitable need to love.

Beginning with his return to school in October 1917 (he was 15, and his brother Jean had been mobilized), the solitude oppressed him so much that he began to play hooky—if that is what you call his pranks in the heart of Paris! He missed class one, two, yes three days, and when he did return, he spoke of a vague malaise and signed his own report. And so his junior year passed in the same way, and then his senior year of rhetoric. He did not have the courage to make a comeback and to set resolutely to work. These unpleasant and sad years left mixed impressions in his memory: a certain pride in his schoolboy pranks, together with the regret of having failed in loyalty to his mother. Added to this was the awareness of gaps in his intellectual formation. At

[24] *Histoire de Paris,* op. cit., 386–87. Courneuve is a commune along the Seine, northeast of Paris. It was destroyed on March 15, 1918, by the explosion of a grenade depot. *Larousse,* op. cit., t. 3, 588.

Stanislas he suffered above all from wasting his time uselessly, while boys two years older than he were risking their lives not far away. Interiorly he did not make any decision concerning this surrender before an obstacle, but he hated himself for it. That is why he reacted so strongly, when anyone questioned him at home or elsewhere. He was condemned in his own eyes without completely admitting it to himself, and he vented his ill temper on other people, when he felt touched at the sensitive point. He seemed to defend himself energetically when anyone reproached him, and there were times when no one would dare say anything more to him. In reality he tried unsuccessfully to justify himself in his own eyes. How could he escape this vicious circle? There was no support for a follow-up effort; he could not find any in himself. At the same time his faith was dormant.

André Sortais had many excuses: a rapid growth that sapped his best energy and provoked the awakening of contradictory tendencies; the heavy atmosphere of the school, where he never succeeded in finding his place; the war that was raging; the universal restlessness; and let us not forget that he was left an orphan at an early age.

Above all his spiritual life lacked depth. Although M. Sortais had a very real piety, his wife only showed an attachment to her "Christian duties," and too often she stopped there. Principles were rigid, with even a Jansenist tendency. God and the king were served with loyalty, despite the Republic and its official anticlericalism. But it was rare in the domain of religious duties that one went beyond the stage of "obligation." Religion primarily consisted of a certain number of "practices," on which, if it pleased God, a life of greater intimacy with him would later be grafted. These practices were Sunday Mass, Friday abstinence, Easter communion and evening prayers in common.

André made his First Communion at Midnight Mass in 1912, not at Stanislas, but at the Cours Valton, 64 Rue d'Assas, where one of his sisters was studying. On the feast of the Ascension, May 21, 1914, he received confirmation at Stanislas and made his solemn Communion after an excellent retreat under the direction of Abbé Thellier de Poncheville. "It is true I do not remember what he said," he admitted in 1952, "but I was so struck by his attitude before the Blessed Sacrament, and by the kind of respect with which he spoke to children who were preparing themselves to meet their Lord."

His life then resumed its former course. There was no noticeable change until the summer of 1917. At that time André was invited to spend his vacation with an aunt. He was 15 at the time. He was a handsome boy, big and strong, with piercing eyes; his turned-up nose gave him a resolute air. Outside of school he recovered his vitality and warmth. While he was staying at this aunt's home, he became acquainted with a relative who was already twice his age. One day, in the course of a walk, he opened his heart and confided in her, telling her of the difficulties he was experiencing in his life as a Christian. Without leaving him time to catch his breath and have second thoughts, his cousin took him to Saint-Malo,[25] to a hospital chaplain she knew, and he went to confession.

In the notebook where, as a young monk, he succinctly wrote down the stages of his spiritual pilgrimage, are found these words: "Became acquainted with X in August 1917. Confession. Little prayer book. Correspondence."

The little prayer book is entirely in his cousin's handwriting. She copied down the Stations of the Cross for her protegé, together with some prayers of a very affective piety, three penitential psalms, some excerpts from the Manual of St. Augustine and from his Soliloquies, the Prayer of St. Thomas and various compositions of Abbé Gerbet, Abbé Perreyve and Père Gratry, as well as some of Claudel's poetry. André took great care of this treasure; it was his devotional book from 1917 until he entered the monastery at Bellefontaine in 1924.

After vacation was over, André and his cousin continued their frequent and close relationship, which had the character of a spiritual friendship. This was not enough, however, to make a zealous pupil of André. As a matter of fact it was just at this time that he began to take his obligations as a student very much at his own ease. At least he did not waste his time, because he profited from his pranks to visit the museums and expositions in Paris, and this is a very effective way to acquire a

[25] St.-Malo is a seaport on the northern coast of Brittany, France. *Larousse*, op. cit., t. 9, 524.

solid education; however, his thoughts were often with his older brother who had been mobilized. He envied him.

The beginning of the year 1918 was a trial for Parisian morale. Alerts succeeded one another, often accompanied by bombardments. Madame Sortais suffered from heart attacks. Her state was such that it was necessary to think of leaving Paris in June, despite André's unwillingness. Moreover she had a serious attack on the train and had to rest at Nantes for six weeks, before they arrived at La Chauminette.

They returned in October and found an excited populace. The German positions were breaking at every point: "On November 11 at 11 o'clock," wrote R. Heron of Bellefosse, "the bells announced the armistice. Students were dismissed from school. They all ran, class by class, to the Champs d'Élysées and La Concorde, where the trench mortars and small cannon recently captured were piled in small rows . . . The effervescence of the crowd in the afternoon on the large boulevards was indescribable . . . They surrounded every soldier they met and carried them in triumph. And we poor rhetoricians kissed more people that day than we were later able to kiss in a whole year."[26]

The atmosphere of a giant country fair prevailed for several days. André took part in it triumphantly and exuberantly. He dreamed more than ever of becoming an officer. Long lines of victorious soldiers confirmed in him this desire. But how could anyone work in this uproar, when politicians were now urging youths to the recovery of the country and to safeguard the gains of victory? He failed the examination in July 1919, as he had expected. In the fall his second year of rhetoric began without fanfare. Soon a family drama administered a rude shock to his personal life.

On January 6, 1920, Madame Sortais succumbed after a heart attack. She was not yet 53. For two years she had been constrained by articular rheumatism to lie down and rest most of the time. Her three younger children (among whom was Jean, still with the occupation force in Germany) were left in the care (theoretical at best) of Marcelle, the oldest, a mere 22.

This grief unsettled André. He suffered intensely from all the reciprocal affection that he had not known how to show his

[26] R. Heron de Villefosse, op. cit., 388.

mother. He reproached himself for his manifestations of independence and his violence. It seems that his faith was then on the brink of ruin, ready to founder in its trial. "I had almost lost my faith," Dom Sortais would later tell a companion in captivity.[27]

This eclipse, to speak truly, lasted only a short time—a few weeks, more or less —during which time André stopped all his religious practices. For a new event occurred, which again revolutionized his life to its very depths. He met a young girl at the house of some cousins in Versailles on February 10, and he immediately fell in love. It was for love of her whom he already considered his future fiancé, whose deep convictions he knew, that he again began to say the rosary. He wanted to show himself worthy of her. Very sweetly, by her own example, she would bring him closer to God, until the day when the love of God, after it had become supreme, would propose a decisive choice to his heart: that of making a home with her, or of renouncing that for a more completely dedicated life.

For the moment André was won over completely by the sweetness of this pure, strong love, which uplifted and ennobled him and from which he drew support to triumph over the anarchical forces and doubts within him.

"I am saying the rosary again," he wrote in his notebook. And since he did nothing by halves, he said it openly in the bus and on the train. He left no room for the objections of self-love or for surrender out of fear of ridicule. Furthermore, he liked to show that he had a tough character, and he needed to affirm himself. His new love was linked to the blossoming of his devotion to the Blessed Virgin, which would only become more intense as the years passed. This devotion took on a character that was both knightly and gentle at the same time, the mark of an ingenuous naiveté. He often called the Virgin Mary "Mother." She took the place of the mother he had just lost. He reproached himself for having failed to have had all the affectionate intimacy he had desired to have with her. He formed the habit of venerating the small statue of the Madonna placed in a niche in the courtyard of the home on the Rue d'Assas. Returning to the house, he would bring a flower, a leaf, or a small bird's feather

[27] Letter of M.P., July 28, 1967.

to place at the feet of the statue. He did the same for the statue of the Virgin which decorated his bedroom, a tiny image with its arms opened wide to the world.

The rhetoric, though, derived no profit from this roughly-sketched idyll. André's mind was decidedly far from dull classes and preparing for examinations. The post-war social climate preoccupied this boy of 17 more than his own future. The collective enthusiasm of victory died down, and people found themselves confronted with the difficult problems of life amid a failing economy. In the workers' world, where the prices kept going up and provoking tragic situations, discontent rumbled, and revolutionary forces had been in motion since the creation at Moscow on March 2, 1919, of the Third International Workers' Union. Strikes were multiplying; there would be 2,000 during the year 1919, and they would involve more than a million workers.

With the new legislature installed in December 1919, the workers' agitation began again, going over the heads of the syndicate presidents, who saw that they would have to follow their troops, or lose all control over them. An order to strike was issued to the railroad workers on May 1, 1920, but it was only partially obeyed. On May 3 the dockworkers, miners and sailors were involved. On the eighth it was the turn of public transportation, metallurgy and the building, automobile and airplane industries. Finally on the twelfth, workers of the light companies and furniture industries were invited to go on strike in their turn. The country could believe it was on the verge of a Bolshevik revolution. The political character of the strikes seems evident. Looking for support from the workers who had not responded to this revolutionary mobilization, the government called on the people, the students of the great schools and finally the volunteers of the civic union to fill the gaps left in the public services.

Happy to find a valid reason to escape the scholastic atmosphere for a few weeks, the rhetorician of Stanislas answered the call with enthusiasm; he took a job as brakeman together with his friend François Brière on the Versailles-Dreux line.[28] He kept some savory memories of this experience. For one thing it

[28] Versailles is 15 miles southwest of Paris, and Dreux is 30 miles west of Versailles. *Life Pictorial Atlas of the World* (New York: Time, 1961) 278.

confirmed him in his conviction that forceful indignation and hard blows on the mouth sometimes have surprising results. He would not forget it in the days of his captivity. After a cramming of this kind, is it any wonder that André Sortais failed the June examinations again?

Vacation began with a pilgrimage to Lourdes.[29] His sisters invited him to accompany them. Although he wished to please them, he found the prospect of this journey anything but bright. The idea of Lourdes that he had formed for himself resembled, in fact, the descriptions of Huysman, not at all attractive. His faith was just convalescing, so the human aspects of the pilgrimage were experienced as a trial. However, he writes in his notebook, "July 1920. First tears at Lourdes, one evening, alone at the torchlight procession." This grace was soon followed by an event which shook him up. While participating in the procession of the Blessed Sacrament, he saw a woman at his side recover her health. In an analogous situation, Alexis Carrel described (in the third person) the intense emotion which took hold of him: "He felt drops of sweat trickle down his forehead. It was as though he had received a blow on the head from someone's fist. His arteries throbbed. He stiffened in absolute insensibility."[30]

André's reaction was a declaration of availability. "I was at Lourdes," he was to say, "when I saw a sick woman at my side get up healed, during the procession of the Blessed Sacrament. I was deeply shaken, and I said, almost despite myself, without even thinking, 'My God, if you wish it, I will consecrate myself to you.'"

But the Lord who had provoked and inspired this act of self-giving did not follow up with a call at that particular time. God did not seem to want André for himself alone, so there was nothing for him to do but continue on the path marked out, and by a serious Christian life, prepare for the establishment of the family he was thinking of.

[29] Lourdes is far to the south of France, at the feet of the Pyrenees, about 30 miles from the border, and 65 miles southwest of Toulouse. See ibid.

[30] A. Carrel, *Le Voyage de Lourdes* (Paris: Plon, 1949) 71.

Chapter 2

THE CISTERCIAN VOCATION

For the second time André Sortais realized he had been "plowed under" during the first part of Baccalaureate. He had no wish at all to continue on this path. Through fidelity to his mother's wish he had already given up on Saint-Cyr.[1] Nevertheless he would have loved the life of an officer in the service of his country. His ardent generosity, his combativeness and his sense of sacrifice predisposed him for it. More than anything else, his innate qualities of leadership and his natural aptitude to command inclined him to it.

So he decided to prepare himself for the field of architecture like his father. His brother Jean was also planning to orientate himself in that direction soon after his discharge. At the time of his own architectural activity, André's father had been interested in the creation of an architectural faculty in the old Catholic circle of Luxembourg,[2] which was filled with memories of Ozanam,[3] Abbé Perreyve[4] and Msgr. de Ségur.[5] Abbé

[1] Saint-Cyr is the name of a commune west of Versailles on the Seine; it is also the name of an officers' school founded there by Napoleon Bonaparte, the French equivalent of West Point. *Larousse,* op. cit., t. 9, 501.

[2] Former national museum in Paris, located in the Medici gallery of the Luxembourg palace. Ibid., t. 6, 915.

[3] Frederic Ozanam was a French Catholic historian, son of an officer in the Italian army. He practiced medicine at Milan and later at Lyons. Concerned about religious renewal, he allied himself with Ampère, Ballanche and the Avenir group. He became doctor of law and doctor of literature. Pope John Paul II beatified him in August 1997. Ibid., t. 8, 70.

[4] Henri Perreyve was a French churchman and friend of Lacordaire; he became a professor of church history at the Sorbonne and had much influence over students. Ibid., t. 8, 350.

[5] Louis Gaston de Segur was a French churchman who gave himself to the apostolate among the people. After he became blind, he devoted himself to spiritual direction. Ibid., t. 9, 717.

Fonssagrives who took charge of the circle in 1887 had, in fact, thought that a preparatory studio for the school of fine arts should be added to the conferences on law, medicine, literature and history. He had asked his friend Louis Cirée to come and take over the direction of it. This architect was an excellent man and a "patron" of good composition, capable of confronting the worst disorders. He was 46 at the time. It was, therefore, to this school that André Sortais went to study.

He prepared his entrance application in his own way, eclectically, or if you prefer, with indifference. The future did not seem to preoccupy André inordinately. He lived in the present intensely and optimistically, careful above all not to waste time on studies, which could be spent more agreeably on other matters. In fact André was very busy—even too busy to be able to devote himself completely to his work.

At this time his life was organized on three principal patterns which sometimes overlapped without becoming confused. It is difficult to harmonize them with one another, but this did not pose a problem for André. He does not seem to have thought of it in that light. He simply lived. From the outside one could distinguish his professional life with its picturesque and tumultuous asides and his political life which was no less so. More important in his eyes (and here he would become very serious, or rather, serious in a unique way) was the life of the heart, beyond which was placed his deep spiritual life which was closely connected with it.

It is certainly necessary to admit that André worked with his comrades in the Louis Cirée Studio without great conviction. He liked to say with a pronounced southern accent, "Work! I'm not against it, but it takes so much time!" Ten boys—all 20-year-old pranksters—formed a closely-knit group at whose center André found himself at complete ease. No one loved to aggravate the townspeople or to stage intricate buffoonery at their expense as much as did André. It would be impossible to recount in full all his escapades or the bets which he always won. You could see him in pink pajamas on the subway or in the Luxembourg Gardens. One day he even succeeded in plucking a button from a policeman's jacket without getting caught. "I was taken to the police station six times: once for threatening to kill someone with a water pistol, once for a nocturnal disturbance," he would later boast. The other "visits" must be chalked up to his political activities. In all of this the eye on his audience was not at all a determining factor, although it was admittedly not absent. André was too spontaneous and honest for that, but he certainly loved to assert himself. He kidded around, first of all, because he needed to, because he was young, strong, imaginative, exuberant, and because it seemed to conform to his real nature. It was not the most profound, as we shall see, but it was one way for him to express his overflowing vitality.

However, he remained in control of himself. "Go in for a minute, but don't act like fools," he told his comrades who wanted to go into a shady café to take a drink. He sometimes went in himself, only to tell the pimps what he thought. For all that, there was nothing about him of a disembodied spirit. His temperament obliged him to a struggle to retain his purity. His self-mastery did not come easily, but he breathed sanity. His reactions were lively and spontaneous, and he still showed little self-restraint or patience, and so some companion at the studio or someone from outside might bring down lashing remarks upon himself or provoke some lesson willingly undergone. For example, one day he was sketching a live model in the studio, and a student permitted himself a verse from an obscene song. It is, of course, mandatory in the fine arts to work silently in the presence of models. André was livid with anger, and he rose to demand silence. Another time he became indignant at seeing an obscene drawing in the studio; he protested violently and demanded that it be removed. "He never allowed himself to engage in idle talk about girls," says one of his companions. His brutal reactions did him no disservice. He naturally aroused sympathy by his simplicity, excitement and sudden enthusiasm. Besides, the essential goodness he hid in himself and his overflowing affection could be discerned by a thousand subtle nuances.

Beginning in 1919 the conferences of the *Institut d'Action Française*[6] were resumed; in this way the Institut proposed to

[6] *L'Action Française* is the name of a newspaper published daily from March 21, 1908, until August 24, 1944, and of the movement which inspired it. It was directed by Charles Maurras and Leon Daudet (co-directed by M. Pujo after

renew thought which had been corrupted, said Bainville, by a century and a half of intellectual subversion based on revolutionary idealism. To reestablish historical facts that had been misrepresented by official propaganda, to return minds to a sane realism formed by an exact perception of the exigencies of the natural order—such was the objective of these courses—to help the French people to think well, in order to act well.

Immediately after the war the 20-year-old movement had expanded rapidly and created a solid organization with, not only its journal and its Institut, but also its reviews, its Federation des Camelots du Roi, its regional secretariats, its divisions and its various services. A permanent residence of the *Etudiants d'Action Française* was opened at 33 Rue Saint-André des Arts in the Latin Quarter.

Leon Daudet fascinated the young by his good humor and wild animation which assured him of success (and enemies as well) in the Chambre and the countryside. What they found attractive were the ideals of order and political propriety extolled by *Action Française*. There were many Catholics who adhered to the movement, and they had no trouble combining Maurras' views with their own. His doctrines contained much that was profoundly in conformity with the nature of things. For him, in fact, it was the observation of the real that permitted the unprejudiced mind to deduce laws from social life, and the fundamental lesson to be learned from this was that every society sees its prosperity and growth conditioned by the permanence of the religious and political forms which assured its blossoming and development. Those Catholics in whose eyes the Republic had, from 1901 to 1914, gone its limit, naturally turned to a doctrine whose conformity with the teaching of Thomist philosophy seemed obvious.

Daudet's death). The movement was started by Henri Vaugeois and M. Pujo at the time of the Dreyfus affair and was first called *Comité d'Action Française* and later *Ligue d'Action Française*. It was Charles Maurras who gave the movement a formative doctrine in his *Conquète sur la Monarchie*. He defended the notion of integral nationalism against the liberal democratic ideas of the Republic and proclaimed the "hereditary, anti-parliamentary and decentralized" monarchy. The conception was largely atheistic, but the movement included many young Catholics, and the Catholic Church was strongly cultivated, because it stood for civic order and cultural traditions. Because of its hold on young Catholics, the movement was condemned by Pope Pius XI in 1928. Ibid., t. 1, 85.

Maurras' theoretical preference for the Greek mind and for ancient humanism mattered little to them, since they saw that he was determined to defend Catholicism as the first and irreplaceable foundation of French society. They were grateful to him for the war he had undertaken against the principles of 1789 and the philosophical doctrines that had permitted their appearance.

With all the enthusiasm of his 20 years, André Sortais was impassioned with the ideas and politics of *Action Française*. It is known that in 1925, when the Cahiers de la Jeunesse Catholique Belge took a survey on the believing younger generation's masters of thought, the results placed Maurras' name at the very top, followed by those of Bourget and Barrès.

Politics, then, will have been the second pole of André's life—politics intelligently understood and based on a conception of life and philosophy which will have served to lessen the gaps in his scholastic formation. His thought will have gained thereby a rigorous logic and clarity. The example of qualified masters will have taught him how to construct his reasoning by basing himself on the real and on life, and how to refine an idea.

One of his companions at "Fine Arts" said of André during this period, "He was very aggressive when he wanted to be, so that what he esteemed as true would win out, and this end was often attained through the force of his arguments." Moreover, André did not have any timidity to overcome, and he unknowingly exerted intellectual charm in favor of the arguments enlisted in the battle.

There is no doubt that André's adherence to *Action Française* had patriotism as the determining factor. He was too young to enlist, even in 1918, and he suffered from not being able to follow the example of those older than he. The struggles of *Action Française* presented themselves to him by way of compensation: he believed he could usefully serve his country by stormily defending her national causes with the Camelots du Roi. The character of their manifestations was not displeasing to him. They kicked up more shinnies in the Latin Quarter than against revolutionary agitation. However, some testimony of this period would tend to show that he was a partisan of violence.

The demonstration he preferred to all others was that which led the devotees of Joan-of-Arc each year from the Place Saint-

Augustin to the Place des Pyramides. Others had a more contrasting character and wound up at the police station where one of his uncles came to find him, after verification of his identity and home. The reason for his first trip to the police station was his cry, "Long live the King!" during the procession in which the ashes of Gambetta's heart were carried to the Pantheon. The other two visits were for booing and whistling at Briand on his return from the international conferences, where he had pursued his own policies instead of those of his government, and for bearing a placard at the Lyons railway station for Briand's return from the conference of Cannes in January 1922; the placard read, "Here comes the blockhead!" The fourth visit occurred after a demonstration of anarchists in which Saint Joan-of-Arc was insulted.

He certainly showed zeal for this saint's honor. It was a tradition among the young recruits of *Action Française*. The concerted action of Maurice Pujo and some Camelots had succeeded in making Thalamas, who had taught contesting any supernatural character in Joan's mission,[7] "lose" his chair at the Sorbonne in 1908. After this first victory a parade was organized on May 16, 1909, from Notre-Dame Cathedral to the statue on the Rue de Rivoli, despite police opposition. The procession of 1914 mobilized 50,000 Parisians. On the day following this victory, in order to prevent the demonstration from taking on a character that would be clearly anti-republican, the celebration was made an official legal holiday. In 1921 the parade surpassed every display that had yet been seen. "I still see André Sortais as he was in May 1921," writes a witness. "He is tall of stature, and he leads a group, brandishing a long cane and crying, 'Long live Maurras!' He is a leader of men."[8]

One day he was with some friends when he had a sudden desire to steal the bronze palm from the feet of Gambetta's statue on the Carousel and offer it at the statue of Saint Joan-of-Arc on the Rue de Rivoli. The attendant tried to stop the reckless person

[7] André Thalamas had already been incriminated for his teaching on St. Joan-of-Arc at the Lycée Condorcet. His little book, *Jeanne d'Arc, l'histoire et la légende* (Paris: P. Paclot, 1904), however, has nothing in it of an injurious character, unlike many pseudo-historical studies.

[8] Letter of M.E., July 11, 1967. Tissier de Malleras, "La fête nationale de Jeanne d'Arc" in *Almanach de l'Action Française pour l'an de grâce, 1922,* 160–63.

who had jumped over the flower bed surrounding the pedestal; the boy threw the palm to another student who passed it to a third, until it got to André who ran full speed and left the forces of the law behind.

Another time, learning that a popular singer had spread some nonsense about the saint in a tavern, "Fursy's Shanty," he descended upon it with catcalls and ripe fruit.

However, when he and some Camelots tried to intervene at a meeting of anarchists, where the speaker took up the subject of Joan-of-Arc, it was more dangerous. If some officers of the law had not intervened, they would have had a rough time of it.

André Sortais' activities in the service of *Action Française* were definitely beneficial to him. He acquired (or strengthened) a sense of discipline freely accepted from it, as well as a religious respect for legitimate authority recognized as such. The strong doctrinal structure of *Action Française*, linked with respect for spontaneity and initiative, channeled his naturally anarchical energies, and without exercising any constraint it conferred a constructive character upon them, which they could only have acquired with difficulty otherwise.

But the most important part of André's life was unknown to his entourage: the interior life of the heart, inseparable from his spiritual progress. Human love was leading him back to God; it would inspire him to grow rapidly toward complete detachment. Almost nothing of this was noticed exteriorly. The young man gave the impression to many of those who met him that he was a bit foolish, and some were concerned about his future: How would he turn out? Appearances were deceptive. His exuberant vitality was hiding a profound interior life, and this ruffian was more serious than the serious people around him.

The small notebook which we have already mentioned shows this entry: "School year 1920–21. Rising early to go to Versailles. Frequent communion." He had questioned a cousin and discovered that the girl of Versailles with whom he was so completely in love went to Mass at the Saint Louis Cathedral every morning. And so he too got up very early, whatever the season, in cold weather, in snow and in rain, and caught the morning train to the suburbs, in order to be at the Cathedral in Versailles at 7:30. "We met in the doorway," she wrote, "and we talked as though we had known each other all our lives, and we were both so timid otherwise!"

God was not the primary motive for these escapades. André thought only of the joy of seeing his friend and returning at once, "his heart full of sunshine for the day." But the girl's behavior made him think. He began to look in the same direction toward the Lord who held so large a place in her life. Little by little his participation in the Mass became more personal and less dependent on his primary motive. His soul received the light and opened up wide. His faith became stronger. André very soon became a daily communicant. His confessor is unknown, but he did go to confession regularly. To the daily rosary he added some practices of mortification, whose value he had discovered. He slept on the floor for a considerable time, using only his bedside carpet as a mattress.

In fact, whatever may have been the opinion of his circle of friends at the time, André's religious crisis seems to have been very brief. There was an eclipse, but this lasted no more than a month or two. After this lapse of time, he began again to say the rosary, and, so it seems, to assist at Mass. It is quite possible that he sometimes suffered relapses of fervor and periods of religious apathy, especially when he was away from Paris or Versailles, but the distant example of his friend was not slow in reminding him of his resolutions. The time would come very soon, when he would experience it as a grievous deprivation to be away from the sacraments, even involuntarily.

And so he was all the more aware that he had to endure great conflicts to remain pure. He was sometimes tempted to lose courage and to let himself go, but the thought of his lovely friend aided him in difficult moments; still, he counted above all on God's grace.

A year passed by in this way, marked by progress and by visible interventions of Our Lady. The future seemed assured. The two young people loved one another tenderly. No difficulty was foreseen on the part of their families.

At the beginning of summer in 1921, the Sortais left Paris for La Chauminette. It was a torrid season. Not a single puff of wind crossed the air above the vines and the short stone walls that surrounded the slope. The Loire flowed idly by, exposing long trails of yellow sand between the aspens of the islands and the willows on the banks. Grass fires and forest fires spread all along the tracks of the Angers[9]-Nantes railroad, started by sparks from the locomotives.

The Sortais were in a hurry to leave the sultry atmosphere of the valley for the fresher air of the Ile of Noirmoutier. They prepared themselves to forsake La Chauminette and to leave their neighbors of La Belle-Touche, the Daviaus, with whom they were very close. The departure had been set for the next day. It was nearly evening, and the fire alarm had already sounded seven times that day. André and his sisters were resting in the garden after dinner, when the bell of La Belle-Touche began to ring again. The 10 o'clock train for Nantes had set the grass afire all along the tracks, and the flames were spreading rapidly towards the hamlet of La Grotte-Chevreune. The people who were in the vicinity ran up and formed a chain to pass buckets back and forth. The well along the road which goes up to the bridge was almost dry. The chain was re-formed to go from the pool-washhouse to the fire, but the water there was very low, and after a short time it gave out in its turn. The flames were six feet from the Macaud house, whose occupants were away. The flames had reached a pile of logs and faggots, and they threatened to spread further.

Then, after a moment of hesitation, André took his rosary, detached the cross with a quick movement, and threw it into the flames. He did not do it without some repugnance. If his act of faith had just been heard, what would God require of him afterwards? Nevertheless he went through with it. The flames twisted and crackled, as though they were going to redouble their violence, then the fire abated, subsided, and finally went out, without even consuming the last of the logs. Someone threw a few shovelfuls of dirt on them.

The next morning, André went down from La Chauminette, got a rake at La Belle-Touche, and went to La Grotte-Chevreune.

[9] Angers is the capitol of the department of Maine-et-Loire in western France. It borders the Maine River and is 48 miles east-northeast of Nantes to which it is joined by a railroad. It has been a diocesan seat since the third century. *Webster's New Geographical Dictionary,* op. cit., 51.

Carefully he raked off the dirt and ashes. There it was! The cross of his rosary had taken on "pathetic" colors. He found it just against the line of the fire. The fire had not gone beyond that point. André bent down and kissed the cross with emotion.[10]

That very day the family left for the Abbaye de la Blanche. "If you want to know at what moment God first asked me to follow him, remember the fire we were watching the evening before our departure for Noirmoutier, where I saw the flames die down at the spot where the cross from my rosary was," he wrote to one of his sisters on September 30, 1923. This was the first sign of his call, not a decisive one, nor by itself a determining one, but others would follow. André sensed God's closeness, and the Lord's personal attentions in his regard provoked a personal response from him. He did not yet discern clearly the form this response would take. He only had a presentiment of it.

Some days later in his Uncle Jeanneau's house at Noirmoutier, in the old monastic domain alongside the ocean, André began to read something that caused him to reflect. It was the novel of Peter the Hermit, *How I Killed My Son,* which had just been published. Edmond Loutil, the curate of Montmartre, later of Saint-François-de-Sales, who wrote under the penname of Peter the Hermit, was a neighbor at Noirmoutier. He came every summer to the Bois de la Clere near the Village de Vieil, where a camp had been founded by his parish. Later he acquired La Garennerie. *How I Killed My Son* is the tragic story of a vocation that the mother herself, through a misguided maternal love, did all she could to destroy. It is a kind of psychological drama whose plot is made up of the young man's interior trials and failures. The book ends on a note of disaster.

André Sortais lived this story intensely. One night before he went to sleep, he promised God that he would follow him, if he heard his call. "The black cassock which haunted the young

[10] Later in the novitiate at Bellefontaine the Father Master of novices noticed the precious rosary with its crucifix in such a pitiful state, and he took it from the young brother, giving him another. André, having become Brother Gabriel, submitted to the exchange without a word of protest for his "relic"; he wished to practice poverty and detachment perfectly. When he became prior some years later, he searched among the effects of his former Father Master in the hope of finding the cross; he never saw it again.

man in the story changed into a white robe and black scapular," he wrote in his notebook. Where had he seen this habit? If he was aware of the existence of the Cistercians, of whose history each detail of the domain would remind him, he had never yet visited a monastery of living monks. The image was a visual reminiscence not adverted to at the time, because he added, "A short time later at La Chauminette, I was looking through some old pictures, and glimpsing a habit, I recognized it." He remembered having seen it before.

The young man's promise remained conditional: "if I hear your call." This call still remained discreet. He would later see a providential indication in this: a sort of premonition of his vocation to Cistercian monastic life.

In autumn André began his second year of preparation for the School of Fine Arts. He renewed his morning trips to Versailles, for no light had been thrown on his true vocation. He began seeing his girlfriend again. When Holy Week of 1922 arrived, he felt the moment had come for a final step that would put an end to his uncertainty. He would ask his girlfriend's family to formalize their engagement through the mediation of a mutual cousin.

On the evening of April 12, Wednesday of Holy Week, since he had not yet received an answer and was keyed up, he presented himself at an aunt's house in Versailles. She was his godmother. He needed to confide in someone, to tell someone he loved what he had on his mind. When he arrived, she was engrossed in writing. He sat down near her, making himself at home, and waited for her to finish. It was then that the full light came, which touched off a great interior struggle, and the struggle became obvious because of his copious tears. God's call was no longer a hypothesis; it was there, pressing, demanding an answer. But, then, could he refuse God? Did God require such a sacrifice? "I found myself suddenly changed interiorly," he wrote in his notebook.[11] His resolution was taken. A peace that

[11] "My poor heart has tentacles which clutch at everything . . . I needed the love of the Holy Virgin to be strong in me at the moment of my vocation, in order that I might renounce at one stroke all that I loved. Oh! This poor loving heart, if only it had loved the good God just once!" Letter to a monk, December 29, 1939.

was at first sad, then sweet, invaded his soul. God could do with him what he wanted. André gave himself to God completely.[12]

His aunt was present, deeply moved at his interior struggle. André told her about it; she listened and encouraged him, allowing him to stay at her house. The next day he left Versailles on foot to make a pilgrimage to Montmartre.

His decision did not concern himself alone. His love was shared, and he considered himself already morally engaged. He did not want to take the final decision of breaking the engagement before speaking to her whom he considered his fiancé and asking her consent. Since he felt this would make her suffer, he waited for a favorable opportunity.

He felt so much repugnance at the thought of dashing her hopes that he delayed for an entire year. He finally did it when he was on leave in March 1923, on the occasion of the marriage of one of his sisters, to which the girl had been invited. After lunch he asked her to dance, then, apart in the hall, he said, "I don't have the courage to tell you, so I have written to you," and he handed her a letter. She read it and answered simply, "I don't wish to stand between you and God." The two young people would never see each other again.

During a stay at Solesmes in September 1843, Louis Veuillot composed a novel in which he inscribed this phrase from Bossuet as a motto: "My brothers, see the flight of this soul wounded by God's love!" It is a story of two young people, engaged, who discovered together that God was calling them to a more perfect life. "One day, Fabian, someone told me just to hurt me, that he had seen you eagerly trying to please one of my friends and wanting to marry her. I did not believe a word of it, but even so the malice made me cry and broke my heart. Another day someone told me that you were talking about entering one of the religious orders; I cried again, but this time I offered you to God in peace. I give you," she said, "to Jesus crucified."[13]

[12] "For a long time I had received many calls up to the moment when I promised God that I would consecrate my life to him. And then what peace, what sweetness." Letter to M., September 30, 1923.

[13] L. Veuillot, *Le vol de l'ame, Oeuvres Completes,* 1re série, t. VII (Paris: Lethielleux, 1926) 149–51.

What provided Veuillot with a subject for poetic fiction, André Sortais and his girlfriend had just lived through in their hearts of flesh. All his life he would know how painful a choice of this kind could be, but also what graces were initiated through it.

"When the devil wants to make us hesitate in our vocation," he wrote, "he raises the spectre of the complete gift. But let us not forget that it is just this that touches the heart of Jesus and makes our life so fruitful: this complete and absolute gift."[14] Another time he said, "Don't you find that, apart from the pain which our nature fears and at which it groans, almost in spite of ourselves, there is immense Joy when we do God's will at our own expense? One is then sure that there is no self-will involved. God has made us, and it seems that the most normal and logical attitude of a creature is to give himself totally to the good pleasure of his Creator. It is to offer to God what he has given to us, to place at his disposal what belongs to us."[15]

[14] Letter to a monk, October 15, 1933. Speaking on the eve of his own death of the woman who had been his fiancée, he said, "I have always considered her since that time as a member of my family, whom I love without desire. I still love her as a sister, so to speak, and that is why I would love to know how she has fared. If you tell me nothing, I will deduce from that that it is better for me to mortify myself on this point, and I will offer it for her and for her family." Letter to X, September 11, 1963.

[15] Letter to a nun, February 19, 1953.

Chapter 3

ON THE BRINK OF MONASTIC LIFE

André Sortais had heard God's call and responded by a heroic sacrifice. Now he let himself be guided by the interior attraction, putting his trust in the Lord. The competitive entrance examinations for the School of Fine Arts drew near with the end of the school year. André was not very worried about them on his own account because he was resolved to leave the world. But he was afraid that, if he failed, he would create the false impression that a failed test was his real reason for leaving the world. On the other hand, if he passed, everyone would know that his intention was guileless. It was a question of the honor of the Holy Virgin, who had led him to the gate of Citeaux! Now, André did not know a single word about descriptive geometry. At a little pub in the Latin Quarter he declared to a friend that he was going to learn just one question on the program, the question about conic sections.

"You would do better, all the same, to learn two. That would be more prudent!"

"More prudent? Oh no! That would show a lack of confidence! I bet you a liqueur that I will be asked just that one!"

He learned the question and went to burn a candle to Our Lady of Victories. He was given the question he had prepared.

"You have answered perfectly," the examiner told him. "In fact, since there is always the possibility of a lucky coincidence, I generally give a second question, after the first one has been answered. But you know your material so well that I need not do it with you!"

So it was that André Sortais passed. He went to claim his liqueur, and he immediately renounced his right to enter the School of Fine Arts.

Since God had faced him with a decisive choice, and he had generously responded with the gift of himself, he was enlightened about the earlier events at Lourdes, La Grotte-Chevreune, and La Blanche. He discerned in them different modalities of the same call. The third seemed to him to indicate the meaning of his vocation. It was for the Cistercian life that God had destined him. But he knew very little about the monastic life[1]—a few scraps of history, some items of folklore[2]—nonetheless, he knew, as did every Christian, that the Cistercian life was a life of contemplation in which prayer alternated with work, and the days unfolded in solitude, separation from others, and intimacy with God. That was enough for him, so far as the decision was concerned, but now he wanted to study the life to which he was called, and so he informed himself about La Trappe without further delay.

A certain book had shown him the concrete realization of this ideal in the person of an officer who became a monk, Captain Gabriel Mossier who became Br. M. Gabriel, a lay brother at the Abbey of Chambarand,[3] who died at the age of 42 on April 10, 1897. His was a very simple life in which devotion to Mary held an important place. His biography was written by Dom du Bourg, Prior of Sainte-Marie in Paris, with the help of documents gathered by Père Nortet.

But let us go on to the phase of complete realization (for André was not a man to confine himself to a simple project, but he needed to go all the way, and that quickly). He had to search out a monastery and try his vocation. He thought immediately of Chambarand, Brother Gabriel's monastery, but that monastery had been closed in 1903, to avoid a forced expulsion and complete expropriation. While some of the monks left for Bra-

[1] "I too went to the Trappists without asking about any details of Trappist life. I was sure only that God wanted me there, and the rest was unimportant." Letter to a Cistercian novice, August 23, 1956.

[2] "I had hardly learned anything on my own, except for an article in an old issue of *l'Illustration.*" Letter of July 30, 1922.

[3] Chambarand, now inhabited by Trappistines, is in the diocese of Grenoble, along the river Isère, about 133 miles north of Marseilles. *Webster's New Geographical Dictionary,* op. cit., 466; see also "Grenoble," *Dictionnaire d'Histoire,* op. cit., col. 330, t. 12.

zil, the rest of the community appealed to Sept-Fons[4] where the abbot, Dom Chautard, gave them a fraternal reception.

So André Sortais thought he would knock at the door of this abbey of Bourbonnais. But Abbé Constantin, curate of Saint-Sulpice, to whom he had confided his project of entering a monastery, spoke to him of Bellefontaine, since he himself was a faithful friend of that abbey.

Bellefontaine was not far from La Chauminette; the abbey was situated in the heart of the *Mauges*,[5] well in the Vendée militaire,[6] for which the militant recruit of *Action Française* had a strong admiration. Memories of the great uprising had filled André's youth: The tomb of Bonchamps[7] was located at St.-Florent-le-Vieil, not far from La Possonnière. It was at Noirmoutier that one of the *Vendéen* armies was massacred by the Blues. Sixty by sixty, the 1200 prisoners who had made up that army, and to whom General Haxo[8] had promised their lives, fell under the bullets of the firing squad. After them the wounded D'Elbée[9] was shot down in

[4] Sept-Fons was the motherhouse of Chambarand. It is located some 60 miles northwest of Macon and over 100 miles southwest of Dijon. Louis J. Lekai, *Cistercians: Ideals and Reality* (Kent, Oh.: Kent State University Press, 1977) 488–89.

[5] The *Mauges* is the southern region of Anjou in northwest France. *Larousse*, op. cit., t. 7, 176.

[6] The Vendée is a department in the region formerly called Poitou in western France, comprising 9,672 square miles. By *Vendée militaire* is meant the whole region of a counterrevolutionary uprising that had taken place in 1793, only part of which corresponds to the present department of Vendée. It includes also parts of Loire-Atlantique, Maine-et-Loire and Deux-Sèvres. The population is predominantly Catholic. The peasants fought for their priests and their churches. Ibid., t. 10, 716.

[7] Charles, Marquis de Bonchamps, was a leader of the *Vendéen* army, chosen by the troops. He was second in command under d'Elbée and took part in numerous battles. Wounded at the battle of Cholet on October 17, 1793, he died the following day. His tomb in the Church of St.-Florent-le-Vieil is the work of David of Angers. Ibid., t. 2, 225–26.

[8] General Nicolas François Haxo of the army of the Revolution pursued Charette and caught up with him but fell into an ambush. Wounded and about to be captured, he took his own life. Ibid., t. 5, 811.

[9] Maurice Gigost d'Elbée was a Scot by birth. Having served in the army, he retired to Anjou, to his estate near Beaupréau. Unlucky in his choices, he accepted the Revolution and was nominated to the third estate. He emigrated in 1791, returned in 1792 and participated in the relief of the West. He joined Stofflet and Cathelineau with his *Mauges* troops and helped take Thouars and Saumur in May and June. Acclaimed Generalissimo by the troops at the death

his armchair, and with him his brother-in-law, d'Hauterive and another officer, and they were buried in a ditch of the chateau. Not far from there, at La Garennerie, a wrought-iron cross facing the ocean registers the fact that the wives and daughters of the men of Noirmoutier passed here, singing the Magnificat, before being shot down on the dune. "Don't cry! We'll have supper tonight with the good God," said one of them to her young 19-year-old sister. André Sortais found himself in complete accord with this heroism whose memory was enshrined at almost every crossroad in this region that saw the uprising of a peasant army to defend its faith, and that army continued the struggle until the religious peace had been won.

The Abbey of Bellefontaine rises in a small valley in the canton of Beaupréau, seven and a half miles north of Cholet.[10] This monastery has a long history behind it, which begins before the year 1100. It saw the white monks succeed the black. Dom Urban Guillet[11] was a disciple of the Abbé de Lestrange;[12]

---

of Cathelineau, he was victor at Coron and Torfou. Gravely wounded at Cholet, he reached Noirmoutier where he was betrayed to a war council and sentenced to death. Ibid., t. 4, 421.

[10] Cholet is the chief city of an *arrondissement* in the department of Maine-et-Loire in the *Mauges* region. It was entirely destroyed during the *Vendéen* wars and its population was dispersed. However, it was gradually rebuilt during the 19th century, under the impetus of the textile industries. It is important in our story because of its proximity to Bellefontaine. *Choletais* = the inhabitants of Cholet, whether considered as a city or an *arrondissement*. Ibid., t. 3, 79.

[11] The group led by Dom Urban arrived in Baltimore, Maryland, in 1803. They established themselves at Pigeon Hill, near Hanover, Pennsylvania; after two years they moved to Casey Creek, Kentucky, where they stayed for four years. Despite their prosperity they moved to Monks Mound, near Cahokia, Illinois. After four years of hardship, they moved to New York City, where they set up a monastery on the Fifth Ave. site now occupied by St. Patrick's Cathedral. The fall of Napoleon in 1814 served to recall the monks to France. *New Catholic Encyclopedia,* 2nd ed. (Farmington Hills, MI: Gale Group, 2003) vol. 14, 162.

[12] Dom Augustin de Lestrange was a religious in the monastery of La Trappe in Soligny, when the order of suppression came from the national assembly. After some initial difficulties, he succeeded in establishing himself at La Val Sainte in Switzerland with 24 monks on June 1, 1791. The story of his various foundations has been told in the article by M. Bernard Brard, ocso (*Catholicisme,* op. cit., t. 7, col. 477–79). After the fall of Napoleon, he took possession of La Trappe on Dec. 6, 1815. Aiguebelle was recovered in 1816, Melleray in 1817, and the Trappistines found a home at Forges, near La Trappe in 1816 and at Lyon-Vaise in 1820. The observances instituted by Dom Augustin de Lestrange

after the collapse of the Empire, he had led the Trappists, after they had been chased from Europe by Napoleon's armies, all the way across the wilderness of the New World, acquired the deserted buildings and some land, before dying of exhaustion in the hospital of Cholet in 1817. Dom Augustin de Lestrange who was having difficulties with the bishop of Séez lost no time in rejoining the religious in their new quarters. Bellefontaine scrupulously preserved the things that belonged to him.

In 1832 the supporters of the Duchess of Berry tried to get the people of the west to revolt. The Abbot of Bellefontaine, Dom Fulgence, was suspected of complicity with them at the time, and because of this he was arrested and imprisoned for some weeks at Angers. Because his features were vaguely Bourbon, he passed in the *Mauges* for the Dauphin, Louis XVII, who had escaped from prison at the Temple and had come to share the Trappist life in the heart of the desert: a beautiful but somber legend of romance.

After the epic expulsions of 1880[13] (these were very important local events), the monks lost no time in returning to their monastery, but the measures taken in view of a longer exile were at the origin of the two Canadian foundations of Our Lady of the Lake near Oka in the province of Quebec in 1881 and Our Lady of the Prairies in Manitoba in 1892.

At about 200 paces from the monastery, there stands outside the enclosure a chapel dear to the inhabitants of the *Mauges:* Notre-Dame de Bon-Secours. The pilgrimage to this chapel goes back to a time before the monastery was founded. Under the Constitutional Church in 1791, the chapel became a rallying place for the faithful who stood firm against the schism; they came in thousands—so many and so strong that 200 men were sent from Cholet with the mission to demolish the chapel and carry the statue back to the city.

---

were characterized by austerity and intransigence, but perhaps this was necessary, due to the political instability of the time and the frequent changes of residence, to say nothing of the cultural and linguistic upheavals, necessitated by it. Dom Augustin is rightly called the savior of the Trappist order.

[13] Actually the monks were only gone for five weeks, but in the beginning the threat of an expulsion like those at the beginning of the century seemed real. *Dictionnaire d'Histoire,* op. cit, t. 7, col. 847.

The first expedition was dealt with and repulsed, for the peasants showed themselves determined to defend their sanctuary. Some days later the revolutionary authorities made another attempt with 500 men and two cannons. The chapel was destroyed within an hour, and the miraculous statue carried to the city "with all deference befitting its veneration." Not long afterwards came the uprising of the Vendée, and the peasants of the *Mauges* took possession of Cholet in August 1793. Their first concern was to regain the venerated statue and to carry it back to the chapel which they rebuilt from the ruins. Afterwards the Virgin served as a safeguard in the great expedition which carried the Vendeen army, defeated in its own region, to Granville. Then the statue was lost during the crossing of the Loire. In 1817 the Trappists renewed the pilgrimage, and Dom Augustin de Lestrange had a large Way of the Cross built with 33 stations, in honor of the years of our Savior's life. As for the chapel, it was entirely rebuilt from 1834–39.

Such were the Abbey of Bellefontaine and the nearby sanctuary of Our Lady of Bon-Secours at the time when André Sortais first heard about them. There were about 45 in the community—almost equally divided between Lay Brothers and Choir Religious. The monastery was governed by an elderly abbot who was both colorful and peevish, Dom Jean-Marie Chouteau, who had been elected back in 1866 (at that now distant time he had been only 26); he had ruled the monks of Bellefontaine for 58 years with an iron hand, and he had become their patriarch in a flowing white beard.

André Sortais made a pretext of a need for a few days rest before beginning military service, and he slipped away from La Chauminette on his bicycle during the second part of July. However, he approached the monastery with a little apprehension. Looking at the monastery from afar one day, he felt the Trappist life was a bit frightening. Soon he was reassured. "The enclosure is wonderful . . . nothing gloomy about it, all is joyful, all is glorious . . . no noise anywhere."

Père Simon, the guest master, met him at the gate, and Père Louis, the prior, took charge of him. Père Louis was a man of experience. Although he was still a "junior," he had attained the status of a "senior." He had fulfilled his office as superior of the minor seminary at Sables-d'Olonne[14] when, in 1917, he had decided to enter the monastery. He was to make his solemn profession within four weeks. "Here is what I see most clearly in the midst of all this joy," wrote our young man a few days later, "I now have a quasi-certitude that God will allow me to follow him. On earth everything has its dark side, but here all is joyful, because it is all done under Mary's gaze. The day will come when I can pray all day long!"[15]

"I am full of joy. I have tasted joys I never expected. To think I once believed a monk's life dark and forbidding! I will not be able to wait very long, before coming back here to pray to the Virgin of Bellefontaine."[16]

André had spoken of his vocation to a few friends, but his immediate family as yet knew nothing about it. For his own part, he was anxious to take the final step, but when he made a second retreat in September, at the end of his vacation, Dom Chouteau told him he would not accept him on the eve of his military service, but he would have to wait until his discharge in 18 months, an eternity for a young man at the age of 20.

And so on November 15 André was summoned to Le Mans[17] to be incorporated into the 104th Regiment of Heavy Artillery. The point has been well made in these days of glory and of ardent, enthusiastic patriotism, that barracks life still constitutes a rude trial. "You have to accept it cheerfully, because a sullen soldier in the regiment soon becomes a 'rotten apple.'" There was fortunately a diversion. "We rode horses for awhile. It was fun, but painful. You know where!"[18] Horseback riding soon became a veritable passion for him. At Cherbourg,[19] where he was to complete his term of service, he would rush out foolishly

[14] Sables-d'Olonne is on the western coast of France, about 50 miles south of Nantes. *Webster's Geographical,* op. cit., 412–13.

[15] Letter to a cousin, July 30, 1922.

[16] Letter to a cousin, postscript dated August 1, 1922.

[17] Le Mans is a city of northwestern France in the dept. of Sarthe. It is, in fact, the capital of Sarthe and borders the Sarthe River. It is 117 miles southwest of Paris and is a manufacturing center. *Websters Geographical,* op. cit., 659, 412.

[18] Letter to a cousin, December 6, 1922.

[19] Cherbourg is on the northwest coast of France, facing the English Channel, at the very edge of the Département of La Manche. *Webster's Geographical,* op. cit., 412.

and gallop down the beach, against all the military regulations, for the sole pleasure of a ride through the sand, lashed by the rushing air.

The "blues" of the 104th were in November 1922 mostly Bretons of the countryside. They would arrive in blue smocks and black caps, with wooden shoes on their feet; many of them had trouble speaking French, and still more in writing it. André did his best to help them, intervening to save them from razzing. Not everyone was happy about this, and it won him some lasting enemies. Since he did not hide the fact that he was a Catholic and had to go to Mass, they usually chose Sunday morning to let him have it. One can guess what his patience in such matters must have cost him at times.

The former militant of *Action Française* had to put a brake on his political activities. The army would not allow them. Nevertheless, Sortais would sometimes react with violence, and some soldier who had insulted the flag would see stars for it; the others would accept the matter as settled.

In order to exert more effective influence, André had himself enrolled in the class for training as non-commissioned officers. His natural aptitude for command served him greatly. In his division the work did not slacken, but the men liked him a lot, and they would have gone through fire just to please him, because he protected them whenever he could from excessive zeal and inept orders on the part of other ungifted non-commissioned officers.

When he was able to go into town, he would attend churches, preferably those dedicated to the Virgin Mary, Notre Dame du Pré or Notre Dame de la Couture. Here he would pray and meditate a long time. He also liked the small church of Saint-Martin de Pontlieue very much.

In September he had the joy of spending a few days at "his" monastery. "You know, I came back to Bellefontaine while I was on furlough," he wrote to his elder sister. "I asked myself what effect a year in the barracks would have on me, and I found that my way of judging things was exactly the same as last year. The life of prayer and immense peace led by the monks of Bellefontaine makes me infinitely happy, and if God continues giving me his graces, I will spend my life here. It was necessary for me to experience this time away from it, in order for me to say that my vocation was really no illusion. I have no way of telling you about all the happiness there is in living in a house of God, very close to him, and in praying for my loved ones."[20]

André's bedside reading on the eve of his becoming a monk was *The Story of a Soul.* Thérèse of the Child Jesus exercised an important influence upon him. She taught him almost his whole interior life. The teaching of the Little Saint was indelibly engraved on his memory and on his heart. He discovered, as she did, that the essence of the Christian life consists in knowing that one is loved by God and in accepting for oneself all the demands of that love.

Thérèse is the apostle of unlimited confidence in God's mercy, and her response was her desire to love Christ by realizing the Lord's will perfectly, certain of cooperating intimately and effectively in this way in the work of salvation of the world and of conversion of souls. Such also became the ideal of the future Trappist. When his military service was over, he determined to make a pilgrimage to Lisieux[21] by way of farewell. Then he renewed the pilgrimage to Lourdes in thanksgiving.

Nevertheless, he lost none of his vitality, and he showed it during the two months he spent with his family after his discharge. As a matter of fact, he delayed his entrance into Bellefontaine, in order to help his brother Jean arrange for his marriage (May–July 1927). He could be seen successfully playing the role of the clown on the stage in Luxembourg Circle in "The Chicago Farmer." The sacristan of the church of St.-Florent-le-Vieil dislodged him one day from the top of a confessional, where he had perched at the best spot from which to take a picture of the statue of Bonchamps. This good chap would one day ask him, "I had to do my duty, didn't I, Reverend Father?" He remained true to his female friends—these were solid friendships of the heart, much like brotherly affection, a necessary adjustment in him to counteract his boyish brusqueness, when relating to

[20] Letter to a sister, September 30, 1923.

[21] Lisieux is about 40 miles from the northwest coast of France, in the Département of Calvados, about 27 miles east of Caen. *Webster's Geographical,* op. cit., 412, 674.

those whose sensibilities were more refined. Friendship was always a point of repose for him, not an obstacle, but a means for revivifying his reaching out for God.

Just before the marriage of his brother Jean, which took place at La Possonnière on July 28, André had said goodbye to the family.

"Uncle, I have some big news to tell you!"

"Are you going to get married?"

"No. I'm going to enter La Trappe!"

"You! Are you completely out of your senses?"

They were all dumbfounded. Afterwards his uncles and aunts tried to get him to reconsider. He would do just as well as a secular priest! At least why not enter the Benedictines? No, the young man's resolution was unshakable.

"Well," said one uncle, "It is a pious thought. Too bad you will be back before three weeks have passed!"

Our Lady cured her knight and servant—almost instantly!—of two slight health impediments that had threatened to delay his entrance of Bellefontaine. On the morning of August 2 he embraced his two sisters tenderly and left them, after giving one of them a letter.

"Let us go where the good God wishes us to go. . . . Let us love him, knowing how to please him. . . . Let us make sacrifices for him, very simple, very humble, very small sacrifices, but let us sacrifice our wills to his love. *Let us imitate St. Thérèse*—that is everything."[22]

[22] Letter to a sister, August 1, 1924.

Chapter 4

NOVICE AT BELLEFONTAINE

"How can I make the reader sense the peace and the special charm we experience living here in this *Mauges* region which remained faithful to Jesus even to its own destruction during the war of the *Vendée,* in the midst of a people who by means of so many sacrifices obtained the grace of remaining profoundly Christian, in a monastery founded in honor of the Virgin Mary, where monks have prayed, loved and made reparation for 900 years, where silence reigns, while nature speaks so loudly of God, in this little valley with the name so fresh and pure of Our Lady of Bellefontaine?"

Father Sortais wrote these lines on Easter 1954, as a preface for a small book on the Abbey where 27 years of his life had been spent, slightly less than half of his life on this earth.

At the moment when he presented himself at the gate of the monastery, he had only one thought and one desire: to live his monastic life intensely, just as Brother Marie Gabriel of Chambarand had done. He aspired to a hidden life, to extreme despoilment, and to be forgotten by all. He wanted to belong to God completely and undistractedly, and he thought he would arrive at that state best, clad in the simple brown habit of a lay brother. He wanted to serve, to be forgotten and to pray. When he would have to choose an abbatial motto, he would take four words from the collect of the feast of the Holy Innocents: *non loquendo, sed moriendo.* He would bear witness to God, not at all by speaking, but by dying, as little children can do. God's call did not make itself heard in the form of a priestly vocation. André wanted simply to be a monk, in the most humble and hidden way.

Two days of waiting at the guest house allowed him to get to know better the Father Master, Father Placid, "a very retiring and sickly man," and to be initiated summarily into the thousand small customs of the Cistercian life, that he would have to put into practice. His first impression was one of immense joy; he compared himself to a "shipwrecked sailor who was able to climb aboard a small boat." His happiness was unmixed. "Leave all? But this was nothing but joy!" he said.[1]

There was, however, a misunderstanding from the day of his arrival. The two monks who had charge of him during his stay in the guest house, Father Louis, the prior, and Father Placid, the novice master, considered the young man whose Latin studies had been carried up to and included rhetoric as a postulant destined to become a choir monk. For two years André, for his part, thought only of the lay brother's life. That went without saying; he thought it understood. It was only at the moment when he joined the community, after his short stay in the guest house, that the problem was raised.

A discussion took place in Father Abbot's office, with Father Placid giving his reasons, and the postulant maintaining his. (After all, he was the one that was becoming a monk, not Father Master who was one already!) Dom Jean-Marie ended the discussion for the time being. André Sortais would begin with the choir monks. Later they would see.

Two weeks later the community was engaged in the threshing of the harvest or "the beatings" as some called it. During a rest period Father Placid took his postulant aside and spoke to him about his clothing day. They could have it on Our Lady's Assumption. "Oh Yes!" But then it would be for the choir religious, because lay brothers had to wait six months before receiving the habit. "Then I would rather wait!" But Father Master had a few more arguments. He explained to the postulant that a brother had to be as strong as iron and to be inured to hard work on the soil for long years, and if he was not strong enough, he would have the door to monastic life closed to him forever. On the other hand, if he entered the choir, he could change to the brothers any time before his profession. "Since it was *ad experi-*

[1] Chat with his sons at Bellefontaine during a jubilee.

mentum, I accepted, and I took the habit on August 15, after having been a postulant eleven days." He was given the name of Brother Marie Gabriel, as he desired: he had chosen it in order the better to be conformed to his model.

The traditions of the Reform begun by Abbot De Rancé at the monastery of La Trappe in the 17th century were still very much alive at Bellefontaine in 1924, despite the mitigations imposed by the Holy See at the end of the 19th century.

De Rancé wanted to bring the Cistercian life back to its primitive simplicity and severity. His whole effort was intended to put into practice as literally as possible what he understood to be the teaching of the desert fathers and of the founders of monasticism, whom the 12th-century Cistercians had taken as models, taking no notice of all the later mitigations. De Rancé, then, tried to return to the most literal observance of the Rule that was possible. In his eyes the only way to sanctity, the unique and obligatory way, was the observance of the Rule, as he understood it, for he firmly believed that he had grasped its essence. He conceived the monastic life as the penitent's return to God. His existence would henceforth be a continuous imitation of the suffering Christ. The monk, then, is, by definition, a penitent, a man of silence and solitude, who tends toward the beyond. Although De Rancé gives first place to the love of God, penitence predominates and impresses its mark on all the monastic virtues, even on prayer and meditation.

This extreme conception of the monastic life, holding to one particular aspect, and not, doubtless, the most important, making it the pole around which all the rest revolved, had its origin in De Rancé's predilection for radical practices. The fact that the site was unhealthy because of the proximity of the marshes which today have been drained, is not enough to account for the problem posed by the Necrology of La Trappe (1667–1737): Two fifths of the monks died before having lived in the monastery more than five years! The personality and the monastic achievement of the reformer have not yet been sufficiently studied, for a definitive judgment to be made. The life seems to have undertaken the employment of measures that were useful in correcting the excesses of the first Trappists. A kind of equilibrium which was more satisfactory appears to have settled into the life by the eve of the Revolution.

The disturbance it raised served at the same time to show the solidity of the monastic tradition of De Rancé and to incite it again towards further austerity. Dom Augustin de Lestrange, the novice master of La Trappe, got together a group of Cistercians at La Val Sainte in Switzerland, a former Carthusian house; and together they established a new form which ended up with an observance still more rigorous than that of La Trappe. The particular circumstances in which the monks found themselves in Europe, and especially in America, led them to sacrifice the solitary life temporarily to the gain of an external apostolate, without abandoning any of their austerities which were considered fundamental. However, once conditions returned to normal, the monks in France took up again their life of silence with prayer and work.

Bellefontaine, then, inherited the double tradition of De Rancé and Abbot de Lestrange. The monastery thenceforth remained faithful to these traditions. There was little place for doctrinal formation, for study of theology and spirituality. The abbey library, enriched by Dom Chouteau's contributions, was not accessible without special permission, except on Sunday. The novitiate had only a very small number of books at its disposal. During hours given to *lectio divina,* the monks read edifying biographies or treatises on prayer. It was essentially the observance which served as support to the spiritual life of the religious. When they were generous in penance, prayed much and worked hard, the abbot who was responsible for their monastic perfection, showed himself satisfied. His preoccupations hardly went beyond that.

The abbot of Bellefontaine, Dom Jean-Marie Chouteau, was, as a matter of fact, "a Trappist of the old school" who missed the primitive rule, as it was before the mitigations of 1892, imposed by Pope Leo XIII. Abbot Chouteau saw in these mitigations a regrettable concession to the weakness of the anemic generation in which "ungenerous natures" predominated. The same intransigence was to be seen on the spiritual side: He did not at all have the style of a Francis de Sales. The exercise of authority in his hands was characterized more by energy and forcefulness than by gentleness. Dom Jean-Marie did not pay much attention to his image, but kept up a rough exterior, like the bark of huge trees against the wind. When there was question of a point of the rule, the culprit was obliged to clutch at the rail until the gust of anger was past. No one thought of holding up his head against him. "His goodness was not effusive, no doubt about that," Père Marie wrote to Dr. Coubard who wrote a pamphlet on the abbot,[2] "but it was real, and it was great." Had he not chosen for his coat-of-arms *In dilectione firmaberis* ("You will be strengthened in love")? Nevertheless, his forcefulness was predominant. For his part, he had always enjoyed good health in every trial, so that, according to him, "sickness ought normally to be a trial that is short as well as severe, and is over in a few days, ending either in healing or in death."[3]

There was no question at all of anyone asking Dom Jean-Marie to work patiently with them through their subtle interior conflicts, or to follow the complicated maze of human psychology. He was very simple himself, he followed a simple way, and he succeeded with those who were simple. His teaching was all of the same vein, nourished by scripture and the fathers which he read often. He was practical and did not encumber himself with the "frills of language," but his native soil of Anjou was not without some influence on him, albeit unconscious, and some of his sayings had the flavor of an apophthegm.

Archaeologists will regret the fact that Dom Chouteau tore down the dilapidated old 12th-century church, a huge and simple edifice. The monastery which he almost completely rebuilt was not without good qualities, especially the church whose apse of rose-colored granite gives favorable witness of his artistic judgment. He knew how to take a large and expansive view.

Dom Jean-Marie very soon became attached to his new novice, without showing it by any particular signs of affection. That was hardly his way.

Brother Gabriel tried at first to adopt the methods of meditation then in use in the novitiate; in the process he almost lost the little Latin he had. Father Placid, the novice master, very wisely counseled him to abandon himself to the attractions of

[2] In the article cited in note 30, Dr. Coubard calls the monk P. M., but the monks of Bellefontaine remember that it is Père Marie.

[3] Dr. Ch. Coubard, "Un Cénobite dans les Mauges au XXe siècle, Dom Jean-Marie Chouteau, Abbé de Bellefontaine et des Gardes, 1841–1929" in *Bull. de la Soc. des Sc., Lettres et Beaux Arts de Cholet* (1931) 62.

grace, and to continue to talk to God spontaneously, as he had done previously, in the very free way that children do. Father Master's teaching was very discreet, just as he was very discreet personally. At his school the novice learned to do all things well and to live in the presence of God, attending to his monastic duties carefully and humbly.

But it was especially Father Louis, the prior, who exercised a lasting influence on Brother Gabriel. He had as yet lived only a few years in the monastery, as we have already had occasion to notice, since he entered Bellefontaine in 1917. When Brother Sortais began to resort to him, he was an old man of 70, slightly bent and walking with a limp. He had courage and optimism in every trial. He was good, open, understanding and sympathetic to the souls who came to him. He had a warm heart; in his presence one felt immediately at ease. During his many years in the ministry, he had acquired much experience in guiding souls; at the time Brother Gabriel entered, Father Louis was still living the monastic life with the fervor of a novice. The monks found in him many human qualities which were lacking in their Abbot. Father Louis' chapter sermons were, in the words of Father Sortais, "an incomparable feast."

Life at Bellefontaine in 1924 was hard. The monks got up at 2:00 A.M. The canonical office was usually not sung. The hours of the canonical office were accompanied by those of the little Office of Our Lady. At the conventual Mass, celebrated at 9:00 A.M. (after Tierce), the harsh, untrained voices of the monks were lifted up to the vaulted ceiling of the church, executing the beautiful slow chants of the Cistercian Gradual sometimes well and sometimes poorly. Manual work took up a considerable time. Sometimes the monks returned from work late, and their spiritual reading suffered from this. Until 1928 the monks had nothing to eat until the noon meal on the numerous fast days. On these days ten long hours had to pass between rising and the first meal of the day. Silence was broken only for the necessary exchanges with the superiors. A novice might pass many days without having occasion to speak. As for family visits, they were limited to three days a year.

Father Gabriel kept shining memories of his novitiate, as though it were a time of courtship. He often avowed, "I found nothing but objects of love."[4] He attributed this to God's compassion and tender love. "I would not have been able to fight," he said. "I would not have known how. So the Lord arranged it that I would have no trials, either as a postulant or as a novice. God keeps the wind away from the shorn lamb."[5] But it is also true that his own generosity was complete and knew no halfway measures. "I was then just about 23 years old, and I was completely given to the good God. I do not remember having searched out anyone or anything except God in my first year of novitiate. I lived with Mary, and she gave me that thirst for God, which is the objective of our observances, as well as of our sacrifices."[6]

This novice felt happy and in perfect accord with the Cistercian life. His days were filled, and they were full of God.[7] After the years of struggle and the sadness of breaking away, he knew for some months an unmixed joy. He felt invaded by a sense of fullness in his continual contact with God, for whose sake the smallest actions of the day were undertaken, who is the reason for every act of cloistered life.

In 1961 Dom Gabriel would have the idea of composing a circular letter to the monks of the order on the middle age crisis. There one can read this passage in which one cannot help seeing an autobiographical tint:

> (When they were novices, these monks) prayed virtually all the time, almost without realizing it. They had been taught methods of meditation, but these seemed forced to them, and to practice them, almost useless. They did not, as a matter of fact, have very far to seek for a subject for their conversation with God, and they had no need to find out from books how a son ought to talk to his Father. They expressed to the Lord their repentance and their thankfulness, and then they told him, well or badly, about their love. And this filial outpouring invariably ended in protestations of

[4] Chat for the occasion of completing 30 years of religious life.

[5] Letter to X, July 23, 1958.

[6] Letter to X, August 13, 1952.

[7] "We had the rule of silence, and it seemed beautiful to me to spend two or three days without saying a word to anyone except to God in the Office." Admission to a niece.

> confidence and of abandonment. "Why have I been seeking my happiness for so long away from you, Lord? It is so good to know that one is loved by his God and to love him in turn with a full heart! Yes Lord, I love you, I trust in you, I abandon myself to you . . ." And at times tears of love would come rolling sweetly down their cheeks to testify in their own way to the truth of these sentiments.[8]

In his subjection to the Rule, Brother Gabriel found liberation from all the constraints experienced elsewhere. Only those remained which he had voluntarily assumed when he came to Bellefontaine. And so he took obedience and dependence as a matter of course, he who not long ago had shown evidence of such independence of character. Peace possessed him completely. His vitality, his native energy, his dynamism found employment within, in the depths of his soul. So he felt an impression of moral health and equilibrium. As often happens in the first weeks of monastic life, Brother Gabriel underwent a rapid transformation, when new conditions liberated profound vital forces, kept below the surface or restrained by the more external forces until that time.

The ardent and tumultuous nature of the young man was rapidly disciplined. The enthusiastic effervescence of his energies changed into a tranquil forcefulness. Those who met him were struck by the novice's interiority. He breathed joy and serenity. One of his old friends said he was "struck by his amiable humility . . . He was a man of God, humble and peaceful."[9] A deep work, then, was undertaken from the very first months of his monastic life. In the absence of autobiographical documents, it is hard to grasp the details of its progress.

Monastic life permitted the novice to experience heart-to-heart solitude with God. The great silence of La Trappe favored this, although the monk was continually among his brothers, even when at his own tasks and during hours of sleep. In September or October 1924 Brother Gabriel spent a week at a hospital in Cholet in very unusual circumstances, and he thus learned something of what the Carthusian life might entail. Because he had a

[8] Notes for a circular letter on the middle-age crisis, 1961.
[9] Letter of July 19, 1967.

contagious disease, he was placed in an isolated room where he saw no one and remained alone; he had only his rosary.

He applied himself to do everything for the love of God in complete purity of intention. "It is for Jesus and for Jesus alone that we came," Father Gabriel was to say in a talk to the novices at the Abbey of Igny,[10] where he was to share some memories of his own novitiate, "not for Mother Mistress or Mother Abbess whom we did not even know a few years ago. They are only creatures . . . ."[11]

Life in the great outdoors pleased him. He loved to find himself among things of nature, and we can discover in his soul on this point something of the Franciscan. Nature "speaks loudly of God" to him. There he finds himself disposed for prayer.

Brother Gabriel took great care to preserve silence, in order to remain intimate with God, even when working with an indiscreet brother who pestered him with questions to get him to talk. Along with that we find a religious respect for obedience, which he gradually learned to make more interior, more supple, and more intelligent. He saw in that above all a way to unite his will to God's and to show the Lord his love.

Until 1943 Father Gabriel kept a little notebook in which he jotted down a certain number of the graces he received in the novitiate: lights on the greatness and perfection of God and on the mystery of the intimate life of the three divine persons. He showed it to the priest who was his confessor at the time, and then he destroyed it. This is regrettable, because this document would certainly give us the key of his spiritual development.

Contemplation of Our Lady and the saying of the rosary gained precious graces for him, with tears of joy and tenderness. He often cried at Vespers, when the monks sang the Magnificat. He also cried during his short visits to the icon of Our Lady of Perpetual Help which was in the little apse which opened on to the north arm of the transept—"almost every time"—he said.

[10] Igny was a monastery founded by St. Bernard about 20 miles west of Reims in northern France. It was completely destroyed in World War I and subsequently rebuilt as an abbey for Trappistines. *Dictionnaire d'Histoire,* op. cit., t. 25, cols. 749–52.

[11] Talk at the novitiate of Igny, May 1963.

The famous "Salve," which is sung after Compline, had made a strong impression on him the first time he came to Bellefontaine. "Picture the church at dusk, the choir in total darkness . . . a 13th-century image of the Virgin illuminated by two large candles. Not a sound. You might think the church is empty. Suddenly you hear the voices of 40 men rise towards their Mother and their Queen. *Salve Regina,* part psalmody, part chant, sung very slowly. . . ."[12]

Another very joyful moment was on his bed during the siesta at the beginning of the afternoon. Instead of sleeping, he was in the habit of saying the rosary, and it was for him a time of interior illumination on the life and mysteries of Our Lady and her Son.

During the first few months of 1925, Dom Jean-Marie Chouteau arranged for Bellefontaine's retreat to be preached by Father Martin.[13] This priest had been a devotee of Thérèse of Lisieux since 1908. He allowed himself to be formed by the spiritual teaching of this saint, who had sweetened everything in his demanding nature that was too absolute or intransigent. In the whole region of the Vendée his name alone was heard, for the crowds were charmed by his eloquence, somewhat like a similar occurrence in the days of Louis Grignion de Montfort.[14] When the war was over Father Martin had been made superior of the diocesan missionaries of Luçon,[15] the Missionaries of the

[12] Letter to a cousin, July 30, 1922.

[13] Gabriel Martin was born at Chavagnes-en-Paillers, a Vendée commune, on April 21, 1873, and ordained priest on Dec. 19, 1896. He became director of the diocesan missionaries in 1904. His reading of the *Story of a Soul* in 1908 launched his career as a preacher of the Little Way. *Catholicisme,* op. cit., t. 8, cols. 758–59.

[14] Saint Louis-Marie Grignion de Montfort is perhaps best known to American Catholics as the author of *True Devotion to the Blessed Virgin Mary.* The French, however, remember him as a devoted missionary and founder of religious orders. He was born at Montfort-sur-Meu in 1673. In 1706 he made a pilgrimage to Rome and was given an audience with the Holy Father, Pope Clement XI, who sent him back to France as an apostolic missionary. He left an indelible impression on the population of the Vendée and the region of Nantes. One of his most characteristic traits was indeed his devotion to Our Lady; others were his penitential life and heroic obedience. He founded the Daughters of Wisdom and the Montfort Fathers and wrote their rules. He died in 1716 at the age of 43. He was canonized in 1947. Ibid., t. 7, cols. 1128–30.

[15] Luçon is on the western coast of France, in the southern part of the Ven-

Plain, whose principal house is at St.-Michel-en-l'Herm,[16] a former monastic property. This was in 1921. He also laid the foundations of the Congregation of the Oblates of St. Thérèse. Louis Chaigne[17] characterized him as a "pilgrim of the Absolute" who "did not live in our dimension."

"Sometimes the florid, expansive, even affected style of his writings are deceptive, because his interior style is fiery. His rhetorical images—those I'm thinking of here at any rate—give a false impression about his deeper feelings which were rarely calm and were easily moved to outbursts of enthusiasm."[18]

Father Martin had all it took to captivate a novice whose temperament was—with some slight differences—parallel to his own. The preacher spoke of the seriousness of the time: In 1924–25 the government seemed disposed to renew the anti-Christian policy of the beginning of the century. All over France, especially in the Vendée, mass movements organized to protest, and Catholics united to safeguard their liberties.

But Father Martin spoke especially about Thérèse of Lisieux who would be canonized by Pius XI the following May 17. He also spoke about abandoned souls who were the torment of his missionary soul.

Brother Gabriel immediately began reading the *Little Way of Spiritual Childhood* which Father Martin had published in 1923. He copied out numerous excerpts from it in his notebook. He also reread *The Story of a Soul* which he had already read before entering Bellefontaine and *Novissima Verba.* Finally he plunged into the *Life of St. Thérèse* by Msgr. Laveille.

As the crowning point of this profound experience, on the very day when the saint of Lisieux was canonized, Brother

---

dée, about 50 miles south of Nantes. *Webster's Geographical,* op. cit., 412–13.

[16] St.-Michel-en-l'Herm is a small commune on a hillock in the marshland of Poitou on the west coast of France. It belongs to the Vendée. *Larousse,* op. cit., t. 9, p. 528.

[17] Louis Chaigne was a poet and critic, another son of the *Vendée,* born at Talmont, near Les Sables d'Olonne. His *Vendéen* origin had a strong influence on his literary art. At least three of his works are devoted to his compatriots. A childhood illness led him to emphasize the interior aspects of the people he wrote about. *Catholicisme,* op. cit., t. 2, cols. 857–58.

[18] L. Chaigne, *Témoin de la vérité vivante, Mgr. Gabriel Martin* (1873–1949) (Paris: B. Grasset, 1961) 217.

Gabriel pronounced the Act of Consecration to Merciful Love. He would feel the effects of this all his life. He did not allow himself to be frightened by the demands of divine love, but delivered himself up without reserve.

> In order that my life may be an act of perfect love, I offer myself as a holocaust victim to your merciful love, beseeching you to consume me without rest and to let the flood of infinite compassion which is confined in your heart flow into my soul, that I may become in this way a martyr of your love, my God. After this martyrdom has prepared me to appear before you, may it end in causing my death, that my soul may throw itself immediately into the eternal embrace of your merciful love.

It was to allow himself to be loved by God, to allow himself to be devoured and consumed by God's love, not to love in his own way or to keep the initiative in this intimate relationship with God, but to abandon himself to the demands of divine love, without program and without self-consideration—this is what Brother Gabriel, following in St. Thérèse's footsteps, wanted to do.

Actually this novice could not yet distinguish what was essential from what was accidental, and his superiors did not watch him closely enough. He was so glad to use up his energy that he exhausted the supply. He did not try to moderate his generosity, and this led him to acts of imprudence. Although his bed was too short for his six-foot-three frame, he did not tell the Father Master about it, and for several nights he could not rest properly; his 24-year-old body was not getting its proper quota of sleep, yet he did not think he needed to sleep during the hour of siesta which the Trappists call "meridian," and which is supposed to make up for the shortened nights in the summer season. His thirst for penance and reparation for souls made him a rival in feats of mortification of food and drink to the most formidable ascetics in the community. This competitive spirit might have made him lose sight of the essential Trappist vocation, had he not been motivated by such a powerful love. As it was, it brought him to the point of physical exhaustion, and it definitely compromised his health. One day in 1926, two months before profession, he was cleaning windows and felt he could do no more. Dr. Coubard was called; he prescribed a complete rest with long hours in bed and a meat diet. But with an abbot like Dom Jean-Marie, the doctor's mind was never at ease. He himself jokingly wrote, "I remember that I was frequently called to Bellefontaine to care for religious who were more or less exhausted. When the visit was over, I had to report to Father Abbot, and it was sometimes necessary to mention rest, bed, and meat diet. . . . Dom Chouteau, with his hand cupped behind his ear would listen indulgently, wagging his head, and he would say, 'Yes, of course, whatever you wish, whatever is necessary!' But the expression on his face would become skeptical, and a wrinkle would take shape between his nose and upper lip. Yes, he would show the sick monk all the fatherly care he could, and he would be ready to relieve him in every possible way, but at the same time in the depth of his being, the mentality of those who have always enjoyed an iron constitution remained unmoved. . . . Really, what are these strange lingering sicknesses that oblige a man, even if he is a Trappist, to lie stretched out on a couch, and to eat like a king?"[19]

No doubt the doctor thought of the case of Brother Gabriel when he wrote these lines. After the latter had spent one brief morning stretched out by the pond in complete rest in the open air, Father Abbot came to him and said, "Well, little brother, is it over? Are you rested? Are you cured?" Dr. Coubard gave up renewing his prescription.

In any case there was now no question of Brother Gabriel's asking to become a lay brother. That door was definitely closed to him now. He was not without regrets, but he saw in it a clear indication of God's will, which he accepted with simplicity, and he entrusted the future to the Lord. "There is more humility in remaining as one is," he would write to a monk years later, "than in thinking up more humiliation, more meekness or more self-effacement."[20]

Neither the abbot nor the community had any difficulty in admitting a sick novice to profession. It was hoped that with rest

[19] Dr. Ch. Coubard, op. cit., 62.

[20] Letter of March 3, 1960, to a religious priest who wanted to transfer to the lay brothers.

Brother Sortais' seemingly strong constitution would return. The date for the ceremony of profession was set for the feast of St. Bernard, August 20, 1926. The novice made two promises to the Blessed Virgin during his retreat, similar to the self-offering suggested by Louis Grignion de Montfort, "to give her the disposal of all my prayers and sacrifices throughout my life, so that she may use for her own purposes whatever I may have done with some other intention in mind"; "to turn over Jesus to her at each communion as soon as I shall have received him, so that she may rejoice in him and love him as though she herself had received Communion." In the spring he had already made over to Our Lady all the merit he might acquire and all the prayers for his intention that would be offered for him after his death. During his novitiate, then, he endeavored to apply the essential spiritual message of St. Thérèse of Lisieux and of St. Louis Grignion de Montfort concretely to his monastic life.

On August 20, 1926, then, the feast of St. Bernard, Brother Gabriel came down laboriously from the infirmary to the Chapter Room for the ceremony of temporary profession. Afterwards he immediately retired to the infirmary again, where he would remain for three more years.

Chapter 5

THE NIGHT OF FAITH

On making temporary profession, Brother Sortais automatically left the novitiate and the jurisdiction of the novice master. It was a cruel parting in the circumstances in which he found himself. From one day to the next he encountered complete solitude. Father Abbot saw him in passing each day, but he never stayed very long, because he did not know what to say. The infirmarians brought his meals, and Father Louis, the prior, came to hear his confession once a week. That was all. Father Prior who was otherwise so attentive thought the novice master would continue visiting and caring for his former charge. This almost complete absence of any signs of affection was a grievous trial for him during the months of his illness. In permitting it, God reached a sensitive point, that part of Sortais' soul which was least prepared for complete renunciation. He was affectionate by nature, and every kind of friendship, often the most intimate and trusting, responded to a need in his heart. The Lord really wanted him for himself alone.

"A centuries-old tradition has it," he would write years later, "that a monk who suffers should be treated in such a way that he should have no reason to regret his mother's absence.[1] Believe me, I have known suffering myself, and I feel deep, fatherly compassion for you. Like St. Bernard to the Abbot of Foigny, I can write to each one of my sons in complete honesty, 'I cannot help suffering when you suffer, and I cannot hear of your grief without sharing it.'"[2]

[1] Dom Sortais, *Les choses qui plaisent à Dieu,* 1st ed. (Bégrolles-en-Mauges: Bellefontaine, 1968) 196.

[2] Ibid., 191. See also Ep. 73.1 in *S. Bernardi Opera,* ed. J. Leclercq and H. Rochais (Rome: Editiones Cistercienses, 1974) vol. VII, 179, ll. 6–8: *Nec enim te*

An echo of the experience of the young professed can be heard in these lines that Dom Gabriel wrote a few years later, "If isolation deprives the sick monk of physical contact with the community and is detrimental in a way we cannot pass off, we must concede that this enforced retreat is not without real advantages. . . . He enjoys more solitude and finds more silence and recollection. And if he accepts all these deprivations, he will even come to see one day that his union with his monastic family, though it may not be as obvious as before, is still more real. For community life does not consist only in physical contact, it is above all a fellowship of souls. If the sick monk in living apart no longer enjoys the physical presence of his brothers, still he knows that his sacrifice will be helpful to them, and that he himself benefits from their prayers."[3]

Every day at Mass Brother Gabriel renewed the offering of his profession at the moment of consecration; he found in that a source of renewed energy. On October 16, 1926, in view of his coming entry into the clerical state, he asked his abbot for permission to make the offering of himself to merciful love again. The Lord did not delay his response long, for he plunged the young professed monk into a night of abandonment similar to that which the saint of Lisieux experienced.

It was easy to find in the works of Maurras many a proposition that a Catholic could not accept and many tendencies which were hard to reconcile with orthodox teaching. Maurras knew this himself, and he had corrected many of his republished works, so that they might not scandalize or simply wound many of his Catholic friends and disciples. Since 1910 or 1911 his works had been undergoing the scrutiny of the Congregation of the Index at the request of certain bishops. In 1913 Cardinal Billot thought a

---

dolente possum non dolere. Foigny was an abbey along the northeastern border of France (*The Cistercians*, op. cit., 488; *Dictionnaire d'Histoire*, op. cit., t. 17, col. 717). In his notes in the *Commentary on the Rule of St. Benedict*, Chap. 36, we read, "I know some monasteries where the abbot reproaches himself if he lets a single day go by without going to see his suffering sons, unless he has a good reason. . . . His suffering sons . . . it is enough to say these two words to understand. If the religious are really like sons to the abbot, and if these sons really suffer, it does not seem that a daily visit is excessive. What mother or father of a family would disagree with what I have just said?"

[3] Dom Sortais, op. cit., 192–93.

condemnation was unavoidable, unless the Holy Father should suspend the decision, on the grounds that it was inopportune. This is what Saint Pius X did, for he saw in Maurras, "a great defender of the Church and of the Holy See," and he saw no point in destroying a movement in which for other reasons he saw many positive aspects. The Pope, then, suspended the decree of January 26, 1914. In April 1915 Benedict XV considered the opportuneness of publishing the decree of the Congregation of the Index; the international situation caused him to come to a negative conclusion. Pius XI would not intervene before 1925. But he was disturbed by the influence exercised on the young by *Action Française,* by the favor the movement enjoyed with the majority of French bishops, and with many rectors of seminaries. The development of Catholic Action in independent milieus did not seem possible, as long as the young people of Maurras' school kept generating enthusiasm for political objectives. Again, Pius XI did not believe at all in the intransigent nationalism of the school; besides, he thought there was a possibility of international conciliation, thanks to the actions of democratic governments and to men like Briand, the bugbear of *Action Française.* He judged that the line taken by its journal was productive of bad results, because it was so aggressive. Of Maurras himself whose works he kept on his shelves for a considerable period the Holy Father said, "He has one of the greatest minds of the epoch. No one knows it better than I. But he has only a mind . . . reason is not enough, and it never has been enough. . . . Christ is a stranger to him. . . . [He sees] the church as an outsider, not as an insider. . . . [His journal] does not understand religion or understands it wrongly; it uses religion, instead of being content to serve it."

Did the Pope foresee that a condemnation would destroy one of the moral resources of the country at a time when other forms of nationalism (and first of all in Italy), which were dangerous and hurtful for other reasons, were affirming themselves? The crisis of conscience undergone by the Catholics in *Action Française* is explained by the interplay of national and international tensions.

Besides, the affair was poorly managed. The Holy See asked Cardinal Andrieu, archbishop of Bordeaux, to inform the faithful about the errors of *Action Française.* The prelate did so in a way that was very approximative in "Response to a Question asked by a Group of Young Catholics about *Action Française.*" This document (August 27, 1926) was full of oversimplifications and inaccurate quotations. On September 5 Pius XI sent a letter of approval, which pointed out certain errors for which the publications of *Action Française* should be blamed, but it did not modify the document of condemnation, so that the Pope seemed to make the response of the cardinal of Bordeaux his own, with all its inexactitudes.

During the last four months of the year, several French bishops and laymen made attempts at conciliation with the Holy See but without success. Some imprudent and controversial declarations provoked a fulminating response from the Holy Father on December 24, on the occasion of his consistorial allocution. Immediately afterward the journal was placed on the Index (December 29). There followed on March 8, 1927, extremely severe sanctions, fixed by the Apostolic Penitentiary. No movement within the church in modern times was dealt with so rigorously. The inflexibility of the leaders of *Action Française* was partly to blame.

It was probably in the first days of January that the abbot of Bellefontaine informed the community about Pius XI's condemnation of the movement. There was hardly any political feeling in the monastery, and the journals were not read habitually. Had there not been an old brother during the expulsions of 1880 who said, "But what have we done to our good King Louis-Philippe, that he should evict us?" Brother Gabriel immediately knew the extent of the drama and the anguish of conscience that it would cause in his friends, to say nothing of their families. That day he went to confide his pain to Father Louis, a stranger to the movement and ignorant of the problems involved: "But all they have to do is submit!"

Feeling sad at the lack of understanding from the one who knew him best, the young monk went to the church, and there in front of the altar of the Sacred Heart, he asked for the grace of complete abandonment, without looking back. His soul was so docile, so used to self-giving already, that it offered no resistance. "The good God made me give up *Action Française*" is what he wrote in his notebook.

But the others! He was overcome with anguish for them. Would they not be lost in the storm? What would become of their adhesion to the church, of their Christian life, and of their faith?

In his generosity, Brother Gabriel felt himself inclined to offer himself for those he loved, that they might receive superabundantly the graces necessary for complete abandonment. At that very moment it seemed to him that his faith was gone, that heaven was shut up, and that God had disappeared from his life. The nonexistence of God appeared to impose itself on him, like an absolute proof, which he rejected with all his might.[4]

It is natural to think at this point of the last trial of Thérèse of Lisieux. "At the joyful season of Easter Jesus made me understand that there truly are souls that have no faith, who, by abusing grace, lose this precious treasure, source of the only pure and true joy. He allowed my soul to be invaded by the thickest darkness, and he permitted the thought of heaven, which was so sweet to me, to become no more than an occasion for struggle and torment. . . . This trial would not last only a few days or a few weeks; indeed, it would not be over until the time chosen by the good God . . . and this time had not yet come . . . you would have to travel in this dreary tunnel to know its darkness."

For Brother Gabriel every reason to go on living seemed to have vanished. Everything was dark. He groped his way along, no longer knowing whether God existed, nor why he had come to the monastery. His life had become devoid of meaning, and his happiness as a novice had disappeared, lost in complete doubt. His faith was untouched, whatever he may have thought about it, but he had been deprived of all awareness of possessing it, and his intelligence was no longer able to contact his faith in that part of his soul where it had retired. Brother Gabriel struggled in revolt against the false evidence that his reason

[4] The sources which allow us to know of this interior drama are essentially his first notebook of intimate records and admissions he later made to certain religious. In his commentary on the Rule, these notes on *Action Française* are found: "The Press. With some very rare exceptions, each one allows himself to be governed by his Journal and takes his votes and attitudes accordingly (Condemnation of *Action Française* because of the influence of the daily reading of a man one loves, who does not admit the supernatural)." Chapter 7, n. 2.

wished to impose upon him. He would not agree to doubt God whose silence was his unbearable torment. He was completely disoriented. The trial of faith, added to the trial of his sickness and the solitude which accompanied it, left him completely helpless. Our Lady also became remote. In this storm he no longer had the recourse of "fixing his eyes on the star."

"You know very well, Lord, that I love you!" he wrote in his notebook. Father Louis helped him by his kindness, understanding and affection, but what could the best spiritual father do in such a case?

Brother Gabriel resolved to remain faithful to his God, to the church, and to the Holy Father, whose severity he did not understand. Over his heart he carried the Pope's picture. "Where Peter is, there is the church," he wrote in his personal notebook. "Anyone who does not have the church for a mother cannot have God for a father." Yet he later confided to one of his monks, "That Pope wounded me." What kept him in the monastery was the fear of disturbing the vocation of any brother by his departure.

In his distress and anguish, he did not hesitate to renew the Consecration to Merciful Love at regular intervals: June 3, 1927 (first Friday of the month); September 30, 1927; October 3, 1928; September 30, 1929.

He decided to become an apostle of complete submission, preaching this to his friends at every opportunity, even at the risk of alienating those who had confidence in him. The drama brought on by the several who refused obedience caused him great distress. Nevertheless, he did have the happiness of leading a few back to the path of duty.

Brother Gabriel's drawn face and sorrowful look betrayed his interior sufferings to those who saw him. They could see he was tense and afflicted. Some monks who noticed it spoke of it to the prior. To them it seemed that he did not flourish in the monastic life, and they wondered if he would persevere. Father Louis was rather perplexed. He was unable to see clearly the trial that his young disciple was undergoing.

Nevertheless, Brother Sortais had begun his philosophical studies. Father Subprior came to give him some classes which did not do him much good, since the professor could hardly get beyond the text of Farges and Barbettes, which he was using. Brother Gabriel's own hard work made up the gap. He studied theology with Father Louis who was a true professor but had only limited time at his disposal. The young professed monk was using Tanquerey to learn Thomistic philosophy and theology.

The three years of temporary vows passed without any notable change in the monk's interior state. His health slowly improved, but his external deportment remained the same. God was leading Brother Gabriel imperceptibly and sustaining him, even if he himself thought he had no faith. Several of the seniors had noticed some slight indications of the predilection Dom Chouteau had for the young monk. They willingly made use of his mediation to let Dom Jean-Marie know what they would not dare tell him to his face, for fear of an outburst.

One day Brother Gabriel was awarded an undeserved scolding in the presence of Father Prior, and the latter ordered him to go find Father Abbot and explain the matter to him, "and then," he added, "you are to tell Reverend Father that everyone is afraid of him, because of his quick temper."

So the monk went to see the abbot at a peaceable hour, and finding him in good humor, told him what had really taken place, then, "Reverend Father, Father Prior asked me to tell you something else."

"What is it, Brother Gabriel?"

"Well, Reverend Father, Father Prior asked me to tell you that the community is afraid of you!"

"Afraid of me? Why?"

"It is because, Reverend Father, you sometimes scold us so harshly!"

Father Abbot reflected a few minutes, then he grasped Brother Gabriel's arm.

"Brother Gabriel," he said, "you are my best friend. Nobody has ever dared tell me what you just told me. I'll keep it in mind."

Next time he saw the young monk, Dom Chouteau told him, "Brother Gabriel, remember what you told me some time ago? You see, I'm working on it!"

Finally came summer 1929, and the three years of temporary vows were almost up. Father Prior did not venture any advice, and Brother Gabriel wondered if making solemn profession in the situation in which he was (without God and without faith, as he thought) was not a mere farce. The matter was placed before Dom Chouteau. "I remember it still. It was evening, and I was alone in a room from which I could see the red lines of sunset on the horizon. I was in utter desolation, and I didn't know what to do. Should I return to the world? This held no attraction for me. What should I do? Commit suicide? What good would that do? In my distress I resolved to obey blindly whatever advice I should receive."[5]

Dom Chouteau advised him to make solemn profession. The feast of St. Bernard in 1929 brought no relief from his trial. Father Sortais made his solemn vows in complete darkness.

Father Abbot had just celebrated his 88th birthday on the feast of SS. Peter and Paul; on December 5 he would celebrate the 63rd anniversary of his abbatial election. "Great oaks fall all at once," wrote Dr. Coubard. "Dom Jean-Marie was sick only a short time."[6] In fact he became exhausted at Christmas. "This time I think the end has come." Nevertheless, he said his three Masses, then on the following day he said the Mass of St. Stephen. Next day, December 27, he went to bed. "You ought to send for the doctor," the prior told him. "I never needed the doctor to stay alive, and I don't need him in order to die." At 11 o'clock on the night of December 28, the feast of the Holy Innocents, his life ended, after he had struggled up until the final breath.

The bishop of Angers, flanked by six abbots of the order, celebrated his funeral Mass on the last day of the year. At Bellefontaine the monastic cemetery is in the préau in the cloister, and there are four great black cypress trees growing in it. The abbot's body went down softly to the bottom of the grave in the thin light of a beautiful winter morning.

Unfortunately, Father Louis, the prior, caught a cold while standing in the cemetery. His 76 years had no resistance to make against the serious influenza which then developed. Brother

[5] Confession to a young female cousin in 1957. He also confided to a nun, "The only temptation I have not had is the temptation against my vocation: that would be terrible."

[6] Dr. Ch. Coubard, op. cit., 73.

Gabriel was in despair. With Father Louis he would lose his last human support. He visited Father Prior in the infirmary and asked him the reason for his trial. "I do not know. Temptations against faith ordinarily come to souls farther advanced than you. Perhaps you are destined to become a superior at a very early age, and in order to guide others, it is necessary for you to undergo this trial."

On the evening of January 4, Father Louis was very sick. "Oh Father, I can't go on any longer!" said the young monk. "When you arrive before God, intercede for me." "I promise you," returned Father Louis, "you are the first one about whom I will speak to God."

Next day the bell for Matins rang at 2:00 A.M. as usual, and Brother Gabriel got out of bed. His anguish was over. Light shone again in his soul. "It was as if you would flick the switch of an electric light," he told one of his relatives, "and it would immediately go on. I recovered my faith completely, with no uncertainty at all, just like a child, and not the least doubt has ever troubled me since."[7] A half-hour earlier Father Louis had breathed his last.

[7] Admission to a young female cousin.

Chapter 6

MONK AND PRIOR

Brother Gabriel's trial of faith had come to an end. It had been painful and had been accompanied by the collapse of all that had excited him in his ardent youth. It had seemed to him that the church had rejected that teaching by means of which alone his country could have found health and balance. No other circumstance could have made the trial harder to bear. It had reached a point where his physical resistance had ceased. He had lived in the infirmary, on the fringe of the community. He had had to deepen his sense of vocation and to realize that the essence of monastic life was to be found much deeper than the observances and external forms with which it was clothed, that it was possible to be a monk even without the choral offices, without fasting, without work, and without common life.

"What God asks of us and what Jesus expects of us is not the more or less perfect execution of such and such a practice, but the realization of that for which the practice has been instituted, namely union with God, resemblance to Jesus by love. . . . Office, private prayer, reading, meditation have the purpose of making God enter our lives. Now God enters our lives mainly by suffering. This suffering which blocks all the acts of piety that give us God, becomes now the act that unites us to God. It is no longer a question of hopelessly trying to overcome a weakness that is not our fault. . . . It is a question of accepting fully the means he has given us of actually being united to him. . . . In the very same measure in which it deprives us of everything, suffering takes the place of everything in us. . . . Remember that unique end that St. Benedict proposes for himself: to lead the monk to perfect love."[1]

[1] Dom Sortais, op. cit., 193–95.

His sickness, far from placing him out of reach of the conditions of sanctification for which he had come to Bellefontaine, effectively led him to God by a way which St. Benedict had clearly foreseen. "You remain solid in your vocation," he would write to sick monks, "when you observe the regulations that have been foreseen for your situation; in order to conform your lives to the prescriptions of your superior, you remain in obedience, and so you are just as authentic monks as your brothers are."[2]

Brother Gabriel's faith also emerged in strength from the dark night which it had undergone. His faith was unmarred, because he had refused the denials that had seemed to his intelligence necessarily to impose themselves. His faith had remained living, and it had inspired, beyond his own perception and awareness, every one of his actions, unceasingly guiding him towards the God he no longer saw. "Trees that grow where there are strong winds," he later told a young monk, "have stronger roots than others. And souls that live and grow amidst temptations against faith are also more deeply rooted. . . . At this moment the good God calls. . . . What about you? What role will you agree to play in the great work of redemption? . . . Will you ask for grace, or will you follow Jesus to Calvary?"[3]

Father Prior's death, just a few days after that of Dom Chouteau, deprived the abbey of Bellefontaine of its leadership. Father Louis was old, but he was also experienced, very wise, and used to governing. He understood the monastery's problems very well. Dom Jean-Marie was used to directing everything himself, and he was, it seems, not worried about the morrow. The future was not prepared.

The community cast their votes on February 10, 1930, for a monk who was still young, Father Jean-Baptiste Auger, a *Vendéen* of delicate health, and by temperament a bit slow. He had entered Bellefontaine in 1911, and had been performing the duties of procurator. The new abbot kept in his office the provisional prior designated by the abbot of La Grande-Trappe at the death of Father Louis, Father Arsène Grimault, the oldest monk

[2] Ibid., 95.

[3] Letter to a young monk.

in the community, who was much preoccupied with his charge of confessor for the guests.

Brother Gabriel continued his theological studies, and while making use of some dispensations, took up the regular life again, from which his ill health had so long kept him. His health grew strong, though it would never again be robust. He would be declared unfit for military service by the board of examiners on May 9, 1932, and relieved of all military obligations.

Following Lacordaire's advice, he tried to be a monk "up to the neck" without reserve, accepting joys and sufferings great and small, which each day might bring. "True happiness here below," he said, "consists in enslaving oneself to God's love. If one truly loves God, one will suffer much—that is understood—but there is also much joy, because, no longer seeking happiness in anything but God, you are always sure that being loved will always make you love, that he will never change, and that you will always discover new depths of tenderness and beauty in him. After having sought your happiness in God alone, you will finish by no longer seeking anything but God's happiness."[4]

"It is a good sign, when you notice that you can no longer resist love, that you are ill at ease and even unhappy, if you did not give everything to him who asks everything. You know very well when you accept one sacrifice, that another one will be asked of you later, but I repeat, it is a good sign, because you know that love is insatiable, and you give it to him, merely because you would be unhappy if you did not give it."[5]

Brother Sortais profited from the time that his studies and manual work left free to do some reading. Saint Teresa of Ávila, St. John of the Cross, St. Francis de Sales, Père Grou,[6] Father

[4] Letter to a young monk, August 26, 1935.

[5] Letter to a nun, November 2, 1958.

[6] Père Jean-Nicolas Grou, born at Calais on Nov. 23, 1731, entered the Jesuits in 1746, at the age of 15. Having completed his studies, he was assigned to teach the humanities at La Flèche. When the Jesuits were suppressed in France, he went to Lorraine. After a year in the novitiate at Nancy, he was assigned to teach Greek (1764) at the University of Pont-à-Mousson. When the Jesuits were suppressed in Lorraine, he returned to Paris. He produced some important translations of Plato's *Republique* (Paris, 1762), *Lois* (Paris, 1769) and *Dialogues* (Amsterdam, 1770). He is best known for his books on the spiritual life: *Caractères de la vrai dévotion; Méditations en forme de retraite sur l'amour de Dieu; Max-*

Faber,[7] Monsignor Gay,[8] and Elizabeth of the Trinity were his favorite authors. He also liked the theology of St. Alphonsus Liguori. There is much uncertainty about the exact period in which he read each of these authors. But they left their mark on him. He constantly referred to them afterwards.

It also appears that he wanted to go deeply into the thought of the great modern spiritual writers of his own order: Dom Vital Lehodey, abbot of Bricquebec, and Dom Jean-Baptiste Chautard, Abbot of Sept-Fons. The former writer's *Ways of Mental Prayer* furnished him with a solid framework on which to place the lectures he was later to give on prayer and his convictions on the primordial place of prayer in a life which claimed to be contemplative. Dom Lehodey would help him to overcome a certain distrust of mysticism, which was too widespread in the order. Dom Chautard was already known to him through Brother Gabriel Mossier's *Life. The Soul of the Apostolate* allowed him to give liturgical prayer its true place in the spiritual life and to see in the "custody of the heart" the keystone of the interior life. He also

---

imes spirituelles; Manuel des ames intérieures, etc. The Jesuits had regrouped in England. Père Grou settled in Lulworth and spent his last years there, until his death in 1803. *Catholicisme,* op. cit., t. 5, col. 313–14.

[7] Frederic William Faber was born of Calvinist parents at Calverley, Yorkshire in 1814. He studied first at Kirby-Stephen, then at Harrow. At Oxford he was strongly influenced by John Henry Newman and the Oxford Movement. Nevertheless, he traveled widely, especially in France and Italy, and had an audience with Pope Gregory XVI in 1843. His conversion to Roman Catholicism took place in November 1845, a month after Newman's. When Newman returned to England in 1847 to set up the Congregation of the Oratory in Birmingham, Faber abandoned the community of converts called Wilfridians, which he had founded, to join Newman. In 1849 he founded the London Oratory. He was much appreciated as a preacher and spiritual writer. He inculcated a very affective, sacrificial piety welcomed by Catholics of the time. His books are: *All for Jesus* (1853); *Growth in Holiness* (1854); *The Blessed Sacrament* (1855); *The Creator and the Creature* (1858); *The Foot of the Cross* (1858); *Spiritual Conferences* (1859); *The Precious Blood* (1860); *Bethlehem* (1860). He died in 1863. Ibid., t. 4, cols. 1031–32.

[8] Charles Louis Gay (1815–92) was a French theologian and spiritual writer. Most of his life was spent in Paris. He was converted by Lacordaire and studied for the priesthood. Ordained in 1845, he became a popular preacher and spiritual director. His books were much appreciated, especially *De la vie et des vertus chrétiennes* (1874) and *Élévations sur la vie et la doctrine de Notre Seigneur Jésus Christ.* His spirituality follows that of Bérulle. He was a theologian at Vatican Council I. *New Catholic Encyclopedia* (New York: McGraw-Hill, 1967) vol. 6, 310.

studied the treatises of prayer by Msgr. Saudreau and Ribet. Later he would gladly go back to the fathers, but they would come to enrich a spirituality that was already formed.

The young monk received the subdiaconate on December 20, 1930, and six months later he was ordained deacon (May 30, 1931). He remained deacon for only one month. On the feast of St. Peter, June 29, 1931, Msgr. Rumeau, the aged bishop of Angers, made him a priest. "The priest ought to be another Christ," he wrote to a nephew in 1944. "But no, that is not the right way to say it. It is less than that. It is less personally *quia pulvis es,* whereas Christ is the eternal Word incarnate. But functionally it is more than another Christ that the priest ought to be. He is Christ himself, an extension of Christ. The priest is Jesus continuing his life in our time; he is Jesus still among us, Jesus made accessible to our senses. The priest, then, since he is Jesus, ought to continue the work of Jesus, in other words, give glory to God and peace to men. That is why the priest has the constant and perpetual duty to look at Jesus and study Jesus, to make him live again in himself. That is the first duty of the priest and the condition for the fruitfulness of all his other actions."[9]

On the next day, the commemoration of St. Paul (June 30), the new priest celebrated his first Mass with his family in the chapel of Notre-Dame de Bon-Secours, among the saints who then surrounded the main altar. He did not like the taste of the furnishings of the sanctuary with its pilasters and cornices, its small back-screens and its false marble. It was not, however, without some charm, and we would perhaps be less severe today toward this neoclassical ensemble, of which some old memorial photographs remain, than he was.

From this day on, Father Gabriel knew the joy of quiet, intimate early morning Masses which the priest-monk celebrated alone in the presence of God and his angels. The consecration was the moment for him to ask graces from the Lord for those for whom he had committed himself to intercede. "At this point of the Mass, you obtain whatever you want. I make no exception: you obtain whatever you want. It is normal."[10] Father Sortais

[9] Letter to a young priest, February 24, 1944.

[10] *Retraite aux Supérieures du Bon-Pasteur d'Angers,* 38.

put great reverence, tenderness and devotion into his gestures. He was convinced that in the gift of the Eucharist are contained all others. "Whatever you ask the Father in my name, I will give you." Commenting on these words of the Lord, Father Sortais said, "I take him at his word which he spoke to us in the Gospel. I tell him, 'If You had not wished to do it, you would not have said it.'"[11] But for his own part, he did not haggle. "I refuse him nothing, so neither can he refuse me."

Father Abbot, beginning in the summer, gave him faculties for confession. He wrote down in his notebook the date of the first absolution he gave: August 14, 1931. For this ministry to guests, he was endowed with special qualities. He was intuitive, and he quickly read the men who addressed themselves to him; he knew how to listen attentively and to inspire confidence; those who approached him understood right away that his was a heart prepared to listen to anything. It was not entirely because of his charm that his penitents were inclined to return. It is possible that they were disconcerted sometimes at his quick spontaneous reactions which surprised them, but they only lasted a moment, and his warm affection immediately returned to disperse the first impression.

Father Gabriel also became the confessor of several members of the community a short time after his ordination. The Christmas sermon of 1931 is probably the first he gave in chapter. Since he was nervous, he wrote it up completely, but soon enough he would acquire some facility and confidence in speaking, and would content himself with a rough outline, informative notes that he would scribble on paper, which he was just about the only one who was able to read.

At the end of February 1932, Dom Jean-Marie Clerc, Father Abbot of La Grande Trappe,[12] came to make the canonical

[11] Confession to a young female cousin.

[12] This name, "La Grande Trappe," goes back to the 19th century and the reform of Dom Augustin de Lestrange. Today the monastery is simply called "La Trappe." The name probably denotes the wilderness or wooded setting. We are familiar with La Trappe as the original monastery of the Trappist reform begun by the Abbot De Rancé. But it actually goes back to the Cistercian origins, having been founded in 1140 and accepted as a filiation of Clairvaux in 1147. It was burned down by the English in the 14th century and became a commendatory

visitation of Bellefontaine, since he was, as they say in the Cistercian order, the Father Immediate of Bellefontaine. It is possible that he suggested to the abbot that he choose a prior who was younger and more resolute than Father Arsène. In any case it so passed that six months later, in the fall of the year, Dom Jean-Baptiste decided to appoint Father Gabriel. However, his timidity kept him from speaking of it to anyone, even to the party most concerned. So one Sunday, toward the end of chapter, Father Abbot declared to the surprise of everyone, his gratitude for the good services of Father Arsène, and made it known that, because of his age and many infirmities, he would have Father Gabriel replace him in the office of prior. The latter had to have the order repeated to him twice, that he was to take the prior's seat. He thought he had heard wrong. He was just 30 years of age.

The duties of prior were never easy with Dom Jean-Baptiste. Father Gabriel made a noble effort to understand the deeper thoughts of his abbot and to conform himself thereto, despite the irritation which some hesitations of his superior must have caused him. His supernatural motivation must have helped him in this, for it made him see the "representative of Christ" in the abbot. When he entered the abbot's quarters in his absence, his first gesture was to kiss the ground as a sign of reverence. By temperament he liked to express his deepest sentiments by eloquent gestures.

"In the monastery," he wrote, "the abbot takes the Lord's place . . .

—He participates in God's authority.

—He participates in God's fatherhood.

—He is called to collaborate closely with God in the sanctification of souls.

"All these prerogatives which manifest the Lord's presence in the Father Abbot are well-fitted to gain him, not only the respect, but the complete filial affection of his religious who know that their union with God depends partly on this superior to whom the Lord has entrusted them. They have need to love him."[13]

---

abbey in the 16th. It is located in the diocese of Séez, in the town of Soligny in Normandy. *New Catholic Encyclopedia*, op. cit., vol. 8, 523–24.

[13] *Les choses qui plaisent à Dieu*, pp. 266–67.

This was certainly his own attitude, inspired by a deep faith. This did not prevent him from seeing the limitations of the man he assisted, nor from sometimes suffering from them. In front of the monks, Father Gabriel always supported the Father Abbot, even if the decision seemed questionable to him. This must have cost him dear many times, for he himself was a man of strong convictions and zealous. In private conversation with Dom Jean-Baptiste he was not afraid to tell him what he thought of some of his decisions, or some of his indecisions. He also kept him from giving in too easily to the whims of his subordinates, or to the fitful moods, from which monks are not exempt. "Nobody knows if he is supernaturally attached to his superiors," he wrote one day, "if he does not have something to suffer from their attitude toward him."[14]

Father Gabriel's firm support of his Father Abbot was proverbial. If the prior had heard the abbot give an order, everyone knew it was useless to try to excuse himself from it, when he was present.

If everyone knew the prior was strict, those who went to him for spiritual direction discovered great understanding and extreme delicacy in the way he tried to help them. He would gently lead their souls to accept difficult situations, trials of obedience, or any other trial. If anyone was away, he would maintain an assiduous correspondence with them, keeping them in touch with the little events of community life, and helping them from afar to preserve the family spirit.

What most surprised monks as well as guests or friends of the monastery who came to him was his availability. He gave himself as if his own life did not belong to him any more.

Before his profession in the spring of 1926, Father Sortais had made Our Lady the beneficiary of all his supernatural acts, "giving up all my merits to her, that she might bestow them on whomever she pleased." He continued to live this consecration to Our Lady, and he never ceased to deepen it. On April 20, 1932, with the permission of, and in submission to his director, he again pronounced his former promises and also made a vow to do always the thing that God would show him to be the most perfect.

[14] Letter to a Prioress, January 17, 1959.

His health, not completely restored since the three years he had spent in the infirmary, suffered from his many occupations. After he became prior, he was extremely careful not to make exceptions for himself. "Besides the sick whose maladies can be seen and whose sufferings are easily understood," he wrote, "there are some religious living in our monasteries whose suffering is less apparent, and whose infirm condition does not always excite a similar compassion. I am thinking of those who, though weak, are not weak enough to go to the infirmary. They continue to live the regular life as well as they can, but it is difficult for them, because everything becomes an occasion of weariness."[15]

His excessive fatigue was related to indigestion. His stomach often forced him "to go on a hunger strike."[16] At the end of the year 1935 the doctor judged it necessary to have his appendix removed. He caught a cold during the blessing of a Lourdes grotto on the infirmary grounds, and the night of the operation he could hardly take the ether. It was feared he would die. "I was threatened with pneumonia, and that would have finished me off in a few days, in view of my general condition. I had developed a serious bronchitis. Jesus allowed me to suffer a lot, for I kept coughing constantly and shaking the wound which was sore. I was so weak that I had no resistance against the frequent returns of the fever day and night, or against the cough which exhausted my strength."[17] He had evaluated his condition exactly. One day he even asked a boyhood friend to come to see him and to recite softly before him the prayers for the dying.

From this period in the clinic dates a letter sent to a young monk on a day when there was adoration of the Most Blessed Sacrament at the monastery. I must quote it, because it is admirable:

> Tell Jesus I want to profit from this adoration to settle accounts with his divine Father. Offer Jesus to his Father in expiation for all my past sins and for all my present failings; then offer Jesus who alone is acceptable to his Father, to repay the good God for all his gifts, especially for the gift of Jesus himself. After you have settled all my debts, you are

[15] Dom Sortais, op. cit., 189.
[16] Letter to a young monk, July 16, 1933.
[17] Ibid., November 20, 1935.

> not to leave it at that. You must make the good God a debtor to the poor little creature that I am. In order to do that, here is what you must say, "Father, on behalf of Father Prior, I offer You Jesus with all His sufferings, all his merits and all his love." After you have completely satisfied the Father in this way (and "satisfied" is not too strong a word), you must then ask him for all that I need. What do I need? Jesus . . .[18]

Is it possible to sum up the economy of the Incarnation better than this? The incessant bargaining of man with God by the medium of the Incarnate Word, whom Father Gabriel tenderly calls by his human name, Jesus.

Taught by St. Bernard, Father Gabriel had a very living love, a very human love, if one may say so, for the humanity of the Son of God, and he found in it the link which allowed his devotion to the Blessed Virgin to join that which was at the heart of his spirituality. "Think of the succession of months, almost like a single unit, which precede Christmas. Think of the instinct of the little child which makes it need the mother so much that it is as though incomplete without her. Remember that Jesus was the Blessed Virgin's child. . . . For nine months Mary's heart was Jesus' motor of life."[19]

The health of Dom Jean-Baptiste, the abbot, became worse and worse. The monastery suffered twice as much from this situation. The shortcomings of the superior made themselves felt all the more, when he was exhausted. When the Father Abbot of La Grande Trappe made the regular visitation in March 1936, he was persuaded that a change was needful for the good order of the community. His conversations with the monks inclined him to think that, if there were an election, Father Gabriel would be elected. He therefore asked Dom Jean-Baptiste to resign his post. The latter then spoke of it to his prior and asked his advice. Father Gabriel gave it in complete frankness. The community's best interests were at stake, he said; it seemed to him that Dom Jean-Baptiste ought to resign.

On April 1, 1936, armed with the acceptance by the abbot general of the resignation of the abbot of Bellefontaine, the visitor

[18] Ibid., December 9, 1935.
[19] Ibid., December 19, 1935.

returned to inform the community and to announce that the election was set for a month from that date, namely May 5. Meanwhile the abbot of La Trappe became responsible for the governing of the community of Bellefontaine. He took advantage of this fact to introduce a certain number of small modifications into the usages. This was not done without some ill feelings. Father Gabriel now applied himself to intercede between a too brusque superior and the community, with various degrees of success. After having had to back up a timid superior in his governing of the abbey, he now had the role of moderating the excessive zeal of a temporary superior for more than a month. This was an opportunity for him to perfect his diplomatic gifts, for which he would find abundant use later. Nevertheless, it made him suffer.

It was with relief that everyone welcomed the day of the scrutiny, everyone, that is, except Father Gabriel. "I have neither knowledge, nor experience nor virtue." Still, it would have been hard for him not to know he was "accepted" by his brothers. But he saw God's will manifested in the vote of the conventual chapter. Was it possible for him to avoid a duty? In responding to this new vocation, he had confidence in God. "If I had had any knowledge, experience or virtue," he wrote, "I would have taken them into account in responding to the community's vote, and that would have been a mistake. So I put my trust in Jesus, in his grace, and in Mary, and I said yes. As long as I count on the Lord alone, it will go well. And so my nothingness, my very real insufficiency forces me to expect everything from God and to be close to him."[20]

Father Gabriel was only 33, so he did not have the age required by canon law. The election could not, then, be effective until a dispensation was obtained from Rome. This done, the new abbot was confirmed on Sunday, June 7, feast of the Blessed Trinity.

For four years Dom Gabriel had made his apprenticeship for the unwelcome task of superior in particularly arduous circumstances, since it fell to him to obey someone in power, who was hardly sure of himself, and at the same time, to be firm in his commands to men who still had the possibility of another recourse.

[20] Letter to X, August 17, 1962.

We do not know in detail what abnegation and humility, what tact and delicacy this program demanded of him. His firmness does not seem to have alienated the monks from him, and he knew how to gain the affection and esteem of everyone. He acquired a deeper knowledge of the house and its special problems. By observing the conduct and weaknesses of the community, he was able to improve his own judgment. The complexity of his new task was clear to him, but he abandoned himself to God with the trust of a child, commended to him his fears and apprehensions, even the awareness of his weakness and limitations, and thought no more of anything but realizing the Lord's designs for him. Is not the Lord able to choose the instruments that he wishes?

"[The good God] is free to make us pass for better than we are. And we have to accept that like all the rest. If he exposes our weaknesses, or if he shows off our virtues, so what? Nothing is changed! All that is necessary is that we love him truly."[21]

[21] Letter to a nun, October 2, 1951.

Chapter 7

ABBOT AT 33

During the period of Brother Gabriel's novitiate, a young monk entered the chapter room unexpectedly one day, and he stopped short at the sight that greeted him. Brother Gabriel was sitting on the abbot's throne, dressed in a professed cowl, with the pectoral cross at his breast, suspended from a violet cord. Was it a dream or a premonitory vision? Not a bit of it.

The Canadian monasteries founded by Bellefontaine had begged to have a portrait of Dom Chouteau. Under protest the aged abbot agreed to pose before M. Livache's canvas. A single sitting was enough to exhaust his patience. He wished all the painters of Choletais and Anjou would go to the dickens. After some diplomacy and appeal, it was definitely decided that the abbot would pose for the hands and the face, provided that a monk of the same height as he would suffice for the remainder of the portrait. This is how it came about that Brother Gabriel posed for the portrait of Dom Jean-Marie.

"This Angevine artist," wrote Dr. Coubard, "painted Dom Chouteau seated. That is perhaps the major criticism we would be inclined to make of the portrait. He was, in fact, one monk who did not know how to sit."[1]

As a novice, then, Brother Gabriel could put up a good appearance as an abbot. Yet, what the confidence of his brothers made him accept as an obedience was difficult to fulfill. It was one of the circumstances in which it is better to close one's eyes and abandon oneself to God's will. "Where faith is weak," said St. Ambrose, "there is trouble; where love is complete, there is

[1] Dr. Ch. Coubard, op. cit., p. 56.

security."[2] Besides, what difference does success make, once one has obeyed God? In a similar situation Dom Sortais would later write, "After all, to have been put in charge, and then to be deposed because of evident incapacity and incompetence, would be a source of sanctification for my soul. God is wise, and he loves me. So I will trust in him and be at peace."[3]

The young abbot was aware of the limitations and gaps in his knowledge. His intellectual baggage was light, because his studies had been eclectic. He was unable to deepen his theological understanding by force of circumstances. It remained at the level of elementary notions, but he had a lively intelligence and an extraordinary faculty of assimilation. Father Sortais' health imposed severe restrictions on his zeal. His health would always be precarious. This was a burden for an abbot like himself, who desired always to give a good example, and not to command something that he had not first accomplished himself. His physical shortcomings had repercussions on his morale. He began to have periods of depression.

He knew that he was impulsive and often enough carried away. He was not always able to overcome his fiery temper, or to prevent an outburst. He remained subject to anger and violent moods. This sometimes kept him from reflecting and planning before taking action, and from listening to advice. His enthusiasm turned his public talks into convincing arguments, and they convinced both himself and those over whom he exercised an irresistible charm. Finally, the abbot did not know well enough how to defend himself against his own heart and his acute sensitiveness. He would hesitate before taking certain steps, or before proposing certain actions which might cause suffering for someone; he would become timid and not take the risk.

"The responsibility of the abbot and of those who share his duties is awesome. There is no doubt about it. No one, then, ought to desire such duties. . . . They are difficult to fulfill. In a community there are persons with free will who must be guided. It is necessary, then, not to impose oneself in any way, or to demand, but

[2] St. Ambrose, *Sur l'evangile de S. Luc* IV.70, cf. Dom G. Tissot in S.C. 45 (Paris: Cerf, 1956) 180.

[3] Letter to Mère Bernard, December 8, 1943.

first of all to convince, and then to get those you have convinced to desire it and to do it. This is painful. In religion to command is to make oneself the servant of all. Religious superiors need a lot of renunciation, because they have to adapt themselves to everyone, and yet to know how to make their rule respected, how to stimulate souls. A superior is sanctified through suffering."[4]

But Father Sortais was too clear headed to belittle his own qualities, the trump cards he possessed to confront the difficulties of his charge. There was no risk of a loss of humility, as long as a man knew how to thank God for the gifts he found in himself. "When you see an especially beautiful sunrise, you glorify God; when you see an act of virtue which seems especially moving, you praise God. . . . Why not admire what the Lord does in us, when we know what we are of ourselves? For my part, I know so well that we bless God for his love, for his works of love, wherever they are found."[5]

The new abbot was a simple and righteous man, endowed with great powers of soul, and practically free of every kind of egoism. He had a horror of small-mindedness. He had going for him youth, energy and a decisive mind, a judgment habitually strong, true, rapid and sure. He had a natural aptitude to command and to govern. On the one hand his willpower, and on the other the charm which he exercised unknown to himself, greatly facilitated his job. He knew how to speak in public, how to express his thoughts clearly, how to share with others the fervor and faith which animated him. His sense of humor kept him from making a tragedy out of situations which were only serious or difficult. Above all, he had a heart of exquisite tenderness, which placed him at every moment at the service of others, attentive to their needs, and able to listen to them and to understand them. Father Sortais' enthusiasm was contagious; one loved to follow him. But all these qualities and gifts could not account for his personal radiance, for the kind of fascination that he exercised. He was already in complete truth a man of God.

I trust I will not anticipate too much if I relate the testimony here, which those who were to share his captivity four years later,

[4] Notes on the *Rule of St. Benedict*, ch. 64.

[5] Letter to X, March 22, 1963.

have given. "Father Sortais," said one of them, "was a permanent subject of veneration and source of courage. But how could I explain it to you? Gestures and obvious actions, there were none, and very few words. Everything seemed to proceed from his interior, without his physical exterior having anything to do with it."[6]

"You felt there was another Christ in him, in constant communion with the Holy Spirit."[7]

"Calmness and tranquil faith radiated from him."[8]

What he would be in the prison camp he was already as a young abbot in the midst of his monks, not unaware of the difficulties of his task, but inclined to give himself without reserve, *non loquendo sed moriendo,* not by preaching but (to freely translate) by witnessing through giving his life. (This is the sense in which he understood the device on his coat of arms.) External regularity, though beautiful, did not interest him of itself. "What pleases God," he wrote, "is not that a monastery 'runs smoothly'; it is rather that the monks who live in it strive for perfection."[9]

Dom Sortais received the abbatial blessing at the hands of Msgr. Rumeau, the elderly bishop of Angers, on July 16 in the abbey church of Bellefontaine. He wanted to take the opportunity to make use of a venerable relic: a 15th-century missal once used by Dom Jean de la Barrière; he it was who began that reform in the order in the 16th century, which finally became the Congregation of Feuillants.[10] Bellefontaine had belonged to this congregation from 1642 to 1791—a century and a half. Afterwards the reception for the invited guests gave him an oppor-

[6] Letter of an officer, May 24, 1966.

[7] Testimony of another officer.

[8] Testimony of an officer.

[9] Dom Sortais, op. cit., 257.

[10] The *Feuillants* were a branch of Cistercian Reform founded in 1577 by Jean de la Barrière. The name comes from the Cistercian Monastery of *Les Feuillants* near Toulouse, which Barrière received *in commendam* and later reformed. Sixtus V approved the Reform and it spread to Italy, where it was known as the Reformed Bernardines. Both branches were suppressed by the Revolution. They were known for their penitential practices, going about barefooted and bareheaded, eating only bread, water, and vegetables, sleeping on planks and using no chairs or tables. Prayer and hard manual labor were their occupation. Unlike the Trappists, they were open to intellectual labor and pastoral duties. *New Catholic Encyclopedia,* op. cit., vol. 5, 905.

tunity to proclaim the simplicity of life and poverty of the white monks, in a way that was far from discreet—such is the unanimous opinion of those who were present. We find in him a feeling for the spectacular on this occasion, and for gestures which proclaim faith. It is the residue of the experiences of his youth, which further experience would do its part to correct.

Now abbot of Bellefontaine, Father Sortais was also responsible for the monastery of Les Gardes.[11] *Posuit me custodem.* ("He appointed me guardian.") At the highest point of the *Mauges,* on a hill from which the whole region resembles a huge checkerboard, there is a sanctuary dedicated to Our Lady. The Augustinians had charge of it before the Revolution. They had built a monastery during the first part of the 17th century, of which a single wing has been preserved. When the Cistercians under Dom Guillet established themselves at Bellefontaine, Dom Augustin de Lestrange acquired this ancient convent of Les Gardes for the Trappistines. For a while the abbey of Les Gardes had been under the paternity of the abbot of Bricquebec, but for some years now the abbot of Bellefontaine had been their Father Immediate.

The community of Les Gardes had just been through a difficult period. Mother Cécile Chauvat, superioress since 1923, had been severely marked by the crisis whose effects were still being felt. It was necessary for the new abbot of Bellefontaine to inform himself immediately about the problems of the Les Gardes community and to meet all the sisters.

Another trip took Dom Sortais to the abbey of Bricquebec[12] whose former abbot, Dom Vital Lehodey, he earnestly wanted to

[11] Les Gardes: In the present diocese of Angers there is a parish called St.-Georges-du-Puy-de-la-Garde and a chapel called Sainte-Marie-du-Genet. It goes back to the 11th century. The hill on which it was built is the highest place in the region. It was entrusted to the Augustinians in 1606. The chapel was burned to the ground in 1794. Restored in 1817, the chapel and other buildings were purchased by Dom Augustin de Lestrange in 1818 for the Trappistines from Forges in the diocese of Séez. They have lived there, except during the expulsions of the Revolution and 1880, continually. *Catholicisme,* op. cit., t. 4, col. 1755.

[12] Bricquebec was founded in 1825, having been endowed by Casimir Lefilastre. It was a parish in the diocese of Coutances, in the department of La Manche on the northern coast of France. The monastery was canonically constituted in 1826. *Dictionnaire d'Histoire,* op. cit., t. 10, col. 684.

meet. He also wished to gather information from him about the affairs of the Les Gardes community. This pilgrimage amounts to a sign indicating the very orientation of his abbatial teaching.[13] The general chapter of 1900 had asked Dom Lehodey to revise and correct the 1869 *Spiritual Directory,* and to prepare a new edition. He had resolutely modified its orientation, outlining a return from De Rancé's conception of the monastic life to the primitive spirit of Citeaux. Habits of thought are not as easy to change as are texts. The return came about slowly, especially in certain monasteries (of which Bellefontaine was one), but the germ of many changes is contained in the work of Dom Vital. The abbot of Bricquebec substituted the vocabulary of mystical theology for a moralizing vocabulary characterized by rigorism. He emphasized the primacy of love over penance, and that of contemplation over austerities. He even took the opposite tack from the old *Directory* and formally invited the Trappists "to give the lie to the bad proverb, according to which holiness would leave the cloister when learning entered it."[14] For Dom Vital, the practice of prayer should normally find its fulfillment and crown in mystical prayer, which presupposes a sound doctrinal formation. It makes little difference that Dom Sortais later expressed some doubts about uncritically applying the doctrine of "holy abandonment" taught by the abbot of Bricquebec, for he had learned from experience. However, that was not Dom Vital's essential message; his message was the return to the authentic Cistercian tradition. Dom Sortais was to resolutely show himself a disciple of Dom Vital in that respect.

As a matter of fact, the new abbot had a well-structured program. His aim was to improve observances by putting a new spirit in them. He wanted to give the soul back to the body of exterior observances, to make them live, that their truth might be more profound. He wanted to rediscover the simple and pure structure of Cistercian liturgy, to give the monks the

[13] "After I had been elected abbot, I went to find Dom Vital, and I told him, 'Give me some advice.' He answered, 'Come back tomorrow morning.' I returned the next day, and he said, 'The good God has many ways of sanctifying souls, but for superiors there is only one: suffering.'" Conference given at the Abbey of Igny, September 22, 1952. Père Bruno Brard also alludes to this in his *Dom Vital Lehodey* (Paris: Gabalda, 1973) 206.

[14] Revised *Directory,* 502, of the French.

taste and possibility for study, that they might acquire a doctrinal formation worthy of the contemplative life, and he wanted to give back to contemplation its absolute priority, to the extent that it had been lost. Besides all this, it was urgent to give temporalities a more solid foundation, and to continue the work of construction, already begun by Dom Chouteau.

Dom Sortais had been advised to wait and see before changing appointments to the monastery's charges. Still, he needed a prior right away, so he took the novice master and made him prior; then he had to find a new novice master. In addition, the brother cellarer had held that post for many years, and in the abbot's judgment he was too overbearing, so after some sharp disagreements, Dom Sortais replaced him. After having maintained that he did not want to make any changes, he found that three of the principal charges of the house had new incumbents.

The many interventions of the Father Abbot of La Grande Trappe while the abbatial seat was still empty had annoyed more than one monk of Bellefontaine. "I will show you how to handle a community," he had said. Dom Sortais' approach was more nuanced, but he did not at first avoid some excesses. St. Bernard's fiery temperament fascinated him; it was in accord with his own. There was too much dash in the inauguration of his program, and it led to some exaggerations. He could have avoided some annoyance by acting with more prudence. The church was quickly relieved of much useless excess baggage of devotion. Some of the senior brothers had regrets, and some of the benefactors outside the community even felt hurt. A bishop's ring was given away to a needy Christian school, and this meant further trouble for him. Dom Sortais was luckier in the liturgical domain.

From the beginning of the Cistercian order, the lay brothers' life has been very different from that of the choir monks. Their time was taken up either by a very simple form of prayer or by manual work and did not include any active participation in the long liturgical office or any intellectual activities. Therefore, when they joined the choir monks in the church at certain times, they had their established place in the nave behind an opaque rood-screen, against which stood two altars. The Cistercian usages remained faithful to this distribution of space, even when it became possible for the lay brothers to participate more actively in the liturgy. Dom Sortais' first concern in the church of Bellefontaine was to open up this screen by taking out the wooden paneling in the lower arches, enabling the two choirs to be effectively joined together. It was not possible to do more than this until the Cistercian legislation was modified.

Dom Sortais had not yet arrived at complete spiritual maturity. One of his companions in captivity was to mention as a sign of human weakness his "emotional outbursts; he was like a big kid." He did not yet have complete control over his imagination, and his combative ardor sometimes played tricks on him. The most typical example is the mobilization of the monastery for armed defense in October 1936. However, if we are careful to take the political atmosphere into consideration, we may the more easily understand his response to it.

The situation of the church in Spain kept deteriorating after the proclamation of the Republic in 1931. Cases were multiplied of attacks on priests, burned churches, and pillaged convents. The election of February 16, 1936, introduced the *Frente Popular* and opened the door to revolution. The left wing constituted by the Anarcho-Syndicalists and Communists practically made the laws. Since mid-July, after the insurrection of the troops stationed at Morocco, and the proclamations of several generals at Aragon, Navarre, Leon and Galicia, the entire peninsula was in a state of civil war, a war without mercy. The forming of a French *Front Populaire* on May 3, thanks to a light turnout of the majority, seemed to many a prelude of similar violence. Revolutionary manifestations and sit-down strikes occurred before the end of the month. Many Frenchmen passionately kept an eye on Spanish events. Communists called for armed intervention, and the U.S.S.R. sent some heavy artillery through France to the Reds in the outer Pyrenees.

In connection with the large gatherings of Communists in Paris and the provinces, a meeting was held at Cholet on Sunday, October 4, in which the local Chairmen attacked the Fascists, employers, and clergy. The monks of Bellefontaine were denounced for hiding weapons and some high officials proposed to go out and look for them.

Dom Sortais was immediately informed, and he took "military" measures to defend his monastery by force, if need be.

Only a few members of the community and three secular farm workers were in on the secret, but the fact remains that the machinery was in place, although fortunately it was not needed. Still, these actions show more signs of the *Feuillant* leagues than of the Rule of St. Benedict. In the 16th century Dom Bernard de Percin de Montgaillard, superior of the *Feuillant* monastery of Paris, violently took the part of the League and was forced to flee to Belgium. He then introduced the Reform at Orval (1606). This was hardly a model of the spirit of the Gospel. Living in constant contact with reminders of the *Vendéen* war, Dom Sortais allowed himself to be duped by the illusion of armed defense of the faith. He still had to grow in his understanding of the Gospel.

God did not allow him to take the usual routes. For three years his faith withdrew to the deepest part of his being, far from the domain of explicit consciousness, leaving him helpless. The temptation that now began would be with him for more than 20 years. It attacked him in his hope, but its exact nature remains mysterious.

A short time after his abbatial election, diocesan officials asked him to look into a case of diabolical possession. A young girl from a *Mauges* parish not far from the monastery seemed to be tormented by a devil. During the exorcisms many times repeated, the devil questioned the Father Abbot, revealing facts about his personal life which the young girl could not have known. This made a deep impression on him. The devil added that he would never leave him in peace again.

From this moment Dom Sortais began to be tormented, as though an invisible evil presence made itself felt near him, inciting him to actions of which he disapproved, and suggesting to him with a kind of certitude that anguished him, that God positively wanted to damn him. It is hard to imagine what distress must have been his at certain times.

All his faith and love revolted against the incomprehensible. He loved God with all his soul, looked for nothing and wanted nothing but him. The powers of his soul inclined toward the accomplishment of God's will in order to respond to his love, and now he seemed to discover irresistible forces in himself, physical constraints forcing him to take attitudes against his will, which he did not want to take at any price. What violence was this inside him? Who had inscribed such a necessity in his nature, which his body wanted to obey against his will? Was it not God himself, God who wanted him lost, and who perversely attracted him, the better to hurl him away? Did the Lord attract his love and then seem not to want it?

His interior battle seemed senseless and absurd to him, and so God himself seemed responsible for the absurdity. The God of predestination could not be good! Still, how could he not want to love God and be completely his? The monk's suffering seems senseless, undeserved and useless. There is no basis for hope. "If I wash myself with snow and scrub my hands with lye, even so you will plunge me in filth, and my very garments will abhor me."[15]

Like a trapped beast he sometimes did not know anymore where to turn. He believed in the mercy of his "Jesus." He saw it constantly at work in others' lives. But for him it was gone. It seemed to him that he was rejected, damned and unable to do anything at all against this irreversible judgment. For his part, he forced himself to do everything possible to remain faithful to God. Why was God unfaithful to his part, and why did he cast him out into the exterior darkness?

Drawn by God, he felt tormented. All security was gone. His interior life was in great disarray, with all the bitterness of hatred and of broken trust. He felt himself the object of an incomprehensible anger, abandoned and alone, face to face with his misery, trying in vain to free himself from his sinful condition. There is something of the drama of Job in all this, except that Job was convinced of his innocence, but Dom Sortais felt and believed that he was a great sinner, despite himself.

There were rumblings of revolt. His aggressiveness would come out suddenly in blasphemous thoughts and actions, but he himself did not will any such outbreak. It was only the leaping out of wounded love, whose violence was in exact proportion to defeated hope. God's apparent refusal made him desperate. At one time he had tangibly felt the Lord's goodness toward him, and his predilection toward him had made itself felt when he had cared little about God. This feeling had been with him

[15] Job 9:31.

wherever he had gone, until he had given himself completely to God. Now God's regard seemed full of hostility.

"God willed to make me go through severe interior trials for many years. It is very hard on a man, when he sees a kind of evidence that heaven, in which he believes with a strong faith, is not meant for him, and that he is doomed to be eternally separated from God and from Mary. This seemed so much in conformity with justice, that I could only acquiesce to the divine will. On some days the only act of love of which I am capable is to accept this terrible fate which I so deserve."[16]

The same searing temptation was to return again and again, at shorter or longer intervals, for many years. Each time it would plunge him into darkness, in which he would sadly argue with himself, amid reactions of revolt, blasphemy, and impurity. At such moments he would take refuge in his own love, all that was left to him. He was resolved to love God despite it all and through it all, whether it be at the bottom of obscurity or in hell itself. Maybe he was condemned? What did it matter? For his part, he would not consent to be separated from God. He would remain faithful to love despite all, despite God himself.

There is no doubt about the time at which this long intermittent crisis began, which left its mark so profoundly upon his interior life. Its first manifestation coincided with the exorcisms he was asked to hold, which impressed him so strongly. But before having recourse to preternatural explanations, which are not of course excluded, there is reason to ask whether the event did not serve to reveal his interior life. Dom Sortais had an iron will, and he imposed severe discipline on an unusually fiery temperament. On the other hand, he had an uncommon vitality which would have led his flesh and blood to assert themselves vigorously, in other circumstances. Outwardly he was almost continually master of himself, but it should not surprise us if there were violent resurgences or outbursts of freedom at first, before the will came into play. Dom Sortais' spontaneous reactions were often very powerful. Vehement sentiments often engender their contraries, at least for a brief moment. It is like a distraction, a lapse of the effort of the will to keep itself fixed

[16] Letter to a prioress, October 16, 1945.

on one course. Fear or apprehension of seeing such movements manifest themselves is often sufficient to excite them. Sad interrogations of culpability appealing to the free will and anguish at having lost one's self-control, even for a moment, come afterward. Such a trial can become terrible, especially when God uses it to purify a soul and to take away all its certitude.

"I am tormented by blasphemy," wrote a saintly prioress of the 17th century, for whom Bremond had a great admiration. "I hear a voice in my soul, and it cries out that I am a deluded fool, running after a God who flees from me and trying to love One who has no love for me."[17]

And so faith responds by hypothetically accepting the pains of hell, if only one may still love God there, and on condition that the cause of this damnation is not one's sin, for sin is the refusal to love God. "If you have decided on my ruin," continued Marie Granger, "I accept the sentence and submit to your divine ordinance. But at least grant me the grace of not taking the least sin with me. I can suffer the pain, but I cannot tolerate the stain of sin. The fires of hell will be agreeable to me, if only I will burn as a victim who has not disgraced you in the least."

St. Francis de Sales underwent similar anguish, and so did the Curé of Ars. As for Dom Sortais, God seems to have used this trial as a long purification of his hope and love. The only solution to the drama of conscience was his ever-renewed, complete abandonment to divine love ("Never despair of the love of God," said St. Benedict) and unconditional acceptance of God's designs in repeated acts of pure love.

"Whatever happens, Lord," said St. Francis de Sales, "All things are in your hands. Whatever you may have decided concerning me, I will at least love you in this life. I will love you here, if it is not given me to love you in eternal life. . . . If my sins merit it, then it is right that I be damned with those who are damned. . . . Only grant that I may not be one of those who blaspheme your name."[18]

[17] Marie Granger, Prioress of Montargis, cf. H. Bremond, *Histoire littéraire du sentiment religieux en France,* t. II (Paris: Bloud et Gay, 1916) 458–63.

[18] Saint Francis de Sales, *Oeuvres complètes,* ed. d'Annecy, t. XII, Opuscules (Annecy: J. Niérat, 1925) 19–20.

Although Dom Sortais' act of abandonment did not end his crisis once and for all, it at least allowed him to surmount it, to overcome the morbid obsession into which the trial could have plunged him for a long time. Far from detaining him on his way to God, the temptation against hope somehow helped him to make his love actual and his faith ever deeper, in the all-powerful mercy of his God. Fortified by his experience, he knew how to guide souls in an admirable way.

"You are a son of God. Nothing can change that. Furthermore, your Father can only will your good, your advancement toward him and your sanctification. He cannot pursue any other objective. His methods seem harsh to you? They are, and God knows it. If he has judged it necessary, why should we doubt? Have we not already had a thousand proofs that God loves us? God is all-powerful. He could have used many other ways, but this is the one that seemed best to him. I am absolutely convinced it is the best, indeed the very best way."[19]

"If someone is faithful to me, I would not want to deceive him or let him go astray. So why should I attribute a thing to God, that I would consider wrong for myself? God is love and truth; his will is love and truth; his ways are love and truth. This should keep me from ever doubting God, even if he seems not to have any love for me or seems to forsake me, even if I should feel that I have been abandoned."[20]

[19] Letter to a nun, January 29, 1956.
[20] Letter to a nun, June 22, 1956.

Chapter 8

BELLEFONTAINE AND LES GARDES

Dom Sortais had a high ideal of the abbatial office. He was incapable of forging a personality for himself, of playing the prelate. Everything in him rebelled against such a conception of the dignity he had received. He was indignant at what he called "smallness" in superiors. "I will say it openly: Some superiors have such infantile vanity about details to which monks ought not to pay the slightest attention! They are such esthetes that they make a show of carelessly allowing their garments to unfold just far enough for the pectoral cross to be seen; then they skillfully wave their hand and display their ring."[1]

Dom Sortais had a very elevated sense of his responsibility, for he had meditated on the Rule and trembled at its demands. He believed he represented God to his sons in all truth, and his power participated in God's authority. He would have no part with those who renounced this authority in false humility, but he surrounded it with veneration and religious reverence, even when he was the one that held it. Yet, as Dom Gabriel saw it, the abbot participated in God's fatherhood, even more than in his authority. His first task was to bring Christ to birth and make him grow in his disciples. "God desires such a birth of Christ in souls, that is always new, and he desires it with special ardor in those of his sons whom he has particularly reserved for himself, whom he has chosen for a higher service. And it is just this very tender and delicate aspect of divine fatherhood that the abbot shares, because his sons are consecrated souls, souls whom God regards with predilection, chosen by love, destined

[1] Conference at the general chapter, September 13, 1955.

to reproduce the qualities of the incarnate Word more perfectly than others."[2]

The work of holiness can only have God for its sole author, but the abbot is one of the privileged instruments the Trinity makes use of to bring it about in those who are called to the monastic life, according to the Rule of St. Benedict. "The abbot is united with the Father, and he works to form the image of his Son in souls; he is also associated with the Holy Spirit who enlightens and strengthens him. He is called to be God's helper in the work, God's interpreter."[3]

St. Benedict thought of the abbot's fatherhood as a sacrament. The abbot is the cornerstone of the monastery. He is Christ's lieutenant and representative; like Christ, he is master, shepherd, spiritual director and physician. He ought to teach by word, but especially by example. His charism is like that of the doctors and teachers of the apostolic church, and it is also much like that of the desert fathers. He has the duty of protecting and interpreting the law, the monastic rule which is the proper way for the monks to realize the vocation to which God has called them. Among his subjects he is the only judge of the way the monastery ought to be governed, which means in sum to organize everything in such a way that souls may be more freely and surely united to God. This is indeed a heavy task, because the abbot's responsibility extends to all domains. Nevertheless, it is exercised principally in two ways: the good order of the house, that each monk may find the most suitable means for his search for God, and effective spiritual direction for each member of the community in his relationship with God.

It is recommended that the abbot share his duties with individual monks whom he can trust, but the responsibility remains his, and his solicitude must extend to all those under his care. The powers St. Benedict invests him with are great enough to inspire those who receive them with a legitimate fear. The author of the Rule sees the Abbot as a man who gives himself to his community and thinks only of how he can be useful to them. He wants the abbot to be a wise man, careful and prudent, who

[2] Dom Sortais, op. cit., 253.
[3] Ibid., 253.

has achieved self-mastery and discernment, a monk above all, having a passionate love for souls, who will consent to any sacrifice for their sake.

Dom Sortais loved to insist on this aspect of the abbot's character. He would have nothing to do with a "love of the will" with regard to the monks "in which the heart seems to have no part."

"We do not love with the will," he would say, "but with our heart of flesh. . . . When our father St. Benedict speaks of the relationship the monks ought to have with the abbot, he uses words that express deep and real affection which unites sons to their father."[4]

For his own part, Dom Sortais had a great desire to show himself a "father" in every way. With watchful tenderness he tried to anticipate the needs of his monks. "Fatherly superiors," he said, "have a kind of sixth sense which makes them go beyond the individual needs of their religious. . . . It is a fatherly intuition which guides them, and guides them with certitude. As true fathers they understand words half-spoken. They feel in their deepest selves what their sons are going through. The sons' sufferings are the father's sufferings, without their having to make any effort at describing them. They share their joys without there being any need to speak of them. Their fatherly instinct has revealed everything to them."[5]

One of the most important duties of the abbot is his spiritual teaching, and Dom Sortais knew it better than anyone. He gave it his full attention. The whole orientation he wanted the monastery to take depended on it. Homilies, commentaries on the Rule, daily remarks to the community—he made maximum use of all these occasions to remind his monks unceasingly of the essence of the monastic life and the Cistercian ideal. Some reforms were necessary at Bellefontaine. The mentality of the community was still very much influenced by the spirit of De Rancé and Dom Augustin de Lestrange (for whom, nevertheless, Dom Sortais cherished a strong admiration). Austerity of life, penance, and particular devotions run the risk of obscuring other more important and fundamental aspects of contemplative

[4] Ibid., 258.
[5] Ibid., 259.

monasticism, by the importance one gives to them. Prayers become more important than prayer, austerities than true penance, and pious reading substitutes for the authentic *lectio divina.* There is a tendency for ascesis to occupy the whole field of vision, so that the primacy of heartfelt contemplation, laid down by St. Bernard and the Cistercian Fathers, in conformity with all the monastic traditions, is lost sight of.

Dom Sortais was certainly convinced of the need for penance with its two dimensions, both personal and communal (the Trappist's penance is for the sake of the entire mystical body), but he still insisted in season and out of season, that the interior life must come before everything else. A man's body can endure harsh external living conditions without the help of the soul, but if on the other hand the primacy is resolutely given to union with God, it will be impossible for anyone to live his monastic life and turn aside from the goal.

"It would be a distortion to become attached to the usages, as the Pharisees were to the Law, to the extent of making them an end, of thinking that all monastic perfection consists in material observances. . . . No, all these things should be kept in their role of helpful means. And so, if it should ever happen that a point of the usages is incompatible with the practice of virtue, remember that the end always takes precedence over the means."[6]

The fact that the interior life is normally transformed into the mystical life did not frighten Dom Sortais. He made Dom Lehodey's point of view in this regard his own. He saw the mystical life as the highest form of the contemplative life to which a monk is called by his Cistercian vocation.

The abbot of Bellefontaine kept the last word of the message of St. Thérèse of Lisieux and made it his own without qualification, "I've said it all . . . it is all done . . . love alone is what counts."

And so Dom Sortais prepared himself for his teaching role. Most of the time it was necessary for him to read and to personally work on his talks, to make his expositions in his own way, simple, spontaneous and unassumed. His teaching was not improvised. He had to take the time for study and reflection,

[6] Letter to the novices of the order, July 16, 1952.

and undoubtedly still more, for recollection and prayer. This is the method he made his own and which he later counseled his young successor to adopt, when he finally had to leave Bellefontaine. "It is desirable that an abbot have solid learning and that he be able to enrich his knowledge over the years, but like other abbots you will surely find that your days pass too swiftly, and that your resolutions to study come to nothing through no fault of your own. I counsel you . . . to read something serious every day, cost what it may, be it only a page, and then ask Jesus to help you to really derive profit from that page. Sometimes there is a treasure hidden in just one page, or even just one line, but only Jesus can help you find it and exploit it. It is possible to read, read, read again and again, but retain nothing. Again, it is possible to read a few lines and to live by them to the extent that they are changed into life for us."

"If your sons are to profit from your reading, it will be necessary for you to keep this daily reading primary and sacrosanct, and it should not be confused with the reading you do as immediate preparation for your talks."[7]

Dom Sortais wanted to be understood by everyone. Therefore he tried to speak in a simple way. There was no need at all to make an intense effort. He loved to illustrate his teaching by using images and stories and by recalling his own experiences. He was serious without pomposity, glad to share his joys on occasion, but horrified by banality. His talks were always sustained by solid, pervasive, and judicious thoughts. He knew what he wanted to say and took constant care to reach those religious who were less gifted intellectually. To speak simply and firmly, one has to be well in possession of what he is teaching. The role of reflection and of enriching his thought was great in the abbot of Bellefontaine, even if it had become easy for him. He knew how to take the time, and would not hesitate to let the officers of the monastery take charge of their own responsibilities, if his personal intervention was unnecessary. "There is a hierarchy among the different abbatial duties," he said, "and instruction of the community is among the foremost of them."[8]

[7] Letter to an abbot, February 29, 1952.
[8] Dom Sortais, op. cit., 294.

Dom Sortais often took notes in the course of his own personal reading, always with the thought of how he might make use of it. Most of the time, it was a phrase or leading idea that struck him. He classified everything in such a way as to find it quickly in case of need, in order to make convenient use of it. There was a wide range of topics to choose from: classics of the spiritual life and commentaries on the Rule kept company with the more solid books that had recently been published.

Father Abbot always tried to avoid a too rigid moralism. "Whatever the subject we intend to speak about, it is better to tell the religious what they should do than to insist on what they should not do."[9]

Bellefontaine's library was a very good one, but it was not too accessible at the time when Dom Sortais became abbot. If a monk wanted a book, he had to write a note to the librarian. In order that the religious might have solid food for their *lectio divina,* Father Abbot had a good number of books brought down to the "common box," thus making them accessible to all the monks.

For Dom Sortais *lectio divina* was not a mental discipline or a means for making use of one's free time after the end of work. *Lectio divina* was indispensable for the monk's spiritual development, one of the expressions of his search for God.

If the soul of the monastic life is constituted by the life of prayer and of conscious union with God, the monk arrives at this goal by means of a kind of communal *ascesis* embodied in what Cistercians call "observances."

"St. Benedict," wrote Dom Sortais, "gives us many occasions for practicing the different virtues by which charity gradually becomes supreme in our souls. These occasions are the observances which our holy legislator, and the Cistercian Fathers after him, organized so well that if we follow them intelligently, sincerely and generously, it will enable us to have an integral development, and to find God in the measure that we renounce ourselves. Observances have no other purpose than to prepare us for the blossoming of charity and to lead us to union with God."[10]

[9] Ibid., p. 295.
[10] Ibid., p. 65.

Dom Sortais was far from being a legalist in any sense of the word. He was never one of those who think of their relationship with God from the point of view of an obligation. Usages did not seem to him to be reduced to a kind of penal code, any more than the Rule or the Gospel did, but the usages are the concrete application of the Rule and the Gospel to the details of everyday life. For Dom Sortais, usages are essentially a guide given to the soul of the monk, to help him discern God's will for him within the concrete circumstances of everyday life in which God's personal call has placed him.

"The title page of the volume that contains the Rule of St. Benedict, the Charter of Charity, the Constitutions and the Usages has this quotation from the prophet Baruch, 'Blessed are we, O Israel, because the things that please God have been made known to us.'[11] If I had to have one of these books reprinted, I would not have it entitled, 'The Holy Rule' or 'The Cistercian Usages,' but *Quae Deo placent,* 'The things that please God.'"[12]

Dom Gabriel had a holy terror of gestures whose full significance has not been assimilated and that have become routine. He detested formalism, but he also thought that forms could be full of meaning and reveal their spiritual riches to whoever would apply himself continually to understand their depth of purpose and to show respect for the spirit they embody.

And so from the beginning of his abbacy Dom Sortais endeavored to renew the spirit of the observances and to liberate the vital force which it is their purpose to free and not to hinder. The risk of automatism run by any regular life is really a facile temptation, and it cannot be overcome by simply suppressing observances.

"Points of the usages are arrows in red ink, which point out opportunities to us, which the Cistercian life offers for the practice of virtue; they are a jewel-box which keeps the spirit of the Rule inviolate, by which the Fathers of Citeaux lived. . . . The smallest observance we keep has no other purpose than this: to urge us to that interior act of virtue by which we give God proof of our love."[13]

[11] Bar. 4:4

[12] Letter to the novices of the order, July 16, 1952.

[13] Ibid.

Dom Gabriel's efforts were directed primarily towards obedience and effective separation from the world. Dom Chouteau had paid most attention to the literal execution of his commands but had shown less interest in the interior dispositions of his monks. The spiritual lives of many were distorted by this material understanding of obedience which St. Benedict had made "the monk's way to God." Dom Sortais had no intention of treating his religious like children, or of refusing to share authority with those who were capable of exercising it: "The mark of a good superior," he wrote, "is that he knows how to make good use of those in his community who have strong characters, and does not repress them."[14] His own authority, though, was not weak, and he could sometimes be pretty stern. Obedience was his life; he thought of it as a way of union with God, as the means of making God's will the model of man's and of finally eliminating egoism, the principal obstacle to the victory of God's love in the soul. Besides his continual availability to his brothers, his own obedience as abbot lay in furnishing them the means to practice the *bonum obedientiae*. His duty, then, was to command firmly and effectively. He showed intransigence in his quick reactions, whenever he thought he saw disrespect or scorn of authority, whether his own or someone else's. The community of Bellefontaine had no difficulty in submitting to him. There was a good spirit, and if there were personal grievances, it did not take much to patch things up. Serious difficulties were rare exceptions.

Father Abbot showed similar intransigence when it came to safeguarding the spirit of solitude, which was especially characteristic of Citeaux since its beginning. Infractions of the rule of silence were the object of severe admonitions and sometimes of penances that might have seemed disproportionate, if the interior life of the monks were not at stake. Permission to speak to guests and trips to town were strictly rationed. In order to allow his monks to work in surroundings that favored the recollection they had come to the monastery to seek, he insisted that they work at different tasks from those confided to farm workers from outside.

He was passionately in love with nature, and so he was alert to the external surroundings of his monastery. To prevent

[14] Dom Sortais, op. cit., 273.

anyone's wanting to leave, it was necessary to have a good home. Dom Sortais had wanted very strongly to add some woods to the north of Bellefontaine to the monastery's property. This wish of his was thwarted, so he was all the more solicitous about the actual monastic property. Woe to anyone who might take the initiative to cut off some branches which seemed unsightly, or who might prune some bushes carelessly. The abbot would be sure to mention it in chapter and be "shocked."

Dom Sortais rigorously maintained the practice of poverty and detachment. For whatever was necessary the monks had to go to him or to those delegated by him. What he regarded superfluous was refused without discussion. Whatever the value of the object in question might be, no monk could dispose of it himself, and Dom Gabriel showed his intransigence on this point more than once. The stringent economy he imposed on the administration of the monastery allowed him to augment the share of the poor. Bellefontaine, of course, was not rich. "Dom Gabriel is a good-hearted guy," the neighbors used to say.

"How good it is to be able to give," he wrote one day. "Suppose I wanted to give something to a needy family. I was going to give a thousand francs, but I didn't think it would be enough. I would rather give two thousand francs. Then someone brought me an envelope. . . . Oh, what a great source of happiness Jesus opened up to us, when he told us this secret, 'Love your neighbor!' I told you this story to bring tears to your eyes. Isn't it a great joy for a superior, if, by giving something away, he can do someone good?"[15]

His extreme generosity was attested by all those who approached him. There was no distress that did not affect him personally. Nothing could keep him from doing all in his power to come to his aid. At the same time he was stringent when it came to himself and those who had chosen voluntary poverty, as he had. There is a story that one of the monks was elected abbot of another monastery, and he asked Dom Gabriel, "What should I take along?" The latter smiled sweetly. "Nothing hard about that," he replied. "Nothing but your toothbrush!"

[15] Letter to Mother Cécile, April 17, 1943.

Father Abbot gradually managed to move ahead with the renovation of the church of Bellefontaine. There was certainly enough to do! There had been too many compromises of the Cistercian spirit of simplicity with the tastes of the 19th century, which were really complicated more than sumptuous. But he could only discard what he was able to replace, and so his budget imposed a very slow pace on his renovation program. Nevertheless, the "Saint-Sulpice"[16] elements were inexorably reduced in number, and Father Gabriel would leave many beautiful accomplishments behind him.

The most important thing of all for Dom Gabriel was the preparation of the souls of the monks for the intelligent and profitable celebration of the Office. And so the community began studying the psalms in groups. There were three groups working separately. Each Monday one of these groups met, and the members discussed a psalm, commenting on those verses which were most profitable for prayer.

On the feast of St. Alberic, second abbot of Citeaux, January 26, 1937, Dom Gabriel made known to the community that he intended to undertake a conventual examination of the manner in which the Rule, Constitutions, Usages, Ritual, and Ceremonial were kept at Bellefontaine. Each one's contributions would be accepted in the way in which St. Benedict directed that the suggestions of monks from other communities visiting the community should be received: "If the monk found anything to point out or to censure with reasonable and humble charity, the abbot should think the matter over prudently, considering that it was perhaps for this very reason that the Lord had sent him to that place."[17]

Suggestions were classified, listed, and discussed by the council according to their importance. Afterwards Father Abbot profited from this work in his decisions and made changes and improvements as the opportunity was offered, bringing about a more stable reform. He tried to discern whether anything had been overlooked, and he also tried to get his monks to want the reform, before proposing it to their generosity. While show-

[16] "Saint-Sulpice" = dealers in religious art in the district.

[17] *Rule of Benedict*, ch. LXI.

ing great discernment, he did not avoid some rigorism at times, for his temperament was inclined to rigorism. He was able to make the chapter of faults more efficient by making changes in accordance with the intentions behind the original institution. There were to be no more all-purpose exhortations and no more routine, stereotyped accusations. The monks formed the habit of accusing themselves of serious acts of negligence as soon as they were committed. Father Abbot imposed penances proportionate to the faults committed and liable to be effective.

The first temporary buildings built by the Trappists at the beginning of the 19th century, at the time of the restoration of Bellefontaine had not all been rebuilt by Dom Chouteau. Notable among them was the east wing, connected to the transept of the church. But the monastery's resources were so limited, that every time there was indispensable rebuilding to be done, it posed serious problems. The abbey's sole source of income was farming. Dom Sortais was not the one to favor the creation of industries that now constitute a permanent temptation of activism for communities, for monks can rarely keep an industry in operation themselves but must hire lay personnel. "The best intentions of establishing and maintaining the peace and quiet necessary for recollection and interior prayer are sometimes thwarted by the realities of everyday existence."[18]

In order to allow the community to meet its necessary expenses without increasing the normal pace of work unduly, Father Sortais got the idea of increasing the livestock. He got his brother to make him the plans for a pigsty and set about its construction. The lay brothers and choir simple-professed did the digging, and it was ready just before the outbreak of World War II.

Bellefontaine was not the only community in Dom Sortais' charge. The nuns of Les Gardes, as has been said, were also under his patronage. He visited them often, especially when he first became abbot, regularly spending several days there every three months. His actions within that community were very much like those he undertook at Bellefontaine during the same period. Mother Cécile was the abbess; she was under Dom Lehodey's direction, and so she saw eye-to-eye with Dom

[18] Dom Sortais, op. cit., 186.

Sortais. In fact it is a moot question whether Dom Sortais' idea of studying the usages communally did not ultimately come from Les Gardes. Mother Cécile had applied herself to that task with her novices, even before replacing Mother Bernarde at the head of the community in 1923. In fact, at the time of the persecution of 1903, only certain former women religious had been "officially" authorized to remain in French monasteries. The latter had lived a semi-clandestine life for 15 years, and many of the observances had had to be abandoned during that time. When she had become novice mistress, Mother Cécile Chauvat had undertaken the full restoration of the regular life according to the style proper to Citeaux, with the consent of the prioress. In order to achieve it, she had come up with the idea of studying with her novices the books on which monastic observances were based. After the discussion was over, she summarized the conclusions, and then she requested the prioress that the forgotten practices be resumed.

Dom Sortais was immediately won over by Mother Cécile; she was older than he, and so she showed him a motherly affection and constant tenderness. She had a wonderful heart and disarming spontaneity; so contagious were her joyful temperament and sonorous laugh that he was soon at ease with her. She loved "the sun and the trees, the blackbirds' song, chickens, white rabbits and sheep."[19] She had a very simple and straightforward manner.

Mother Cécile placed all her confidence in Dom Gabriel for the reunion of her community after the incidents mentioned in the last chapter. He himself was taken by her rich, attractive personality and saw only the positive aspects of the situation, without taking the shortcomings of her government sufficiently into account. The sisters at Les Gardes were eager for Father Abbot's simple, practical, and colorful talks. His visits always left a deep impression. Little by little the unity of the community became less precarious and more certain.

The friends of the two communities also formed part of the abbot's family, and he extended his solicitude to them as well.

[19] *La Réverénde Mère Cécile Chauvat, 1886–1943, Abbesse du monastère cistercien de Notre-Dame des Gardes* (Angers: Siraudeau, 1951) 113.

He gave his unconditional support to the members of "Remember the *Vendée*," an organization whose aim was to maintain the Christian traditions of the area and the cult of the heroes of the 1793 epic. For his part he constantly reminded himself that the root cause of the *Vendée* War was religious. In 1937 he proposed to bless the monument of Real del Sarte, which was erected at Cholet. The monument pictured a peasant armed with a sickle, standing in front of the cross and holding a heart in his right hand. The bishops' judgment was that the affair would compromise the church now that the *Front Populaire* had begun, and they positively requested him not to do it. Maxime Real del Sarte had been the president of the *Camelots du Roi* in the good old days of *Action Française*, and one of their founders. Dom Gabriel knew him personally.

The intense activity Father Abbot had imposed on himself at the beginning of his abbacy soon undermined his health, still precarious since his novitiate days. By the spring of 1938 he could hold out no longer. He had too habitually cheated his hours of sleep in order to face the demands of his charge. Besides this there was the interior trial he was undergoing; it often left him worn out and exhausted, and this further undermined his health. In the course of his regular visitation, Father Abbot of La Grande Trappe ordered him to take a real rest. If he wanted to avoid tuberculosis, he must go to the mountains and have many long hours of complete rest. For the mountains he would content himself with the hill of Les Gardes, battered by the wind. Mother Cécile's affectionate, motherly devotion and simple joy would be the best thing for the abbot of Bellefontaine, and he would forget the pressing weight of his charge and his interior trials for a time. He spent the brightest part of the days up in the tower, all bundled up, with only his eyes showing. He finished them in the parlor. This was a beneficial rest period for him, a long period of quiet intimacy with God and human companionship.[20]

[20] "From the top of his 144-foot tower, he thought of Jesus on the mountain. Certain images helped his meditation: The sun that hides behind the clouds but is always there; the limits of human action; their sphere of influence, even though apparently extensive, is always reduced; the sacramental presence of Christ beneath each of the bell-towers, which were in the vicinity." Manuscript notes.

The past two years had enabled Dom Sortais to understand both the beauty and the problems of his abbatial charge. His initial difficulties had rendered him more prudent and less anxious for immediate tangible results. He realized that God's work bears fruit slowly, and that pulling on the trunk of a tree will not make it grow. He lost none of his ideals nor of the absolute demands implied by them (are they not God's demands?), but he began to lose some of the excessive zeal of his approach. For St. Benedict one of the most important qualities of the abbot is discernment, and discernment is that interior quality that makes the soul attentive to the inspiration of the Holy Spirit and docile to his prompting; this permits the abbot to discover the will of God in the details of everyday life and enables him to imitate God's judgment in everything. And so, at the end of this first trial of actual government with its minor errors and great achievements, Dom Sortais found himself closer to the portrait painted by the Father of monks.

Chapter 9

WAR, 1939–40

In order to launch his project in Central Europe of bringing all the German minorities closer to his great Reich, Hitler had played his game of intimidation and had plunged the masses into pacifism, both in France and in England. This policy had been successful since 1936. He meant it to end in unlimited capitulation on the part of the nations of Western Europe and in their sober acceptance of every new situation.

The declaration of war on September 3, 1939, had at least one advantage: that of clarifying the situation and ending the era of flight, but by that time France no longer had the ability to stand firm. "If you must pay again the same price as at Munich last year," wrote Dom Gabriel to one of the monks recalled to active service, "do not pay it; if France must surrender her honor in order to gain a shameful peace, I don't want it. Besides, such a peace would not last, but defeat would certainly follow a peace easily gained."[1]

The abbot of Bellefontaine did not know the actual state of the opposing forces. Still under the influence of his memories of 1918, he could not believe in a rapid military collapse of the armed forces of his country.

He saw 20 of his 50 monks leave inside of a few days at the beginning of September. This was a grievous trial for this loving abbot and spiritual father, and it tore moving cries from his heart. "Oh how I think of you all! Yes, I think of you constantly! If I wake up at night my thoughts are immediately of you, and I offer you to God, and he sees my prayer. Sometimes my eyes are full of tears. Yes I weep, because I reflect that you may be in

[1] Letter to a monk, August 29, 1939.

danger, and I, your father, am safe at home. You simply cannot imagine how much this hurts me. It would be easier to bear, if I myself were exposed to danger."[2]

To one of his sons he wrote these surprising words, "I don't want to answer you, I want to write to you. Don't ask me if I have other work waiting for me, or if I have slept well; no, I need to come and chat with you. I have a poor heart which bleeds from the absence of my sons."[3]

"My thoughts never leave you. Your mother who surely thinks of you constantly does not think about you more often than I do. I did not know I loved my sons so much!"[4]

"It would be easier to bear, if I myself were exposed to danger." In these words we have the key to the explanation of his actions during the following months. He felt the imperious and irresistible need to share the living conditions of those of his sons who were the most exposed. Every other consideration would give place to this one. It would end by occupying his whole field of awareness and covering up every other aspect of the question. He who was not quite 37 had to be in the same situation as his young monks. "I no longer know who that famous imbecile was who claimed to know that monks live side by side in the cloister without loving one another."[5] "If you only knew how it hurts me to have sons who are in danger! It would be easier for me to be in danger myself."[6]

This would continue until he rejoined them at the front. Meanwhile he organized the monastery to meet the new situation. Although they had not finished the harvest, the strongest workers had left, and so it was necessary to adapt the observance to the special situation of an aged community reduced in numbers. Dom Sortais also prepared to welcome those whom events would force to seek asylum at Bellefontaine. He was thinking of the monks of Mont-des-Cats[7] in Flanders and of

[2] Circular letter, September 18, 1939.

[3] Letter to a monk, August 29, 1939.

[4] Letter to a monk, September 10, 1939.

[5] Circular letter, October 14, 1939.

[6] Letter to a monk, October 9, 1939.

[7] Mont-des-Cats is between Dunkirk and Lille. It was founded in 1826 on a hill at an altitude of 518 ft. *Catholicisme,* op. cit., t. 9, col. 597.

the students at the minor seminary of Beaupréau, who had lost their building through requisition, and of possible refugees.

But the abbot was thinking above all of his absent sons. He wanted to write to each one frequently, every eight days if possible. Sheer volume eventually forced him to make his personal letters fewer and to content himself with a circular letter, one copy to each, a substitute for the spoken word which he dispensed in chapter. He would add some personal note to each copy, which would, at times, amount to a mini-letter itself.

He insisted on fidelity to the monastic vocation. It was necessary to respond in a new, unexpected way. "We should not regard the war . . . as a period of wasted time or as an unexpected delay; it is not a kind of digression in our life of contemplation and penance."[8]

He earnestly asked his monks to see that they keep their religious spirit, "Jesus has given you this spirit, and it is very precious; it is your pledge of special favors in eternity, but it may itself be lost or become stale."[9] It is necessary, then, to persevere in living in God's presence, and be attentive to him alone. "Our life is still what it was or at least should be: a constant search for God. Oh how privileged we are to be called to so simple and bare a life: seeking the good God, tending towards him, and trying to reach him; there in that contact, in that brief vision, we give him our whole being. Yes, our whole being, but not only our whole being; that would be a mockery. We give him what we are in Jesus, ourselves united to Jesus, Jesus and ourselves with him, ourselves as part of the package."[10]

The monk outside the cloister, away from his abbot, is not dispensed from his vow of obedience; he should try to fulfill it in some other way, by accepting the difficulties of military life and the orders of commanding officers. A Christian and a monk should know how to joyfully assume the role of suffering, which enables him to be united to the passion of Christ.

What is needed is to continue the pursuit of perfection, far from the help accorded by striving together, which is the sweet

[8] Circular letter, November 5, 1939.
[9] Circular letter, September 23, 1939.
[10] Ibid.

fraternity of the monastery. "I do not think you will have any sudden falls," he said to his draftees. "We have formed good habits in the monastery, and this will save you a lot of trouble; one of these habits is that we do not trust in our own strength, but we put all our confidence in God alone. What we do have to fear in the long run is a certain half-heartedness, a kind of weariness that will come over us willy-nilly, on certain days or at certain hours; a kind of laziness or stupor will invade our lives, if we are too inactive, or even if we are overworked. This stupor will lead us unawares to see ways to take things easy and to do like the others. That is what we must avoid . . . we should never, from one point of view, do 'like the others,' because we aren't 'like the others' any more, after we have made our profession. We were taken out of the world, given many graces, and called to make vows by which we renounced many things. When we made our vows, those vows which are our pledge of special tenderness reserved for us in heaven, we made no exception, not even 'except in wartime' or 'except at the front.' No, we made our vows until death."[11]

In order to be sure to get his sons back, all his sons, without loss to their ideal, he confided them to Our Lady. As for himself, he thought only of joining them in conditions like their own. If there was any time when he listened only to his heart, this was it. He did not even seem to perceive the obvious objections: what would become of his monastery? How long would he be gone? What was the hierarchy of his duties? Would he not really be more useful to his sons in the army by remaining at his post as abbot, than by going to join them (in other words, by being with them morally, rather than physically)?

It must be said in his defense that he was anticipating an eventual call-up. Those declared unfit for military service in peacetime would be called up one after the other by the wartime recruiting boards. That is what happened in the First World War (1914–18). What was the difference if he went sooner or later? And he was inclined to prefer that it be as soon as possible. "I am suffering, because I am not suffering what you suffer. It is a question of my affection for you. Friendship demands a certain

[11] Circular letter, December 3, 1939.

resemblance of the friends to one another. And I love you so much that I cannot bear to be well off, when you are bad off . . . No I cannot, and if someone does not understand, it is because he has never been a father."[12]

Dom Sortais did not posit his old nationalism as a determining factor, but it did play an unconscious part in his reasoning; neither did he seem to be sufficiently aware that his abbatial paternity was just as real for the older religious as for the younger: a too natural reaction, for our spontaneous affection goes to the latter. An abbot should know how to correct this tendency. Dom Gabriel salved his conscience by using hypothetical considerations. "I said to myself that I could count on a more abundant grace of state as superior, if I acted in this way, and that if one or the other of you had given up his vocation after the war, using as pretext the fact that his mind had evolved under the influence of events, I could guide him back to the right path more easily, because I would be the more able to understand his trials . . . A superior is sometimes very clumsy, when he tries to overcome trials in others, that he has not experienced himself."[13]

In point of fact, Father Abbot was in no position to pass an objective judgment in his own case; reasons of the heart spoke too loudly and forced him to act. He did not want to risk being called up as a pen-pusher or censor, a revolting prospect for him; he chose to request a place at the front as a military chaplain, and he took advice on how to obtain it. "If stripes must be worn, as in the last war, I find it distasteful, but I suppose I'll have to accept it."[14]

It seems that all this took less than four weeks to decide, since he applied at Angers to make his request on September 26. At his request the recruiting office at Cholet declared him fit for military service, and on September 29 he agreed to enlist for the duration of the war, a necessary preliminary step for obtaining the post of military chaplain. As a matter of fact he was three years below the legal age. While awaiting his marching orders, he went to Les Gardes and spoke to each nun individually.

[12] Circular letter, November 5, 1939.

[13] Circular letter, October 28, 1939.

[14] Letter to a monk, September 25, 1939.

Not long before this he had had to go to the abbey of Bricquebec twice; this abbey had been placed under the care of Dom Corentin Guyader, abbot of Melleray,[15] since the resignation of Dom Maur Daniel who had gone to Bellefontaine for his retirement.

Dom Sortais' appointment as military chaplain of the Eighth Army would not reach him until December 21, and it would make him rejoin his regiment in an obscure village near Le Mans called Souligné-sur-Ballon. He had received an erroneous order summoning him to the 106th Regiment of Heavy Artillery, stationed at Le Mans. He had left Bellefontaine on November 6; leaving his abbatial ring in the care of the Child Jesus who was resting in his mother's arms. This statuette remains permanently on the abbot's desk.

He began his life as a soldier in his monastic habit, in the barracks of Paixhans, for there were no army uniforms in his size. He was exempted from battery duty, given his particular rank, but he took his turn at the guardhouse. This was at his own request, for the other noncommissioned officers thoughtfully offered to replace him. "I have many friends here," he wrote. "All the poor devils love me. There is a little old man from Nantes, whom I managed to get released from prison, and he has followed me like a dog."

"I won over an ex-convict who has 21 convictions against him in the civil court, and who was on the point of being court-martialed. No one dared come near him, except with two soldiers armed with fixed bayonets, and I know that many of the non-commissioned officers who had been on guard duty said they would ask for bullets, if they had to go near him again. Well, I treated him just as I pleased without bayonets. He told me I was 'the best guy he had met in his life.' Even so, I had the prison regulations literally applied in his case."[16]

Although they may have thought him a "good guy," he did suffer much from "guardhouse jokes" and the rest. Another time he had written, "It is extremely painful to love God and know

[15] Melleray is a Cistercian abbey in the department of Loire-Atlantique, near the city of Chateaubriant. *Webster's Geographic,* op. cit., 412; *Catholicisme,* op. cit., t. 8, col. 1131.

[16] Letter to a monk, November 25, 1939.

how he is offended, hated and blasphemed, and it is also very distressing to notice that we do not serve him ourselves, as we could and should do. Expect to suffer in the most profound part of your being, when you see the sins committed in the world and your own half-heartedness. There are times when it is too painful for words."[17]

He took refuge in his devotion to Our Lady. "Here in this rough place, I certainly see Mary as mother, but especially as virgin. I love her as the ideal virgin, the *dulcis virgo* of the *Salve Regina,* the virgin of incomparable charm, who entices my heart away from all the evil that surrounds me."[18] He also thought of Joan of Arc "who was sanctified in this same life that we are living, surrounded by soldiers, the business of war, the din of camp life, and the fatigue and danger of battle. . . . I thought about her when I was visiting the prisoners last week. The prison walls are covered with immodest drawings and graffiti, and the prison where this daughter of France was held must have had similar horrors, yet Joan was sanctified there."[19]

Despite Dom Gabriel's wish to pass undetected, his presence at Le Mans had been noticed by the bishop of Angers, and he had to appear at the chancellery. He went to the seminary to say Mass, and here indeed he managed to avoid making himself known. One outcome was the intervention of Msgr. Grente with the Commandant to hasten his appointment as chaplain. Father Abbot feared the proposal that he should be made "army chaplain." He did not want to be given a "safe job," far from any danger, 30 miles away from the front. "I suppose you think I am not practicing abandonment. . . . Well it is all right with me, if I seem imperfect to you, if being worried about not being in danger like the rest, like my sons, is imperfect."[20] This obsession with sharing the conditions of his sons who were the most exposed never left him. "I am not at all fit for military chores in the rear guard. . . . I am no master of ceremonies or choirmaster for sung Masses. . . . Can you picture me directing a choir or getting the soldiers to

[17] Letter to a monk, August 26, 1935.
[18] Letter to a priest, November 25, 1939.
[19] Letter to a monk, November 1939.
[20] Letter to a monk, November 21, 1939.

sing? That would be nothing but a joke." He continues with that moving sincerity so characteristic of him. "Well then, I will abandon all that; I have promised Jesus, but my soul is sad. Must I tell you everything? . . . I hoped, or rather I thought I would have been killed at the front, and a glorious death would have ended a very mediocre life. I will not lie to you. I would have gone to absolve a dying soldier, with the grace of God, in one of the most exposed positions. It seems to me, despite the weakness of my flesh, that I would have had no fear of death. I would not commit suicide, have no fear of that; still, it seems to me that I would have been full of courage. But all that is no more than a dream. My virtue is feeble. If I take up the abbatial crosier again, will it keep me on the right road for the rest of my life? . . . Will it not be better for me and for Bellefontaine if I die a good death?"[21]

It was in fact the fancies of his own imagination, always ready to break loose, that Dom Gabriel was struggling against. The post suggested to him was just as exposed as the one he wanted: the difference lay in certain responsibilities towards division chaplains. After having received his appointment as chaplain to the Eighth Army, the abbot of Bellefontaine would be allocated to the 25th Infantry Division without any other responsibility. He spent Christmas happily at the monastery; then he set off for Belfort.

He had two hats: One, he explained, was a tramway conductor's kepi on which he had three stripes sewn at a hatter's shop in Le Mans, in order to speed up proceedings in divisional offices; the other was an unadorned beret "for every day, to avoid intimidating anyone." He arrived at Belfort[22] on December 29 in a bus, traveling third class "with an old soldier, dirty as a little pig, and I was as happy as a child."[23] From Belfort he continued to Giromagny where the headquarters of the Eighth Army was situated. "The country is gorgeous; we are at the foot of mountains covered with forests, and the snow gives them shades of color that are unspeakably precious. The mountains,

[21] Letter to a monk, December 1, 1939.

[22] Belfort is a city and department of eastern France, near the Swiss mountains, about 88 miles east of Dijon. *Webster's Geographic*, op. cit., 130, 412.

[23] Letter to a monk, December 29, 1939.

the snow, the cold, the quiet surroundings all contribute to give the soul the peace it needs to find God. I find pleasure in everything here, even the cold which bites the fingers. Only one thing is missing: Bellefontaine."[24]

Dom Gabriel's contact with the general headquarters of the Eighth Army was brisk. He did not even see the commanding general. He was told that this personage was violently anticlerical. On the evening of January 1 he said goodbye to the Vosges[25] and set off for foggy Flanders to join the 25th Division to which he had been assigned in the interval: Surprises are traditional in military travel! Again to Belfort, then to Vesoul,[26] Paris, Calais,[27] and Bourbourg.[28] The men of the 25th Division of Motorized Infantry were mainly from Auvergne[29] and Forez;[30] these southerners were astonished to be addressed as *tu* instead of *vous* by the northern women and girls: It was an invitation to still greater familiarity! Three infantry regiments and two of artillery, together with the services and the armored scout unit were placed under the direction of General Molinié, an exacting but steadfast leader, aware of his responsibilities and wishing to make his unit "the best division in France." It was he who, by the intermediary of Lieutenant Mazerat (future bishop of Angers) had asked the general director of chaplains for "someone who would make an active and devoted chaplain." "We will send you the best we have" was the answer he received. And so Father Sortais was welcomed with open arms. He immediately won over his commanding officer who said he had discovered "the exceptional riches of his intelligence and compassionate

[24] Letter to a monk, December 31, 1939.

[25] Vosges is a mountain range in eastern France, northwest of Belfort. *Webster's Geographic,* op. cit., 1304.

[26] Vesoul is a commune of Haute-Saone in eastern France, about 50 miles east of Belfort. Ibid., 412.

[27] Calais is a city on the northern coast of France, about 60 miles northwest of Arras. Ibid.

[28] Bourbourg is a city in Flanders, near Dunkirk. *Larousse,* op. cit., t. 2, p. 292.

[29] Auvergne is a mountainous region in central France. *Webster's Geographic,* op. cit., 97.

[30] Forez is a plain and mountain range in central France between the upper Loire River and the Allier. Ibid., 404.

nature . . . the moving generosity of his exuberant heart . . . not only did I appreciate the support of his valued friendship in the course of his frequent visits, but also the rich wisdom of his reflections. In silence I often profited from them."[31]

Three chaplains were assigned to the division. Father Gabriel was responsible for the 38th Infantry Regiment (whose leader, Colonel Denis, became one of his dearest friends), an artillery regiment, an anti-tank battery and some other small units. General Molinié's concern was to distribute the mobilized priests among the units to the best advantage, in order that all the men could have recourse to them.

The abbot of Bellefontaine admired the Christian qualities of many of the higher officials in the division. Reciprocally, almost everyone was won over by his kindness, simplicity, and unlimited dedication. "My predecessor was always on the move, and I will do the same, spending one day a week at the division headquarters, 20 days a month with the infantry and 10 with the artillery which is half as numerous. What I have just written amounts to at least 34 days a month, but you will know what I mean."[32]

At the end of October the services of the German engineering corps had drawn up a plan proposing an attack of the French front through Belgium and the Netherlands. The order to go ahead had been signed on November 5 by Hitler, who had specified November 12 as the launching date. Bad weather had delayed execution, but the French command had received information and made preparations. The 25th Division, belonging to the Giraud Army (the Seventh) had been placed along the shore in the proximity of Dunkirk[33] and the Belgian frontier, just to the left of the Allied dispositions. If Germany violated the neutrality of Belgium and Holland, the division would have to meet the enemy while facing the coast. Meanwhile its leader tried to maintain a state of alert and readiness, in order that the long months of inactivity would not make it lose its ability to fight.

[31] Letter of General Molinié, June 3, 1966.

[32] Letter to a monk, January 5, 1940.

[33] Dunkirk is a seaport of northern France on the Strait of Dover, 44 miles northwest of Lille. *Webster's Geographic,* op. cit., 346.

He counted on his officers, but also on the chaplains to keep the morale high.

All winter, in the strong gusts of wind that blew from the North Sea, in rain and in slush, Father Abbot went from one unit to the next on a bicycle, with the luggage rack covered, in order not to depend on anyone. His imposing stature was seen emerging from the darkness. He arrived exhausted but happy, his gaze straight ahead, with a big smile on his face. His ardor tempered by a delightful shyness and his cheerfulness had the ability of winning the hearts of all. One of those who knew him then calls him a "born charmer." He was in great demand. He was very soon at ease with the officers. He loved to have anyone ask him about the Trappists; it allowed him to speak about his brothers and about God. One day he brought back from leave a bottle of brandy. "Do the monks drink that?" asked someone. "We make a lot of brandy," he said, "but it is for nursing our calves!"

Dom Gabriel encountered more difficulty among the men. He had to be hard on himself. Long years of silence and taste for solitude and contact with God had not prepared him for this apostolate. "Well," he said, "I would rather go barefoot in the snow than enter a crowd of soldiers or a house where soldiers are quartered and say, 'Well, boys, how is it going?' . . . I must learn to do it! With God's grace I will overcome my timidity and the sort of horror I feel of saying to each one a meaningless word and giving out a hundred handshakes, cigarettes, and *Pelerins*.[34] I know, however, that it is expected, and I ought to do it."[35]

Some reserve had to be overcome on both sides, because the soldiers were impressed by this bright-eyed giant. Father Gabriel forced himself to spend all the long winter nights with the men on the straw, in the barns where they were quartered. These *Saint-Étienne* people often have a strong leftist trend which does not make them easy to approach. Little by little the ice was broken. "I bless the good God for having prepared me for my ministry here by permitting me to make regular visitations. What I do here is a little bit along the same line. I receive grievances. Someone talks to me about one person and another (officers, to be sure), and I try to refute their objections and make the officer

[34] *Pelerins* is probably a literary magazine no longer current.

[35] Letter to a monk, January 8, 1940.

well-liked, whoever he may be, as well as the specific officer in command here and now."[36] The Frenchman is a born grumbler! There is no fault, however, which displeased Dom Gabriel more.

By the end of January, not having taken care of himself, Father Abbot was exhausted. For some time he suffered from intestinal pains. Dysentery kept him tied to his bed for eight days without food and almost without being able to pray. His morale suffered from this: "Do you know what would please me now? To have a little child like Annick here beside me, so that I might marvel at her innocent eyes, her simple soul and her spontaneous, unaffected love. We must become like these little ones in order to participate in the joy of heaven—how far I am from that! Yet I love little children, the *parvuli,* so much!"[37]

Back on his feet after this warning, he returned to his work, hardly disturbed for a moment by apprehension about being named chaplain of the Eighth Army again. He paid careful attention to mobilized priests and seminarians in his division: "I go to see them again and again; I go to their meetings, and I hear the confessions of many of them; I put them back on their feet and give them back to Jesus with the 'old one-two,' and they know I don't want to see them either gloomy or especially moaning or grumbling."[38]

Easter found him redoubling his activities; he was everywhere with his "muddy shoes, his wet and dirty raincoat, his cap so out of shape from the rain that it no longer had any but a faint resemblance to the caps worn by conductors on the train." He was supported by the prayers of Bellefontaine and Les Gardes and all the communities that knew him. But he acted much more by what he was than by what he did: "It wasn't difficult to grasp that the real key to his influence lay in his union with God. We had from the first a monk who lived intensely his life with God in his heart. To approach him gave us, as it were,

[36] Letter to a monk, February 3, 1940. The following passage is found among his notes on the Rule: "Even in the case of a superior who seems to take sides or act unwisely, we should not murmur. Just because a superior commits a fault, we are not authorized to commit one ourselves." *Notes sur la Règle de St. Benoit,* ch. 34.

[37] Letter to a monk, February 3, 1940.

[38] Ibid., March 3, 1940.

a sensible presence of God. No one was mistaken in this, and he had no need for many words."[39]

Soon after Easter he obtained one last leave for Bellefontaine (April 10–20), where he saw seven of his mobilized monks again. Then he was suddenly plunged into the storm. His aspiration had been to give himself in battle to the service of the soldiers. Events were rushing forward to furnish him ample opportunity for this.

On the other side of the front, Von Rundstedt's chief of staff, Erich von Manstein, had succeeded in getting his remarkable plan adopted; it was a maneuver which consisted in concentrating all the armored divisions at Germany's disposal on the weak point in the French defense, while drawing the majority of the French Divisions toward the battlefields of Belgium and the Netherlands; they would then be isolated from the rest of the Front by the breach made by the German army towards the North Sea.

Hitler had adopted the plan at the beginning of February, but it could not be put into execution on account of the Norwegian diversion. Finally a favorable opportunity presented itself on May 10.

The attack by the German troops on the Netherlands, Belgium, and Luxembourg was announced for the night of May 9–10, and the French command ordered the Anglo-French armies located between the Ardennes[40] and the sea to arrange themselves in a line from Dinant,[41] along Namur,[42] Gembloux[43] and Louvain[44] to Bréda.[45] The Twenty-fifth Division was to get to Anvers,[46] and from there to take its position in Holland.

[39] Testimony of an officer.

[40] The Ardennes is a large wooded region at the border of France and Belgium. *Webster's Geographic*, op. cit., 68.

[41] Dinant is a city in south Belgium, along the river Meuse. Ibid., 332.

[42] Namur is a city along the Meuse in south Belgium, about 20 miles north of Dinant. Ibid., 843.

[43] Gembloux is a city of south Belgium, 10 miles northwest of Namur. Ibid., 43.

[44] Louvain is a city of central Belgium along the Djile River, 15 miles east of Brussels. Ibid., 690.

[45] Breda is a city in the southern part of the Netherlands, along the Merk River, 14 miles west of Tilburg. Ibid., 171.

[46] Anvers, Antwerp, Antwerpen is a city east of the river Scheldt, 23 miles north of Brussels. Ibid., 58.

Father Sortais was informed of the order at 7:00 a.m., returning from his Mass. He immediately wrote a few words to his sons at Bellefontaine: "I certainly hope to perform all my duties, thanks to God and to Mary. . . . Long live France who fights for God!"[47] He was, in fact, convinced that he was fighting for Christian civilization. In the opposite camp (as had been seen in the Polish campaign) were ranged the two large nations which professed militant atheism, both of which brutally persecuted the church: Nazi Germany and Communist Russia.

Already on the evening of May 10, the vanguard of the 25th Division had arrived at the city of Anvers, and scouts had been sent to Bréda. Father Sortais was in the company of the medical corps, one of the last to leave. It was only on the evening of May 11 that he was also at Anvers where he found General Molinié and his Division already sorely tried by machine gun fire and hedge-hopping aerial bombardments. It was useless to try to move by day. Sunday was utilized to visit the wounded. Taking advantage of the night between Sunday, May 12, and Monday, May 13, the chaplain rejoined the troops in contact with the enemy, crossing a ruined countryside.

The combat on May 13 was fierce. The intervention of a German armored division forced the French troops who had pushed ahead towards Bréda to fall back. The surrender of Holland seemed only a matter of hours. The next day, May 14, the Giraud Army was ordered to entrench itself behind the river Scheldt in Anvers. On May 13 and 14 Dom Sortais shared the lot of the combatants at Putten,[48] Kapelle,[49] Kalmthout[50] and Sainte-Mariaburg. He went among the men giving general absolution, from one section to the next, raising the morale which continuous machine gun fire had severely tried.

On May 15 the Dutch Army had stopped all fighting. Runaways threw the French ranks into confusion, but it was

[47] Letter to his monks, May 10, 1940.

[48] Putte or Putten is on the border between Belgium and the Netherlands, east of the river Scheldt. *Larousse,* op. cit., t. 8, p. 914.

[49] Kapelle or Kapellen is a commune northeast of Antwerp in Belgium. Ibid., t. 6, 440.

[50] Kalmthout is a commune about 25 miles north of Antwerp in Belgium. Ibid., t. 6, 433.

especially far away in the Ardennes that the concentration of Guderian's armored divisions had literally broken up the Ninth Army, and a dangerous pocket had taken shape. The success of the breach was so complete, that it surprised the German general headquarters, and Guderian had to rant and rave, in order to obtain permission to exploit it more thoroughly. His initiative would be decisive.

For the Seventh Army these events completely changed the way things looked. While the battle was raging its commander, Giraud, was taken away to command the Army of the Ardennes, which was in distress. His large units were added to those in the Blanchard army or placed at the disposal of Admiral Abrial, who had to defend the fortified town of Dunkirk. Other units were brought back to the south of the Somme, in order to be integrated into a new battle corps placed under the command of General Frère. The 25th Division itself remained in Flanders, together with the First Army (that of General Blanchard) and retreated from one river to another towards the coast, while the Panzer Divisions charging toward the sea in the direction of St.-Valéry,[51] Boulogne[52] and Calais, succeeded in cutting the French army in two. Father Sortais had participated in the retreat; several times, when the main body of the troops broke off the action, a section left as rear guard begged him, "Father, stay with us." And he stayed. At general headquarters of the division he was thought to be a prisoner at one time. These tragic days he had no news of his sons: "I am thinking with anguish of my soldier sons. For eight days I have not received a single letter. . . . It is a long time to be without news of my sons, many of whom would be in the thick of the fight. We have had some fierce moments, and this evening we are going towards other sectors. I say Mass often but not every day, because we are always on the move. Once we marched 13 and a half hours at a stretch, after an already tiresome day."[53] And a few days later: "How are we still alive? That is God's secret. Humanly

[51] St.-Valéry-sur-Somme is a town on the south side of the mouth of the Somme River in northern France. *Webster's Geographic,* op. cit., 1051.

[52] Boulogne is a seaport on the English Channel in northern France, 61 miles northwest of Arras. Ibid., 166.

[53] Card of May 18, 1940.

speaking, I have no hope of returning, but God can do what he wishes, and he can protect us, as he protected the children in the furnace. . . . I am writing to you amid the noise of machine gun fire and airplanes. . . . In a second I could be before God: I will all that he wills, I love him, I love his will. . . . If I return from the furnace, I believe I will be greatly changed. The proximity of death makes us understand many things."[54]

On May 19 the 25th Division changed sectors; it left the region of Gand[55] and the coast. It seemed to the French High Command that the German pocket forming like a finger against the sea could still be cut off at its base. Guderian's Panzer Divisions, in fact, were spaced out at 124 miles in a relatively narrow passageway from the Ardennes to La Manche; the motorized infantry had a hard time occupying the ground behind it. General Molinié's Division, then, was assigned to join the Anglo-French units whose mission was to sever the corridor conquered by the enemy by attacking from the north.

Unfortunately, the transport was hopelessly slow, due to bombardments, machine gun fire and sabotage, and the English were eager to evacuate instead of attacking. Finally on the evening of May 20 the division arrived south of Lille.[56] At Courcelle Father Abbot witnessed a frightful drama. The psychosis of the Fifth Column was so bad among the soldiers and the civilian population, that spies were seen everywhere. Rumors were spread (and they made their way even to places most remote from the battlefield), that spies were disguised as priests and religious. And so on the morning of May 21, after he had said Mass, someone came to tell Dom Gabriel that two nuns had been killed not far away, and that the crowd had mutilated their bodies. He hurried to the place. "Ten people surrounded the bodies, abusing the 'spies.' Some trampled on them. . . . I was indignant at this conduct. Then it was I who was attacked and abused in my turn. I was treated as a friend of the Germans and of the spies, as a Fifth Columnist, as a parachutist." He had

[54] Letter to his prior, May 21, 1940.

[55] Gand, Gent, Ghent is a city of Belgium at the confluence of the Scheldt and Lys Rivers, about 20 miles west of Brussels. *Webster's Geographic,* op. cit., 432.

[56] Lille is a city of Flanders near the Belgian border. Ibid., 670.

an ambulance called. "When we lifted the second body, much of the inside of the head remained on the ground, because the skull had been broken by the blows from the heels of shoes. All the brains were there in the grass. A dog pounced on them. I pushed the dog away, and amidst the jeers of the spectators, I picked up with my own hands all the brains which were there in the grass, thinking of that nun who had loved and served the good God, whose body would be glorified some day."

That very evening the division was engaged in the offensive. On May 22 Generals Altmayer and Molinié attacked in the direction of Cambrai,[57] pushing on to the suburbs of the city, but the German armored divisions, reversing their positions, threatened to take the counter-offensive from the rear. Fierce combat continued for four days, then came the order to retreat toward the sea (May 26). It was already too late. Rommel's division occupied the roads giving access to Dunkirk. It was the Battle of Lille in which four French divisions, one of which was the 25th, sustained the assault of eight enemy divisions, three of which were Panzers. General Molinié, the oldest, took command and tried in vain to slacken the noose. The attempt at a sortie on May 28 ended in failure: Only a few tanks and motorcycles succeeded in forcing a passage to the other French troops. Then the commander of the 25th Division decided to resist as long as possible, in order to keep the enemy he was holding at bay from participating in the attack on Dunkirk.

For the units the chaplain was accompanying, the withdrawal to Lille and the River Lys was achieved in two stages of 28 miles during the night on bypaths, each soldier, besides his own pack, loaded with 600 cartridges. Dom Sortais stayed with the rear-guard, the most exposed, helping any soldier to carry his crushing burden without hesitation. These were nights of nightmare with shells and bombs, crossing villages in flames.

With the 38th Infantry Regiment, which he was accompanying, Dom Sortais had thought it possible to skirt the city through the suburb on the west, but the Germans were already in front of Haubourdin. They skirted around the city, then through the

[57] Cambrai is a city of northern France on the Scheldt River, 34 miles southeast of Lille. Ibid., 206.

nearer suburb of Loos and Canteleu. The Armentières Road to the northwest had been cut off by Rommel's tanks. Other German troops had followed them, and Lille was surrounded. The enemy had even penetrated into certain parts of the center of the city. The citadel was occupied. Unaware of this, the 38th Infantry Regiment tried to cross a bridge dominated by it less than 218 yards away. Thanks to a thunderstorm which momentarily took away all visibility, two sections managed to get through, but they lost men, and it was necessary to cross the bridge under fire from the citadel in order to go and help the wounded. Dom Sortais did not hesitate to volunteer: "The four stretcher-bearers hurled themselves onto the bridge; then they walked bent over in order to be shielded by the bridge's parapet; from a certain point they ran, one waiting for the other to arrive behind a metal electric post; they crouched down, then ran again and went down along the bank." Dom Sortais with a companion was last. A burst of gunfire got them both. Father Abbot fell first, and the stretcher-bearer collapsed on top of him. Father Abbot took a direct hit. He thought it had penetrated his chest, but in fact the bullet had hit his chaplain's pectoral cross, and the latter had become embedded in his flesh. "I remained about an hour in the rain, without being able to move because of the weight of the body which was lying on top of me, and because of the Germans, who would have taken me away immediately. I was exposed to their bullets, which were whistling over me without a break, and the fire of their antitank cannon which was 131 yards away and was fired five times in my direction. I cried out toward the other bank that no one should come looking for me, because it would have been foolhardy to come to that place."

What could be done? Wait for the darkness of night to relieve the wounded? Major Bredeau, commanding officer of the Second Battalion of the 38th Infantry Regiment did not agree. He organized a dangerous rescue mission executed by four stretcher-bearers protected from enemy fire by the side of a tracked vehicle; it was done in the midst of explosions, under fire from the enemy who did not even relent at sight of the arm bands of the Red Cross. The priest was brought back on a stretcher at a run by Major Gay, a chaplain named Lafay and two other volunteers. Dom Gabriel seemed lifeless and unconscious. His chest was "all chewed up because of the force of the blow," but his chaplain's cross had saved him. On the evening of May 28, in the shelters, cellars and trench sections of the suburb, the men spoke in low voices about the "miracle of the chaplain whom bullets could not wound."

When combat ceased three days later for lack of ammunition, Father Sortais had been up for 48 hours assisting the wounded, in spite of the pain in his chest.

Chapter 10

WATCHTOWERS AND BARBED WIRE

German airplanes had dropped pamphlets on Lille to invite the French divisions to surrender; bombs had followed the pamphlets, and shells had followed the bombs. Struck by #150 shells, entire districts had collapsed. The German General Wagner, a true soldier and a good-hearted man, wanted to avoid a general massacre in which women and children would be involved. He tried to slow down bombardments and multiplied peaceful offensives.

On May 21 at 4:00 p.m. in the suburb of Canteleu the northern fortified position gave ground. There was no choice but to accept the ceasefire. Papers were burned, vehicles were sabotaged, and ammunition was blown up. Rifles were thrown into the canal. Many officers wept. Some soldiers imitated them.

In the part of the city occupied by him General Molinié still held his ground and refused the offer of the German commandant, who nevertheless recognized the bravery of the troops and proposed war honors. At 9:00 p.m., however, General Molinié's situation was desperate, and he had to lay down his arms in his turn.

On the next day, June 1, at 9:00 a.m. in the central square of Lille, General Wagner was present at the parade of French troops bearing arms for the last time. A German infantry battalion did the honors. Those defeated at the suburb of Canteleu did not participate. They surrendered a few hours too early!

Dom Sortais had been cited by order of the division before the fighting stopped. So he could console himself for losing the honors of war, but he regretted the deprivation for his companions' sake. During these painful hours the population multiplied its marks of sympathy for the prisoners who were conducted under escort into the fairground building. The bitter captivity was beginning. "This Friday May 31 was the feast of the Sacred Heart. Lord, I did not have a moment's doubt about your love for us and your love for me! But what a day!"

Such was their exhaustion that the captives did not have the strength at first to take full stock of their new situation. They collapsed on the ground and fell fast asleep. They awoke in pain: The truth became clear in all its tragic horror, without the least hope for the future.

At this point a brusque change of attitude could be seen in Dom Sortais. He would show the conquerors an inflexibility and aggressiveness that we had not been in the habit of associating with the monk. Toward his companions he would always be the same, satisfied with everything, forgetful of himself, neither difficult nor exacting on the necessities of everyday life. But the Germans always found him offended, ready to demand the prisoners' rights, refusing to submit his pride to humiliation. A characteristic signal: He congratulated himself at the moment of surrender that the Germans did not oblige him to raise his arms; he would never have done it, he said, even if threatened with death! Another very characteristic fact: At Tournai[1] a German officer requisitioned him with some prisoners to conduct the interment of several English soldiers whose corpses were lying on the ground some distance from the city. This medical officer was a fervent Catholic, and he wished to have a priest say the prayers over the bodies. He invited Father Abbot to accompany him in his automobile. When Dom Sortais learned from his companion that he was a Nazi and one of the first to become a follower of Hitler, he could not control himself, but poured out all the feelings of his heart to the officer. How could a Catholic become a party of the nightmares, cruelty, and crimes of the Führer?

So far did he take his rank obstinacy that he tended to see vexation and abuse everywhere: In his mind everything coming from the Germans came from bad faith. He was stubborn on this point, he who was otherwise so open and understanding. The

[1] Tournai is a city of Belgium near the French border. *Larousse,* op. cit., t. 10, 412.

authority of the victors, imposed by force, was necessarily illegitimate, and he submitted to it without accepting it. He would find fault with their conduct at every opportunity; his reactions were violent. In this way he meant to give his companions new confidence and courage, depressed as they were by the ordeal, to incite them to recovery and keep them from moral surrender. But this fact kept him from perfectly recognizing loyalty in his adversaries, a loyalty of which they gave many proofs. Dom Sortais had the merit of sincerity: He never kept his opinions to himself, even if he had to pay for them. His protests, often vehement, also had positive results for the prisoners.

The first stages of exile took him to Tournai and Enghien,[2] where he stayed for a few days at a small Poor Clare Monastery transformed into a prison. He acted boldly at Tournai: passing a Belgian army clothing store which prisoners were dismantling under the watchful eyes of armed guards, he entered and took a new pair of pants to replace one of Major Bredeau's which was torn at the knee: "Well, Major, I thought your pants were torn, so I brought you a good pair."[3] As for himself, all he possessed was a portable altar kit left him by Abbé Lefay, his reserve supply of hosts and his wine for Mass. Neither clothing nor food. God would provide. From the Poor Clare Convent the prisoners were transferred to the large Jesuit high school where Dom Sortais found a spiritual book in the library, which he would keep during the whole captivity; afterward he would return it to its owners. A young Dominican officer, himself a prisoner, presented him with a Cistercian *diurnale*[4] from the same source, so he could say his Office: "Father, guess what I have brought you." These days of rest were necessary after the heavy fatigue of combat and wounds.

On June 11 they left for Beverloo[5] via Nivelles and Hasselt;[6] one day all the food they had were some rhubarb stalks. It was a

[2] Enghien is a city of Belgium about 25 miles south of Brussels. Ibid., t. 4, 552.

[3] Testimony of an officer.

[4] A *diurnale* is a small breviary containing only the day hours (Lauds to Compline).

[5] Beverlo or Beverloo is a commune near Hasselt in the province of Limbourg in Belgium. *Larousse,* op. cit., t. 2, 111.

[6] Hasselt is the chief city of Limbourg in Belgium. Ibid., t. 5, 798.

long journey, first by bus, then by train, followed by exhausting stages of 25 miles on foot under an extremely hot sun in a particularly hot summer. Exchanges with the citizens were strictly forbidden; an officer was brought down by a bullet in the neck for having stopped a few seconds near a woman who offered him a few lumps of sugar. Nevertheless, the Belgians did what they could for the prisoners. "I remember the wonderful example of a certain old lady who tried many times to provide a line of prisoners with fresh supplies, despite the shots from a guard."[7]

Dom Sortais suffered much from the long marches. His breathing was still laborious. "We arranged it among ourselves never to be too far from him in the column," wrote an officer, "and we kept an eye on him. When we saw from his pallor or excessive perspiration that he was weakening, we drew near and tried to relieve him of his pack or of his blanket, but it was not easy. He grew angry and would not listen. I think we did not succeed very often in persuading him. This did not keep him, when one of our companions was growing weak, from being the first to rush forward to relieve him of his burden. Not content to carry his own cross like Christ, he wanted also, like Simon, to carry those of others."[8]

The stop at the camp of Beverloo lasted ten days. Father Sortais immediately succeeded in obtaining the concession of a room which he transformed into a chapel where he held exposition of the Blessed Sacrament in order to allow the prisoners to come and pray. Hunger was felt bitterly by all. The only nourishment granted to the captives was potatoes, rotten, unpeeled, prepared in the open air in a washing machine and stirred with a broomstick. The departure for Germany was made in padlocked cattle trucks, replaced after Dortmund by passenger trains. The further they got from the front, the more aggressive the guards became. Regular prison guards took over from the soldiers the job of incarcerating the prisoners. Father Sortais took advantage of the great influence he exercised over his companions to appease their anger and revolt. Firmness is not imprudence!

[7] Conference for prisoners' wives.
[8] Testimony of an officer.

Magdeburg,[9] Brandenburg,[10] Berlin, Kustrin, Kreuz, the Polish frontier was in sight. Obviously the intention was to take away all desire of escape from the prisoners. It was dismal Pomerania with its lakes, its pines and birch trees, until you can see no further. The former Poland begins 25 miles further on.

Gross-Born was a training camp for the German army. At the center of a vast plot, nine miles to a side, reserved for maneuvers, was a stone camp for Hitler's troops and a mass of plank barracks surrounded by watch towers built on the sand: It was Oflag[11] IID, an enclosure of 11 hectares, divided into three blocks whose environment left much to be desired. The officers would live there in rabbit-hutches placed on the sand, where they would be crowded together to the number of 6,000. At the end of June the congestion at the Oflag was such that the Germans considered the building of another larger camp one or two miles away. At the end of August there were still 4,700 officers. The following months—September, October, November—would be marked by some collective departures: 80 young officers and the oldest of the officers up to a total of about 150 of them; 80 priests, ministers and rabbis; then the Alsatians on the morning of November 21. During Father Sortais' captivity the total number of prisoners crowded together in the camp would fluctuate between 6,000 at the end of June and 3,700 in January 1941.

The number of priests, chaplains, or soldiers, was considerable at first: More than 120 until the massive departure of October 16; afterward it remained at about 30 until January 29, 1941, the date of the repatriation of the division chaplains (in virtue of the Geneva accords).

There were very important priests in the camp united by a common misfortune: Abbé Garrone, the future Cardinal, then rector of the major seminary of Chambéry; Père Des Places, a Jesuit, first chaplain of the block; Dom Colliot, future abbot of Landévennec; Abbé Didier, professor at the Catholic faculty of Lille; Abbé Froidevaux, professor at the Institut Catholique in Paris; Canon

[9] Magdeburg is a city along the Elbe River in E. Germany. *Larousse,* ibid., t. 6, 962.

[10] Brandenburg is a city between Magdeburg and Berlin in E. Germany. Ibid., t. 2, 336.

[11] An *oflag* is a prison camp for officers only.

Chanson, rector of the major seminary at Arras, who was responsible for the seminarians in the camp. Dom Sortais found three monks of his order.

The registering ritual followed soon after the arrival at camp on June 30. The prisoners had to present all their meager baggage, and they were quickly searched. Next they put down their money if they had any. Those who had waged the campaign in Belgium were often for that reason stripped of everything. Then the examiner wrote their names, surnames, rank, religion, regiment, date and place of capture, and state of health in a register. Each officer received an identity tag of aluminum, which he wore around the neck. The last operation was the prisoner's identity photograph, bearing his number inscribed in slate in large digits.

Each section of the camp formed a whole, without regular communication with the other blocks. And so religious life was organized autonomously in each of the three sectors in which the Oflag was divided (blocks I and IV, blocks II and III). Father Sortais was assigned to block II, and he found lodging with some friends from his escapades in Belgium in stube[12] I of barrack II: The room was six and a half by 19 feet, containing 16 beds in three tiers.

The German authorities reserved for themselves the right of authorizing religious manifestations of a public character. And so in the beginning the first celebrations, especially of Mass, took place in half-secrecy. In the first evenings some former scouts grouped themselves around some priests for sung prayer, as they had done in camps on French soil. Masses were celebrated with very restricted congregations at first, because of the absence of authorized places for religious gatherings, and because liturgical furnishings were almost totally lacking. Thanks to some portable altars brought along with great difficulty, a Mass-list was arranged. There was no question of each priest celebrating Mass daily. The priests said Mass by turns every ten days, later every eight. Toward the end of summer, when hosts and Mass-wine could be obtained, the schedule picked up, and the frequency was twice a week. The first high

[12] *Stube* = barracks room

Masses were celebrated in open air on a stage formed by four or five tables.

The division chaplains who wore a short black cassock as a uniform over their khaki pants were easily recognizable. The men formed groups around them. In block II there were Father Sortais and another chaplain of the 25th Division, Abbé Bréchard of Limoges.

Two factors would contribute to make Father Sortais the most striking personality of the block (the various parts of the camp were too partitioned for him to be able to act effectively outside of this sphere): his place in the hierarchy of the church—he was Abbot of a large monastery—and his exceptional personal radiance. The testimony on that is unanimous:

"The Abbot of Bellefontaine was universally admired," wrote Abbé Pierre Flamant in his thesis on life at Oflag IID. "He left an undying memory among the prisoners. How often they regretted his departure! A sojourn of a few months had given him an extraordinary influence over them. Beaming with the supernatural each time he spoke, he incarnated . . . the ideal military chaplain. He was very human, and he knew how to gain the affection of his companions in exile, by his radiant goodness."[13] These lines, written for a book finished in 1956, well before Dom Sortais' death, do not have a hagiographical character. It is direct and sincere testimony to a living man, and it should be taken literally.

Testimony gathered after 1963 is very similar. Here is one witness among a hundred others: "It was during the first days of captivity . . . the dejection of defeat, the state of almost complete destitution in which we lived for 15 days, the total inactivity had put us in a moral and physical state of extreme lassitude, very close to anarchy. No rank existed for us any more, especially the military, and the higher-ranked officers, although certain ones were distinguished, aware of this situation, seemed ashamed of their stripes. I see myself still, sprawled on the sand with some comrades, waiting, no doubt, for the meager evening repast, when a group of new arrivals passed close by, among

[13] Abbé Pierre Flament, *La vie dans un camp d'offiçiers français en Poméranio, l'Oflag II D–II B* (Paris: Amicale l'Oflag, 1957) 543.

whom was Father Sortais, whom I had never seen before. What reflex did I obey? I do not know, but the attitude of the abbot, so full of dignity and simplicity at the same time, in his poor cassock, worn but immaculate, made such an impression on me, that I spontaneously arose and saluted. Perhaps I was not the only one to be moved by his appearance, for the conversation in my group turned immediately to him."[14]

This was an exceptional influence which facilitated Father Abbot's task greatly; he immediately guessed its urgency: to put these demoralized officers back on their feet, to return to them the sense of their dignity, the taste for existence, then to turn them resolutely to God and open them up to spiritual preoccupations which ought to have primacy in any life. He knew the bitter questions these young men were asking because he had asked them himself: Why this defeat? How could we have come to this? Career officers especially saw their ideal shattered at one blow. Now they had no more social ground. The most intense personal problems were grafted on this knot, already inextricable. These 6,000 officers represented almost as many families in distress: They lived by the thought of those whom they loved, whom they could not protect, and from whom they were separated for how long a time? The absence of news augmented the disarray. How had their loved ones gone through this torment?

Dom Sortais took advantage of the Mass on July 14 to recall the reasons that had made France decide to enter the war: fidelity to her obligations to Poland. The German propaganda was used to give our soldiers a guilty conscience, to make the responsibility for the war fall on France.

Father Abbot thought, in fact, that he ought to aid his companions in every need that they had: materially (he could not go very far in this), in their personal problems, in their quest for God—this is where his principal field of action lay—but also in their condition as officers and combatants. In this regard the captivity was only an accident of war in his opinion. The soldier in enemy hands was not therefore discharged; he had to preserve the soul of a combatant.

[14] Testimony of an officer.

In this period of his life, Dom Gabriel seemed to some too harsh toward the Germans. He seemed to include them all in his reprobation. There were cutting words and reactions in which his violent temperament broke through. But this attitude was dictated by his chivalrous need to oppose injustice. Force did not intimidate him in any way. He denounced oppression at his own risk and peril.

Yet there was not the least amount of hate. In 1952, having become Abbot General of the Cistercians, he would begin the series of visitations of his monasteries with Germany. He wished, he said, to carry his affection first and foremost to those of his sons who had had the most to suffer. And the monks of Mariawald in the Rhineland entered the following lines in their chronicle: "The common father of all the Trappists has conquered all our hearts. He spoke to us twice in chapter with the elegance and facility that give his majestic bearing something so tender and candid, that we are no longer afraid to approach him."[15] The distance between the prisoner of 1940 and the Abbot General in 1952 is less than one might believe.

At the camp of Gross-Born he did not show any more tenderness for those who played ball with Germany and thought that Europe's future was on their side. The Germans distributed a paper printed in French in the prisoners' camps, which was completely devoted to them: *Le Trait d'Union.* Taking advantage of the Mass on August 15, at which some of the guards were present, he vehemently took exception to a picture that had appeared in the paper: a tomb of a French soldier with the caption, "Unnecessary Sacrifice." "There is no wasted sacrifice for anyone who knows how to unite his sacrifice with the redeeming sacrifice of Calvary," he loudly proclaimed. "Joan of Arc was also sacrificed, and the *Vendéens* of 1793!"

This jarring homily was delivered in the large canteen of block II, a theater which was used as a chapel on feast days. It was not always easy to create a proper atmosphere there for liturgical celebrations, but it was spacious, and it provided a relatively grandiose environment. Father Sortais, no doubt, counted

[15] "Chroniques de nos abbayes" in *Collectanea Ordinis Cist. Ref.* XIV (1952) 146.

for something in this temporary appropriation, because he knew how to impose his will, even on the camp authorities. "He often decided on religious celebrations, against the will of the Germans, which he knew how to bend by showing them that he would not give in to them."[16]

Sermons usually did not get much publicity, nor did they have much effect in the camp. The officers liked them short. They indicated their preference for the courses given in the skeleton university of the camp and for conferences. All fields were tackled by those who wished to profit from the enforced leisure of captivity to increase their knowledge, complete their education, or occupy the otherwise interminable hours in an interesting and useful way. Religious studies had their place. During the first few months the specialists had to prepare their lectures from memory, for there was no possibility of consulting the least book—*docti sine libro!* Before there was free circulation among the different sectors of the camp, they were able to obtain permission from the camp authorities for the professors to come and give the same lectures in the different blocks. Such was the regime until spring 1941. Father Sortais spoke of what he knew. He gave a lecture on Cistercian monastic life, which left a strong impression on his hearers. He also gave two series of conferences on the liturgy and the Divine Office, showing the place of the latter in the scheme of things and sketching out a short history of the breviary. His lectures on prayer and presentation of times of prayer that, by searching the heart and by way of loving knowledge, lead the soul to intimacy with the living God, were especially listened to.

On the occasion of All Saints and All Souls Day, the abbot of Bellefontaine gave a description of the liturgy of the sick, the dying, and the dead as it was celebrated in Cistercian monasteries.

During the "phony war" he had attended with partiality to the mobilized priests in his division. In the camp he tried to help the priest-prisoners (about 40 for block II until the massive departure of October 16). It was organized spontaneously. After having overcome the first shock, which was bitter for some, the priests

[16] Testimony of an officer.

would feel the need to live in contact with each other and to work at their own perfection. There was a total lack of books from the first. Spiritual reading was done in common. The Divine Office, too, was often recited in common. Necessity had imposed a practice which some would perhaps not have adopted by themselves. Dom Sortais applied himself more particularly to the meetings of priests on the occasion of the novena preceding the Assumption.

Since Enghien, by way of a personal pack, he had carried four liters of wine and a large quantity of hosts. It was a providence for his block. When the supply was gone he had recourse to the canteen-keeper. "For a fortune, she sold me some wine which she affirmed was strictly pure. A good many Masses were celebrated with that wine. One day I became suspicious, so I asked an officer who understood German very well to inquire discreetly about the origin of the Mass wine. The good woman told him confidentially that it was her father who had made the wine with some elderberries! All the Masses celebrated with this so-called wine had been invalid!"

In mid-October, when the congestion of the camp was relieved, Father Sortais obtained the favor of moving into a small room with three other priests. From then on the Blessed Sacrament presided over their days from the top of a wooden cupboard. Up until then the priests in the camp had taken turns carrying the sacrament in a pyx hanging from their neck.

In his sermons and brief remarks at the rosary or Evening Prayer, the abbot of Bellefontaine recalled the redemptive value of sacrifice and of suffering accepted in a generous spirit, as well as of the ability the Christian has of sublimating his most ordinary actions.

But mostly he heard confessions, despite the prohibitions of the Germans and the interference of the guards. To disarm suspicion he used the method of walking confessions as private talks: "I am not hearing confessions; I am administering the sacrament of penance." On certain days it obliged him to walk for whole hours, despite fatigue and cold. Officers came to him ten at a time to confide their cares and anguish to him and to beg his counsel. He gave evidence of unlimited and indefatigable goodness. A small group of fervent disciples who desired a deeper interior life addressed itself regularly to him. This would be the start of the St. Francis de Sales Group. In block II from July 1940 on, instigated by M. Champetier de Ribes, a formation group of Catholic Action was also organized, and Dom Sortais was its chaplain. The two groups seem to have been distinct.

In all his actions, what struck the witnesses was his insistence on the interior life, on prayer, on contemplation to be frank. In this he remained profoundly a monk, despite the total absence of solitude. No nonsense with him. It was useless. But he was not afraid to talk, if the service of God required it. Some of his conversations ended, it is said, in miraculous catches. A certain conference on confession given in block I had brought about 150 returns to sacramental practice.

The abbot himself was in admiration at the work which was accomplished: "The religious life here is surprising. God is certainly good."[17]

"I cannot express my joy at so many returns. Sometimes at night on my bed I weep with happiness, when the conversations are over, and I am alone with God."[18]

Dom Sortais only wanted to be one priest among the others. He practiced great discretion in order to facilitate the ministry of his brother priests, but his personality imposed itself. He dominated without wishing to do so. In this regard the Mass of Christmas 1940 is a good example. Father Abbot celebrated as he would have in his own monastery, with crozier and mitre. Everyone had worked for this. An artist had carved a shepherd's staff from a bedboard. Liturgical furniture had been created out of every sort. Officers had made albs and learned the liturgical functions. Nothing was missing, thanks to the treasures of ingenuity and patience displayed by all.

Father Sortais still had his violent reactions (sometimes) and his intransigence. When he noticed them, he humiliated himself in a way that surprised everyone. The extreme kindness he showed in everything caused the shadows to be forgotten. He had an extraordinary talent for hearing and understanding. It was as though he instinctively knew the proper answer. "We considered him a man who was not like other men."

[17] Letter to his community, November 18, 1940.

[18] Admission made to an officer.

Giving himself thus to all, careless of the fatigue that undernourishment aggravated in an alarming way, his health did not hold up. Dysentery returned in August. He treated it with charcoal produced at the place. In order that he might recover, the officers of his barracks each set aside a ladle of soup from their ration to augment his. When lying down or getting up, Father Abbot often found under his pillow a morsel of bread which he accepted simply.

But he was himself a father of a family too, and he had his own cares. He often asked himself about Bellefontaine. What had become of his monastery? As the months passed, his presence there became more and more indispensable. It had been a year in November since he had left the abbey. In principle he ought to be repatriated fairly soon in virtue of the Geneva accords. Chaplains are non-combatants.

Dom Sortais could ascertain that the religious service of the camp continued to be largely assured, even after the massive departure of October. There would still be 20 priests once the chaplains were repatriated to France. On this side, then, there was no moral obligation to remain. But Father Abbot would not have been himself, if his heart had not suffered from not being able to give himself at one and the same time to his companions in captivity and to his monks. Since the two duties were absolutely irreconcilable, he opted for the most urgent: serving in his monastery but at the price of real interior torture. And so he accepted his repatriation when finally there was question of processing it.

The list of those leaving was put up on January 25, 1941. Dom Sortais left the camp on the 29th, his heart upset by the confidential information he had received during the last few hours. "From France, from the monastery to which I am returning, I will pray for your families and for you, dear friends, believers and unbelievers," he wrote. "I will pray that all may understand that the captivity will not be in vain, for every sacrifice has its effect. Suffering is as active as any other act."

Chapter 11

WATCHMAN, WHAT OF THE NIGHT?

Father Sortais' haste to see his monks of Bellefontaine and his nuns of Les Gardes again was soon put to a severe test. He left Gross-Born on January 29, but before he knocked at the ancient portal of his monastery, a month and a half would have elapsed. He would have been repatriated through Switzerland and the free zone. The formalities of demobilization would have been long. Dom Sortais would have profited from this to present himself at the abbey of Dombes and plunge with delight into the Cistercian great silence. How this stopover in the midst of his brother white-monks did him good! The greeting of Father Guest master, however, who could not believe that this half-vagrant skeleton bore any resemblance to the abbot of Bellefontaine, had not been very encouraging!

His companions of the Oflag had loaded him with a thousand errands for their families. Father had written everything down in a small notebook: addresses, the most necessary things to send, requests to let them know the prisoner was okay. He began to keep himself busy with those of the region of Lyons, while waiting to receive the necessary papers to cross the boundary line.

On March 11, at the beginning of the afternoon, the community of Bellefontaine welcomed its abbot, returned at last to its midst, in front of the church door. Only the brothers who were captives were missing. "I can hardly write, so great is my emotion," he had written from Switzerland on February 7. "How good it will be to see the ancient portal of our gatehouse from the end of the avenue and to see the fine bell-tower of our church, outlined against the sky . . . how refreshing to look on the red roofs of our farm buildings from afar and the forest against which they are outlined, the trees around the pond. . . . The happiness of coming to the inside of the monastery, into the cloister which has never seemed so peaceful. . . . Oh! How you can really pray in your own monastery church, near the venerable statue at whose feet so many prayers have been laid."[1] These impressions of his return from captivity translate the sentiments of Dom Gabriel's return very well, even if they are written beforehand.

On the next day he was up at 2:00 a.m. for Vigils. Father Prior and the monks had to insist that he agree to take his rest.

Even though officially demobilized and "returned to his hearth," Dom Gabriel did not feel that he was liberated from his obligations toward the prisoners. Duties imposed by the heart are exacting. Every opportunity was a good one for him to occupy himself with the captives and their families and to support them with his friendship from afar.

Beginning in June 1941 and for a large part of the following year, all his Sundays were taken up by "trips for the prisoners" in *Mauges* parishes. This bothered him a bit: Was he not absent too often from his monastery? The abbot of Sept-Fons reassured him on that point; circumstances sometimes demand a broad interpretation of monastic stability. And so Dom Sortais spoke of the prisoners and reminded everyone of their distress and of the need to come to their aid. In addition he continued the work begun among them and preached unity among the French. If the year 1939–40 remained and would remain one of the most lamentable episodes in the country's history, it was because France had entered the war without the capability of doing so and without the positive will of waging it. Her domestic politics present an overwhelming picture in which the powerlessness of the parliamentary system confronted by a dramatic situation imposes itself upon the historian as a proof. The parliament was unable to unite, and it did not want to. The pre-war rancor remained a determining factor, and it held a larger place than the problems raised by external hostilities. Ultra-pacifism bleating from the left joined the pacifism that had developed on the right

[1] Circular Letter, December 28, 1939.

after 1934–35 among anti-Communists and many Catholics and took from the country all possibility of efficacious action for maintaining peace. The awakening had been brutal, and the bill to be paid extremely high. Recovery became imperative after the defeat. If there was to be unity, it was only possible with Marshal Pétain,[2] who had undertaken an attempt at national renewal by combating that which had been the cause of demoralization in the country, and then of defeat.

The real free France for Dom Sortais was found beyond the line of demarcation and in North Africa. He was absolutely convinced of this, and he resolutely combated whatever could disunite the French. They were being pulled in two directions. Some thought that Germany had already virtually won the war, and that it was necessary to envisage the new Europe of the future in collaboration with her; others, and these were more numerous, had given their allegiance to General De Gaulle[3] and easily canonized all his initiatives. On the other hand they considered the members of the legal government of France simply as puppets whose strings were pulled by Germany.

Father Abbot, with the great majority of the prisoners and a good proportion of the population, gave Marshal Pétain a

[2] Philippe Pétain (1856–1951) was a French marshal and statesman. He was a general in World War I. Ambassador to Spain in 1939, he was recalled by Paul Renaud to be vice president of the council in May 1940. He believed the war was already lost. He became president and asked for an armistice on the night of June 16. On July 1 he set up the government at Vichy. He believed France's only option lay in limited collaboration with Germany. An act of Parliament made him chief of state on July 11. The high court of liberated France sentenced him to death in 1945, but the sentence was commuted to life imprisonment. He died at the Iled'Yeu in 1951. *Le Petit Robert dictionnaire universel des noms propers,* ed. Alain Rey (Paris: Dictionnaires Le Robert, 1995) 1611.

[3] General Charles de Gaulle is well-known as the leader of the French Resistance in World War II and French president from 1958 to 1969. He was born at Lille in 1890 of a Catholic family of liberal culture. After military training at Saint-Cyr he joined the 33rd Infantry Regiment under Col. Petain. He served in World War I and was taken prisoner by the Germans in 1916. He served in Poland in the war against Russia in 1920. He was made chief of staff of the Army of the Rhine and served as a member of Pétain's cabinet (who was then vice president of the Supreme War Council). Charles de Gaulle was a quite prolific writer, and at that time modern warfare was as yet little developed. He set forth his theories on armored motorized warfare in *Vers l'armée de metier.* In 1940 he left Pétain's government to continue the fight from England and Africa. Ibid., 813.

vote of confidence; he saw a warlord in him who had accepted the armistice against his will while secretly preparing to renew hostilities. He proclaimed, then, very strongly the necessity of gathering around him and obeying him by adopting his program of social renewal heart and soul. The occupying army, however, had no rights whatsoever. They exercised a de facto power which of itself could claim "neither respect, nor esteem, nor obedience." He said this in public before vast crowds who trembled for his safety. So important did the correct conception of the Catholic's duties towards the legitimate government seem to him, that he made it the object of a mimeographed tract of three pages, which the bureau of documentation at Cholet distributed. He even tried to have it printed, after revising it, but the printer was unable to see it through for lack of paper. In the same spirit he prepared two other tracts, one on the family, the other on the attitude of the episcopate toward the government of Vichy[4] ("Frenchmen, your Bishops are speaking to you . . . ").

The invasion of the free zone in November 1942 would modify Dom Gabriel's attitude toward the government. From then on he would be more circumspect and would doubt that the leaders of occupied France were entirely free. Marshal Pétain more and more seemed to him to be dominated by an entourage that was in large part pro-German and unable to act. And so the abbot of Bellefontaine stopped speaking in his favor and abstained from wearing the Frankish battle axe that he had been awarded by Marshal Pétain at the beginning of 1942.

And so it was the prisoners who had led Father Sortais to assume an activity external to cloistered life. He had sensed its danger with great acuity, and he had been able of himself to measure the difficulty experienced in tearing oneself away from the action of the gears once one is enmeshed in them. After becoming Abbot General, he would often insist on effective separation from the world: "Our trips outside, even those most justified, are never without danger for us, because they easily create a habit

[4] *Vichy* refers both to the seat of the government headed by Marshal Pétain and to that government itself. The city is in the department of Allier on the Allier River. The department of Allier is located roughly in central France, and Vichy is about 100 miles southeast of Dijon. Ibid., 2159.

which carries with it the risk of changing into a kind of need, prejudicial, without any doubt, to our interior life."[5]

When he returned to his abbey, there were still four absentees: three brothers who were prisoners and would not return until 1945, and one severely wounded, who had been hospitalized at Val-de-Grace in Paris after his repatriation from Belgium. He would return in autumn 1941. The monastery had passed through the first part of the war without great harm, but it had suffered from the prolonged absence of its abbot. There are things in a house governed by the Rule of St. Benedict that only the abbot can do. His presence is necessary to imprint a sure and permanent direction on the community.

Refugees had invaded the guest house in May and June 1940. Everything had been provided in advance by Dom Sortais. They had departed again. Conventual life had again taken its normal course, hardly ruffled by external events. In the country, except for the absence of many of the men who had not returned, it could almost be believed that pre-war habits again governed everything. Green uniforms were rarely seen. Privations were less felt than in the city. Life seemed only to go on at a slower pace and, as it were, to become sluggish. No more motors, no more construction sites, electricity that was unreliable, no more quick exchanges with the city and nearby villages. The solitary conditions wonderfully favored the tranquil and recollected life of the monks. Father Abbot continued his commentary on the Rule. He spoke of the Mass, of the Office and of prayer.

The war's great lesson had helped many vocations to mature. The austerities and difficulties of the life, which were imposed upon all, gave to the young a sense of the primacy of the spiritual and of renunciation. During these years Father Abbot had the joy of receiving many postulants.

At Les Gardes Dom Sortais had found the abbess, Mother Cécile, in pain. During the tragic spring of 1940 she had undergone an operation for the extraction of a kind of cyst, and the wound had healed poorly. Ganglions had afterwards formed on her arm the following year. The tests made in July revealed cancer of a particularly malignant kind. Father Abbot was responsible

[5] Dom Sortais, op. cit., 160.

for the monastery's future, so he decided to warn her as delicately as possible, but with complete sincerity, and he advised her to resign her role; a new abbess chosen by the community could be at her side, aided by her advice, beginning right away; in this way the transition from one regime to another would take place without difficulty. Mother Cécile accepted everything with admirable self-renunciation: the prospect of atrocious suffering and the immediate renunciation of her function as abbess, which she had exercised for almost 20 years, and which had responded to an inclination of her nature. "It was as though my heart were torn out. I did not think I loved you all so much!"[6] she confided to some of her daughters. She wrote her letter of resignation on October 9. The election of a new abbess was held on November 6.

Dom Sortais knew how painful were the sacrifices he had asked. He wished to surround the community with his care and affection, to guide the first steps of the new abbess, and to help Mother Cécile bear the severe physical and moral suffering that awaited her. He loved her as a mother and would soon venerate her as a saint. In order to get to Les Gardes, Dom Sortais used a wagon or a bicycle. The abbey was 12 miles from Bellefontaine, at the end of the earth! When he was unable to get to the bedside of the sick woman, Father Abbot sent a card, a few encouraging words, direct, austere, yet full of the most tender affection. "My desire is your sanctification. All my other cares are subordinate to this. Become holy by abandonment; become holy by self-forgetfulness and by complete dedication to your monastery."[7] "Suffering is a kind of sacrament which brings you the grace of God. I ask Jesus to make you profit from this sacrament."[8] "May God be blessed for everything, for sanctifying you and even for making you suffer. Everything comes from his love for us: suffering as well as his divine smile. I am so happy to see you climb towards God!"[9] "It is time for you to place all your good in the road to sanctity, because the time draws near when you will go to rest close to God. The first bell has already rung!"[10]

[6] *Mère Cécile Chauvat,* op. cit., 130.

[7] Letter to Mother Cécile, December 21, 1941.

[8] Letter to Mother Cécile, September 23, 1942.

[9] Letter to Mother Cécile, written on a Monday the 29th.

[10] Letter to Mother Cécile, February 14, 1942.

Weeks followed weeks, months followed months, and half-years followed half-years. The martyrdom of Mother Cécile would last almost two years. Her hand lost all human resemblance, then her arm became a monstrous thing; it reached a circumference of six inches. "Come see the swelling of the proud!" she said one day as Dom Gabriel entered the infirmary. Suffering had established itself permanently in this limb, and it was diffused all about in the chest; each heartbeat reechoed in pain in the part that it touched. "My arm is growing fat in a truly scandalous way," declared the sick woman to her entourage.

"I have the feelings of a father for you, my dear daughter, and that is why I will, no doubt, surprise you at Les Gardes without fail," wrote Father Sortais to her, "because I love you as a dear daughter, a daughter whom I love more than the others. I know your dedication to Les Gardes, I know your heart, I know your good will and your attachment to Jesus, and that is why I love you more. I certainly can tell you this now, because you will soon be leaving us. . . . I embrace you like a daughter, like a mother, and also like a messenger who is going to Jesus and Mary."[11]

"I want you to be completely beautiful and completely pure, because I will need you after you leave us, and for that you must be in heaven."[12]

Father Sortais' visits brought Mother Cécile much joy. But they did not bring relief. The temptation to rebel against the God who allowed such torment had been added to her physical torture. Everything was gloom, darkness, distaste, interior groaning. The abbess died on Ascension Day, June 3, 1943. "To meet him whom one has loved more than oneself! To see him for whom one has searched all one's life! To possess him who will be our eternal joy! To be united to him who is our divine friend, as well as our Creator! To know him to the very core, who has loved us to the point of becoming our Savior and our heavenly food! . . . Oh! What blessed moments are those which give us heaven!" Dom Gabriel had written to her a few months earlier.

It seemed to Father Abbot that he had lost a second mother, but his suffering was calm and peaceful, and he had to put it

[11] Letter to Mother Cécile, written on a Tuesday.

[12] Letter to Mother Cécile, written on a Wednesday the 28th.

aside quickly in order to look after the new abbess. He guided her step by step in her difficult responsibility.

Dom Sortais' position did not require him to have regular contacts with the German authorities. For his part he had no worries, and his attitude of extreme frankness could have gotten him into serious trouble. Seven months had gone by since his return to France, when a drama was played out in Nantes, whose vestiges have not disappeared.

The Feldkommandant of the city was Colonel Hotz, a veteran officer whom the Gestapo considered pro-French. He was a doctoral candidate working on a doctorate in history at Tübingen. He was extremely courteous, and his relations with the French authorities were marked by great understanding. On Monday, October 20, 1941, at about 7:00 a.m., he arrived on foot to check in at the Feldkommandant's office, accompanied by an officer. The streets were still in semi-darkness, for dawn had not yet broken. At the entrance of the Rue du Roi Albert, two men came up behind him and killed him with two shots from a revolver. Other similar crimes had been perpetrated. The first one had coincided with the declaration of war by Nazi Germany on the U.S.S.R. (July 1941). Subsequent inquiries would reveal that they were to be imputed to a terrorist group belonging to the international brigades of the Spanish Civil War, of which the principal members were named Brustlein, Zalkinov, Gueusquin, and Pierre Georges.

The Führer's reaction was brutal. At the first crime committed in August in Paris he spoke of publicly hanging in the Place de la Concorde a hundred hostages previously taken from the prisons. The Vichy government intervened and succeeded in averting the blow. But two days after the attempt at Nantes, October 22, the terrorists having escaped arrest, General Von Stülpnagel, military commandant of France, had 50 hostages executed by order of Berlin: at Nantes 16 inhabitants of the city and two Polish soldiers; in Paris at Mont-Valerien five Resisters from Nantes; finally at Chateaubriand 27 Communists or trade-unionists taken from the camp where the party elite were interned.

"Due to the seriousness of the crime," read the proclamation of Von Stülpnagel, "50 other hostages will be shot unless the guilty ones have been arrested before October 23, 1941, at midnight. I offer a reward of a total of 15 million francs to the citizens of the country who will assist the capture of those guilty. Useful information can be placed at the disposal of any German or French police station. If requested, such information will be treated as confidential."

The French authorities, who had not been able to stop the first executions, immediately multiplied their attempts to avoid more bloodshed. The mayor, M. Rondeau, offered himself as a hostage. Mlle. Landois from Nantes had asked for execution in place of a father of a family during the first round of executions. Her request had been refused. The regional prefect of the lower Loire, the mayor, the bishop, the families of the first massacred hostages pleaded with the new Feldkommandant to intervene. For its part the government of Marshal Pétain asked the German ambassador to France, Otto Abets, to intervene. He thought he could obtain a delay of 48 hours, and this was, in fact, granted: the deadline was postponed until October 27 at midnight.

Some French had come to offer themselves to be shot in place of the hostages: Mlle. Benoît, a teacher at the Nantes Conservatory; Mme. Patou from Yerres (S & O); other names were added to the list, including two priests and four leading citizens or ex-servicemen.

When he read the details of the drama in the news, Father Sortais became upset. On Sunday, October 26, he was at Cholet where he had promised to participate in the consecration of the new Sacré-Coeur Church, but he had made his decision; he would go to Nantes the following day. He spent the night sorting papers. He got off at Nantes station at a very early hour and went to Sainte-Croix Church to pray before Our Lady of Bon-Secours. He could not expect to be received so early in the morning. Having stood before the Virgin a long time, he went to the Hotel d'Aux at the Place Louis-XVI, where the Kommandant was installed.

"I handed over my card on which I had written that I was able to give the German colonel useful information on the identity of his predecessor's assassin."

Father Abbot was then allowed to enter, and an officer presented himself to interrogate him. Dom Gabriel refused to answer to any other than Feldkommandant Von und zu Bodman.

He was told that the Feldkommandant was away. By dint of earnest entreaties the abbot of Bellefontaine succeeded, nevertheless, in being led into his presence. "I then handed a letter to the colonel." It conveyed the following message:

"Commandant, you are an officer, and you certainly should understand our pain at seeing 50 Frenchmen die. For mercy's sake, spare the lives of those whose disappearance will again create implacable hatred in the hearts of the families wounded by legitimate sorrow.

"For the love of your mother, have pity on these 50 men, guilty in your eyes, but for crimes which normally, according to your system of justice, would not require the death penalty.

"I was military chaplain during the recent war. Among the wounded French I found wounded Germans. I treated them all with the same charity. I had pity on all, and I tried to relieve the sufferings of those whom, perhaps, at the risk of my life, I had gone to pick up while the battle was raging.

"Commandant, I do not wish to have you fail in that which you consider your duty. Therefore, since you judge that your safety requires the shedding of French blood again, I do not dispute your decision, but I offer you my own blood.

"Consider me the guilty one, the assassin of Lieutenant Colonel Hotz, and sacrifice me, but only me.

"I accept your sentence without complaint. I accept it even with joy."

The Feldkommandant of Nantes was only a simple subordinate in the matter. He could not make any decision. The decision depended on the Führer, who dictated to General Von Stülpnagel the conduct he was to follow. But Colonel Von und zu Bodman was very moved on reading this document. Father Sortais added a warm plea to it by word of mouth, in which he employed all his powers of persuasion. When he had finished speaking, the Kommandant told him that the letter would be telephoned immediately to Paris in its entirety, and he gave him grounds for hope.

Father Abbot went out. He spent the day in front of the statue of Our Lady of Bon-Secours, praying and pleading. Before boarding the train for Cholet, he went again to the Hotel d'Aux: "The Germans told me to keep on hoping."

At 10:00 p.m. the radio announced that a respite *sine die* had been granted to the hostages, and the next day, October 28, 1941, Von Stülpnagel published the following proclamation: "To the people of France: I am letting the French government know that the Führer of the Reich has decided to suspend the execution of the other hostages in reprisal for the attacks in Nantes and Bordeaux."[13]

Father Sortais had been heard. Only those close to him knew of his intervention at the time.

The entrance of Russia into the war had, at a later date, an unexpected consequence. Lost at the end of its forest, the abbey had lived ignored by the occupying armies, but at the beginning of August 1942 a Panzer Division returning from the eastern front was sent to the *Mauges* for a rest. The prospect of having to provide lodging for German troops, as one can well imagine, was not a bright one for the former division chaplain. Every village received its contingent, and the abbey had to lodge a certain number of men at the guest house.

Father Abbot introduced himself to the new arrivals: "I am the Führer here!" he said. Then he capitalized on the impression he produced to impose conditions: a line of demarcation not to be crossed, a prohibition against allowing women to enter the cloister, the guarding of the gatehouse assured by a monk who would open and close the gate for the vehicles of the occupying army. By treating him condescendingly and with an authoritative tone, he got the upper hand on the German lieutenant in charge of the quarters. Only the most indispensable equipment was left at the guest house: "You see, I have taken away all that might embarrass you: I am seeing that you are quite comfortable, and that nothing bothers you." The occupation lasted three months. Father Bruno, like the sergeant of a barracks, watched over the observance of the rule and complained about every infraction of it. "It is too much," declared a soldier. "Europe is ours; it is only at Bellefontaine that we cannot go where we wish!"

[13] Reimers, the administrative counselor, had been assassinated at Bordeaux on the Place Pey-Berland on the 21st, the day after the assassination of Hotz. The perpetrator of the attack was the Communist Pierre Rabière, formerly of the International Brigade of the Spanish War.

Father Abbot's position vis-à-vis the organization of the S.T.O.[14] in Germany was unequivocal. Having occasion to preach in the hospital chapel of Saint-Antoine des Quinze-Vingts in Paris to the families of prisoners, he had bluntly expressed his thoughts. The essential thing was for all the young to serve France in the place where they were. If anyone thought he ought to answer the appeals of the S.T.O., it should not be in order to place themselves, even indirectly, at the service of Germany, for Germany had no rights over the French, but only to combat Nazi influence in Germany itself. If anyone thought it better to choose the side of the Resisters, he should disappear inside France among the clandestine operators or go to North Africa and fight.

There is certainly reason for surprise that such free speech had not aroused reprisals on the part of the Gestapo. Georges Suarez, former member of *Action Française,* threatened Father Abbot that, if he repeated the offense, he would quote "these infamous words" in the newspaper *Aujourd'hui,* which he directed. If he had not done so, it was because he was a Catholic, and it was a case of a priest.

His private counsel was even clearer, if that is possible. Dom Gabriel thought at first that, according to the promises made by Germany, prisoners would be freed as the workers arrived and in numbers equal to them. That is why he let two of his young religious, requested by the service, leave the monastery. He did not allow himself to be caught again. Quite the contrary, he lodged at Bellefontaine all those to whom he was able to give work, thus shielding them from pursuit. There had been more than a dozen of them.

He even welcomed escapees and Resisters sought by the Gestapo. It was difficult to cover up such activity. Father Abbot was the object of several denunciations. The first was to the subprefect at Cholet, who turned a deaf ear; the second was to the police commissioner who knew what to believe, since he also belonged to the Resistance. One day, returning from a journey, Dom Gabriel found two French policemen at the depot. They

[14] S.T.O. = *Service du travail obligatoire* or forced labor in the service of Germany.

warned him that they had orders to go to Bellefontaine, to see if he was there. Father Abbot went to Les Gardes, in order to permit the police to conduct a fruitless search calmly and legally.

With the Gestapo of Angers, one could not count on practical jokes of this kind. A quite complete dossier of Father Abbot's activities was being gathered, and it seems to have been damning; it should have infallibly led Dom Sortais to Buchenwald[15] or Dachau.[16] An employee opened it one day by chance, cast a glance at it and caused it to disappear. The police never laid their hands on it again. Even at the Gestapo, agents of the Resistance were sometimes to be found.

Dom Gabriel would not have been himself, if he had not suffered from the interminable slaughter at the very bottom of his heart. He desired the liberation of France, but he did not know the meaning of hate. Every morning he sent up a prayer to the Lord for the German soldiers who had fallen in battle the day before. "I think that is why we have not been bothered," he confided.

After the homecoming of October 1943, Bellefontaine's guest house was transformed into a major seminary. Since the buildings of Angers had been requisitioned by the German troops, Dom Sortais proposed to Msgr. Costes to take in the students at Bellefontaine. On great feast days and during Holy Week the monks and seminarians united in a common liturgy. Some Capuchins from Angers, whose convent was destroyed by the bombardment of May 28, 1944, joined the seminarians.

Any distress or inextricable situation found an effective helper in the abbot of Bellefontaine. We would never finish the list of all those who appealed to him during the tragic hours of the war, or implored his counsel in difficult situations. Mgr. Costes jokingly gave Father Abbot the title: "Bishop of the Mauges."

The Allies landed in Normandy on June 6, 1944, and the German divisions from Bavaria immediately poured into the

[15] Buchenwald was a Nazi concentration camp northwest of Weimar in Thuringia, Germany. It had been built in 1937 for political prisoners. *Larousse*, op. cit., t. 2, col. 422.

[16] Dachau was a Nazi concentration camp northwest of Munich, Germany. It was first built in 1933 for political prisoners. In 1939 it was made a deportation center. It is estimated that about 250,000 prisoners from 23 nations passed through its gates between 1933 and 1945. Ibid., t. 3, col. 750.

beachhead which the British and Americans methodically enlarged until July 20; at this date it surrounded the Cotentin peninsula and the coastal region between the Vire and the Dive, 19 miles wide. Having concentrated their forces in this way, the Allies were ready at the end of July to launch their offensive.

On July 30 and 31 Eisenhower with the First American Army crushed the 70th German Division, making a large breach between Granville and Avranches. The Second Army of General Patton, held in reserve until this moment, rushed into the breach on August 2, in the direction of Rennes. The army arrived at the city on the following day. According to the original plan, the whole army would have been used in Brittany. The intervention of the F.F.I.[17] would permit the American General to engage only the Eighth Corps and send the two others to Laval and Angers respectively. On August 11 the 20th Corps entered Angers and Nantes simultaneously. But the Allies had no intention of moving south of the Loire. And so the *Mauges* remained in the German zone three weeks longer. The liberation of Southwest and Central France was left to the initiative of the insurrection movements of the Resistance, and these are the regions where the most violence would occur.

For the Communist or communizing leaders the liberation of territory was actually only one phase of the revolution which would end in the creation of a Marxist state and society. They had their own autonomous troops, the F.T.P.,[18] and they tried to infiltrate all the movements in the Resistance, especially the Front National into whose committee they had a certain number of priests or right-wing conservatives admitted, in order to fool public opinion.

General De Gaulle, however, did not think he was letting himself be outflanked. His strategy for limiting Communist

[17] F.F.I. = *Forces Françaises de l'intérieur,* name given in 1944 by the French National Committee of Liberation to all the units which carried on the fight against the Germans. Ibid., t. 5, p. 115.

[18] F.T.P. = *Francs-Tireurs Partisans,* troops of the Front National in the French Resistance during the Second World War originated in the defense organization of the communist party and was made up mostly of Communists. Their tactics consisted in constant harassment of the enemy through sabotage or sorties. Ibid., t. 5, 249–50.

penetration had always been to set up a substitute organization created for the occasion or restructured, every time the leadership was about to be overrun by the Communists.

At Cholet, as elsewhere, the tendency toward the extreme left dominated 80 percent of the actual Resistance workers. During the month of August, in fact, there were no regular soldiers at Cholet, except the Third Company of the Third Regiment of French Parachutists, assigned to lead harassing and sabotage operations between the Loire and the Charente Department. A small group, "Jeannette 74" was first installed at the farm of Lavau in Trementines and later between Beaupréau and Chemillé[19] at the Chaperonnière; they were forced to seek a more secure refuge by the arrest of the mill owner of Cholet, who had brought them there. Father Sortais agreed to give them lodging for as long as they wished. They arrived at the monastery on August 10 and stayed two days.

The Departmental Committee of Liberation of Maine-et-Loire[20] was organized at Angers on August 11, shortly after the American troops arrived. One of its members, M. Le Bault de la Morinière, had the duty of sounding out the important people of the *Mauges* who would agree to sit on the departmental and regional Committees of Liberation, after the liberation of Cholet. Cholet was already represented on the departmental Committee by its archpriest, Canon Douillard, future bishop of Soissons,[21] who had been arrested by the Germans, then kept under house arrest at Angers until the liberation of the city. So M. Le Bault de la Morinière crossed the Loire and got through into occupied territory. There was no front on either side of the river; the two enemy armies regularly avoided coming into contact with each

[19] Chemillé is a canton-seat in the arrondissement of Cholet, in the department of Maine-et-Loire in the *Mauges* region.

[20] The department of Maine-et-Loire forms part of the region called Pays-de-la-Loire in western France. Its largest cities *(arrondissements)* are Angers, Cholet, Saumur, and Segré. The canton seat, Chemillé, is located about 15 1/2 miles northeast of Cholet. Montfaucon, also a canton seat, is about 10 miles to the west of Cholet. *Larousse,* op. cit., t. 6, 986.

[21] Soissons is a city in the Aisne department on the Aisne River, about 15 miles west of Reims and about 60 miles northeast of Paris. The cathedral was badly damaged in the two World Wars because of the proximity of Soissons to the front. Ibid., t. 9, col. 886.

other's flank. He went to the house of M. Pellaumail, a Cholet manufacturer and repatriated prisoner. The latter did not wish to agree to join the departmental committee before asking the advice of Father Sortais.

Now Dom Gabriel was precisely one of the personalities whom M. de la Morinière had to try to invite to join the regional committee. And so the two men presented themselves at Bellefontaine one fine morning about August 20. When Father Abbot was informed, he made it a duty for M. Pellaumail to accept. It was impossible in conscience to leave the control of the committees to the leftist parties. Disorder was inevitable; unless someone was there to restrain them, they would quickly lead to a really revolutionary situation. The manufacturer agreed. But Father Sortais' argument turned against himself, when M. Le Bault de la Morinière pressed him in his turn to accept a seat on the regional committee! It was morally impossible for Father Abbot to extricate himself. His popularity in the *Mauges* and at Cholet was immense. He was in a better position than anyone to exercise a moderating influence within the Committee of Liberation.

A first secret meeting was held on August 28 with the president of the departmental committee, M. Le Tétour, who had come from Angers under the Germans' nose. Other meetings were envisaged for September 1 or 2, in order to prepare concretely for the liberation of the city, which wasn't far away.

But the Germans left Cholet sooner than expected, without any fanfare, during the night of August 29 and 30. Without delay a member of the Committee of Resistance, who wished to derive some advantage for himself from the situation, proclaimed the liberation of the city on the morning of August 31, unknown to the regularly constituted Committee of Liberation. The latter, convoked in an emergency session, would have to act energetically in order to establish its authority and then to exert it. By evening of this great day, the situation was thoroughly confused; no serious military measures had been taken against an offensive return of the enemy. The passage of an enemy column retreating towards Berry could be expected at any moment. The Americans refused to send the smallest detachment to Cholet, and the F.F.I. of Saint-Florent-le-Vieil did not think they had enough men to spare any of their troops. Cholet, then, was left to her own minimal resources: half a dozen parachutists, some F.T.P. and a handful of F.F.I. without battle experience.

The delirium of the crowd gave way in an instant to a horrible panic, because an alert was sounded. Fortunately it was a false alarm. A few small groups of the enemy were taken prisoners during the day.

After having waited in vain for the arrival of the official authorities, who were charged with investing the committee and choosing a president, the members decided to nominate one themselves. On a motion of Father Abbot, they chose a levelheaded individual in whom they had confidence: M. Gourdon.

The committee would be in session and be effective until October 1945, about 13 months. Dom Gabriel constantly occupied himself with limiting damage, disarming accusations, recalling the sense of legality, preventing arbitrary arrests and all the abuses that accompanied the installation of the Fourth Republic.

Many had wondered what the abbot of Bellefontaine was doing there; others had asked him outright, more or less politely. The particular religious situation of the *Mauges* and the influence exercised by Father Abbot over the population had removed from him the moral possibility to escape the entreaties addressed to him. Within the committee he gained the esteem of all his colleagues, whatever may have been their political options. But for his part his contribution was essentially to prevent irregularities, arbitrary acts, and reprisals, at least to limit them to extreme cases. He did not succeed in preventing all violence, but it is a significant fact that at Cholet not a single prostitute was shorn. Almost all the mayors and town councilmen were retained in office. There were hardly, then, any petty local quarrels, such as those that ended tragically elsewhere. Purges remained moderate. There were a little more than 100 internments at Cholet (70 for the city itself), which is still a lot, against more than 2,300 for the rest of the department. The proportion is revealing. And only 20 of these internees were detained to appear before courts of justice. No bloodshed marked the liberation of Cholet.

When Dom Gabriel died in 1963, one of the Communists on the Committee of Liberation gave him this eulogy: "The strong personality of Father Sortais had surprised me, and his so human and so delicate feelings had won me over. He will always remain engraved in my memory and in my heart. . . . He remains for me a figure of great intelligence and of careful thought. Shortly after the great political storm I sensed in him the need to know and understand all the elements, all the social classes, and especially the most humble. He was a moderating element, but not a braking element. He sensed that a new situation was coming and he wished the church to be present; he was profoundly right. . . ."[22] "In the materialism and obscurantism that today invade our world where the most sordid enjoyment sometimes seems to become the goal of human action, Dom Sortais will remain for me as a light for the mind. . . . It was good for a man of the church to be present among us at that time. Such was Dom Sortais. What he did he did well in Christian thought that is eternally true."[23]

Father Abbot, then, traversed the tragic events of his time, which awoke painful resonances in him. He presented to all the image of a man who knows no lack of courage, hesitation or fear, who goes straight ahead on the path marked out for him by duty. As soon as he saw clearly, he in fact went ahead decisively, approaching difficulties with courage, whatever they might be, without caring about the consequences of which he might be the victim. He didn't care about the apprehension of men, because his gaze was fixed on God. There was no bravado or pride or wasted imprudent actions with him; just tranquil certainty, calm, self-mastery, a well-balanced mind; he appeared as a humble, but powerful and irresistible force which nothing could stop.

[22] Letter of December 12, 1963.
[23] Letter of July 24, 1964.

Chapter 12

AT THE SERVICE OF THE CISTERCIAN ORDER

By virtue of the structure of the Cistercian Order, the abbot of Bellefontaine is the Father Immediate of the monasteries descended from his abbey. To him falls the duty of the regular visitation. And so Dom Gabriel made his first trip to Canada since 1937. "On your first visit," he would confide to a young abbot, "content yourself with observing, but at the second it will be time to act."

For himself, he had not wished to rely upon his natural gifts alone. Conscious of the effort to be made in order to link up with the mentality of another world, he had spared nothing in order to be informed on the history, geography, and customs of the country he was going to. A relationship of race and language unites Canada to old France, but this would not always be so in the communities he would have to occupy himself with.

In his difficult task, Father Abbot profited from several trump cards. He naturally inspired people to take a liking to him; they felt attracted to him. His nature and natural dignity were imposing, even intimidating. You could sense in him a man of authority, a leader whose prestige affirmed itself, without the need to raise his voice. He hardly perceived it himself. One could only obey a man like this. The idea of contesting it did not come to mind. But this natural greatness was immediately corrected by simplicity, by the direct manner with which he approached those who had been strangers to him yesterday, by his unique ability to listen. When he was at somebody's disposal, nothing else in the world mattered; his presence was felt. He was all eyes, all ears, even for the most uninteresting stories.

No one had the impression of annoying or tiring him. He produced confidence by the abandonment with which he himself confided in anyone, asking advice or seeking approval.

Very quickly he discerned the heart of problems, and through his human contacts he attained a clear vision of a given situation, even one wantonly confused. He had declared that the principal difficulty lay, not in the decisions to be made, but in discernment: to form for oneself an adequate image of reality; to manage to ascertain; afterwards the decisions would assert themselves, with the appropriate remedies.

His first contact with the New World surprised him. He was then the strict, uncompromising young abbot, the often excessive zealot for poverty and penance. The search for ease and comfort pained him in Christians and still more in religious. But he did not wish to judge. His first care was to understand and to form correct ideas.

Twice, then, before the war, he had visited the great Canadian abbey of Notre-Dame du Lac, located in a small hollow of a valley along the small chain of Deux-Montagnes, which gave its name to the lake: two small mountains, hardly more than hills. The community counted 170 members, with their very odd manner of speaking as one of the Frenchmen of the old country. He met the monks here for the first time at the beginning of summer in 1937. He saw them a second time in January 1939, in the heart of the great white silence of the Canadian winter, where *lectio divina* could reclaim its rights.

On the eve of the war, Father Abbot of Melleray, Dom Corentin Guyader, charged him with a mission to Bricquebec whose abbot, Dom Maur, had just resigned.

The apparent facility with which Dom Gabriel fulfilled these mandates, the judicious character of the measures he proposed, as well as his interventions at the general chapter, where he fulfilled the difficult function of promoter, would move Dom Dominique Nogues, abbot of Thymadeuc and abbot-vicar of the order, to make use of him often.

The Father General, Dom Hermann-Joseph Smets, died on January 4, 1943, and since a general chapter is impossible in wartime, it was Dom Dominique who *de facto* found himself at the head of the order.

Dom Nogues was a Trappist of the old school, humble and austere, a friend of silence and self-effacement, hard on himself, intractable on the question of usages which he thought were all equally important. Timid and jovial at the same time, reserved and a lover of witty remarks, his flashes of wit allowed him to overcome his natural timidity. He had sharp impatience, momentary bluntness, and was no lover of discussion. He admired Dom Gabriel for his zeal for the Rule, for the amplitude of his conceptions, and for his firmness. He liked his youthful enthusiasm and his great devotion to the Virgin, whom he himself called his Lady, *"Domina mea!"*

On November 14, 1943, Dom Gabriel sent a note from the monastery of Les Gardes to one of his monks, "Knowing that you are very obedient . . . I ask you not to murmur but rather to bless God, when you learn that the Reverend Vicar General wants to take me with him to La Grande Trappe. . . . Obedience is always lovable."[1]

When the war began, Dom Jean-Marie Clerc, the abbot, had resigned his office. It had not been possible on account of events to proceed with the election of his successor. Since that time the monastery had been governed by a *Superior ad nutum,* Father Raymond, under the watchful eye of the abbot of Sept-Fons. Now Father Raymond had fallen gravely ill, and the abbot of Sept-Fons had desired to be relieved. The vicar general hoped the young abbot of Bellefontaine could aid the monastery to get past this difficult stage. He counted heavily on his invincible goodness, on the accuracy of his observation and on his firmness.

"A monastery is a spiritual infirmary where souls come to be cured, to repair the damage done by original sin, and to win the fullness of the spiritual life," wrote Dom Vital Lehodey in his autobiography. "Until they become perfect, they have, like the sick, their feverish periods that they do not always succeed in overcoming."[2]

In this case the infirmarian himself was on the verge of being very sick. His health was in a deplorable state, and the doctor who attended him had threatened him with dire complications

[1] Letter to a monk, November 14, 1943

[2] Dom Vital Lehodey, *Autobiographie,* ms., 67.

if he did not agree to take some rest and some more substantial food. "It will be enough, if I take a little butter at breakfast!"

At La Trappe Dom Sortais was glad to find reminders of De Rancé: the large pond, the old guest house of the 13th century, the abbot's house built in 1680, the promenade where the abbot had his long conversations with Bossuet, the marshal of Bellefonds, Mabillon, James II of England and Saint-Simon.

Despite this, his first contact with the community caused him some apprehension: Would he have to leave Bellefontaine someday in the future in order to accept the leadership of the monks of La Trappe? "My soul has much need for humiliation, detachment, renunciation, solitude, abandonment of everything, and the responsibility in question would bring me all that in abundance. . . . God is wise, and he loves me: so I am confident, and I am at peace."[3]

This thought would preoccupy him constantly, even torture him. What was the limit of his duties in respect to the two abbeys? But it seemed to him in all loyalty that Bellefontaine could not do without him. There was as yet no one who was ready to take his place. A large number of young men were arriving, and it was important that they receive a good formation. But was he seeing things with enough objectivity? Was not his heart drawing him unconsciously toward the solution he preferred? Was not even his love for Bellefontaine another reason to sacrifice the bonds that united him to the monastery of his novitiate and profession?

Those who do not understand to how great an extent each monastery constitutes an authentic family with its traditions, its personal ties and its common life will hardly understand the anguish which now held Dom Gabriel in its grip: "My thoughts go out to Bellefontaine. I feel that I am such an *amator loci et fratrum* that I see clearly the sacrifice and spiritual profit I would find in leaving everything and staying here."[4] "He who loves father or mother more than me is not worthy of me. He who loves son or daughter more than me is not worthy of me" (Matt 10:37). One can leave a boarding house without difficulty, but a family is something else! But does not the love of God demand

[3] Letter to Mère Bernard, December 8, 1943.

[4] Letter to a monk, December 17, 1943.

at certain times the renunciation of even the most excellent gifts that he himself has given?

What La Trappe needed most was continuous direction, the presence of an abbatial authority capable of stamping a general orientation by governing effectively. Father Sortais would, then, divide his time between La Trappe and Bellefontaine until it would be possible to proceed to a regular election. His mission would last almost two years, hindered for a few months by the traveling difficulties brought about by the battle of Normandy.

Dom Gabriel had decided to show great respect for the personality of the monastery, to maintain the legitimate usages of La Grande Trappe, but certainly not the small abuses which had crept in, because of the practical absence of a superior for 16 months. Affectionate, confident, attentive, he quickly gained the hearts of the younger monks. The older ones esteemed him, too, but less unanimously. Could it be otherwise? They sometimes disputed his decisions, and this caused him suffering. Dom Sortais had thought at first that a rapid solution could be found, which would free him from this new responsibility, but there was none. Dom Dominique asked him to contribute his time and care generously to La Grande Trappe, while continuing to watch over Bellefontaine.

Despite his reluctance ("You do not know how fed up I get"), Father Gabriel resolutely set himself to the task. He saw to reorganizing the monastery, appointing a new prior and a new novice master, but he proceeded with great tact in order to keep people from suffering fruitlessly, and that the changes might be accepted by all: "At the beginning they were surprised that I asked so much, and then it was okay. The community is always very kind to me, but they knew that I would ask a lot."[5]

The affection which he left behind him at Bellefontaine was a powerful encouragement to him: "The good God is also a Father, and he should certainly know what I go through, when I look for a hoped-for letter at each mail, and return empty-handed from my chase. . . . I will never doubt your affection, even if you never write to me again, even if I knew you had climbed up onto the abbot's seat, after having publicly burned my effigy."[6]

[5] Letter to a monk, March 6, 1944.

[6] Letter to a monk, February 24, 1944.

However, traveling became difficult because of a renewed outbreak of bombardments and because of the scarcity of railway supplies. Trips between Paris, La Trappe, Thymadeuc, and Bellefontaine took on the form of the travels of discovery: "I believe they are going to attempt the invasion," he wrote on May 4. "In any case, if the event happens, it cannot be delayed very long: May 15 to June 15, for the weather governs any operation of this kind. The Germans are acting as if the thing were imminent. Here the monastery is clearly making progress, especially the novitiate. But I am obliged to stand my ground on various points. My nature is more inclined to peace than to battle in affairs of this kind, but I believe that God's interests demand these efforts."[7] To be an occasion of pain to others, even legitimately, was in fact painful for him, and he had to take his heart in both hands, in order to "dare to say things before it is too late." His sense of duty helped him to win the victory over his heart.

Dom Gabriel was also occupied with temporal matters; he tried to improve the property by increasing the cultivation of the land and by draining the swampy parts. On the advice of the father of one of the monks, former engineer of the forestry commission, he decided to clean the peat bogs by digging drainage ditches, and then planting resinous trees in them.

Fortunately for Bellefontaine, Father Abbot was back in the *Mauges* when the Allied invasion took place in June. He wished to get back to La Grande Trappe, which was in more immediate danger, and with this intention, he tried to take the train on June 8 at Trémentines. The locomotive was machine-gunned right at the station. He had to give up going any further.

In the course of the following weeks all travel in the direction of Normandy became impossible, for all transport was commandeered for the German troops. Then came the liberation with the necessity of Father Abbot's remaining in the *Mauges* at his post in order to fulfill the mission of moderation and pacification that he had accepted. He was unable to return to La Grande Trappe until November 1944, between two weekly sessions of the Committee of Liberation at Cholet. The community in Normandy had not suffered from his long absence, thanks to

[7] Letter to a monk, May 4, 1944.

Father Prior, Father Edmond de Cocq, whom he had appointed in February.

During his visits in 1945, he prepared the community for the abbatial election which would take place on November 7. His chapter conferences gave him the opportunity to describe the qualities necessary in the abbot, and the spiritual state of mind of those who had the duty and responsibility to choose him, as well as the climate of peace and silence which should reign over the days preceding the election.

He usually preached abandonment to others: "Life is too short and serious to waste the present by thinking of the future."[8] He did his best to practice this counsel as well.

Besides, at the time he did not think that a majority of votes would be cast for him; at most his name might occur to a few; it was only five days before the election that he was confronted with a decisive choice.

Suddenly he recognized that their minds were inclined in a different way than he had thought: "I had arrived here with my mind free, never suspecting a crisis like the one that awaited me. . . . but then, just at the time when Father Hubert was being buried, I felt God was asking me to abandon myself completely into his hands. I had recognized, despite my great unworthiness, that God was asking something of me. I answered, 'Yes.' We cannot resist God. I felt that all I loved here below was breaking into pieces. Perhaps God only wished this death to all that I love. Formerly there was the sacrifice of Abraham, and God can be satisfied with my offering, with my acquiescence. But I have been delivered into the Father's hands."[9]

It was, in fact, the sacrifice of Abraham, for God's will was not made clear. He did not discern it clearly, except in this invitation to abandonment and despoilment of any personal project: "When I answered the good God that I accepted everything, I felt so many things that I loved cut away. But I regretted nothing. It is good that that is the way it is. . . . I sensed that I would have so much to suffer in leaving Bellefontaine, that I would not be surprised, if the good God imposed that sacrifice on me."[10]

[8] Letter to a monk, April 18, 1945.

[9] Letter to a monk, November 3, 1945.

[10] Letter to friends, November 3, 1945.

However, in order that God's will might appear clearly, Dom Gabriel wanted something more evident than the vote of the community. He needed positive arguments whose cogency was absolutely decisive. At least he did not feel he had the right to abandon Bellefontaine, for which he had responsibility and whose future without him remained uncertain.

In fact Dom Dominique Nogues tackled the affair half-jokingly, arguing that ancient Cistercian law made it a duty for the abbot of a daughter house to accept the election to be abbot of the motherhouse, under pain of being deposed: "I am leaving you free," he said. "In fact I have no right to oblige you to accept, because today these texts have no binding force. Besides, you have excellent reasons. You can, then, refuse the election. But after your refusal I will read the text of the ancient usages to the community . . . not in the least to reproach you, but to recall the facts of our history."[11]

A juridical argument and, more to the point, one depending on an obsolete law! All that was quite insufficient in Dom Gabriel's eyes to constitute a clear sign of the divine will. And so, after the scrutiny in which he received a majority of the votes, he believed he was authorized to refuse the election. To make him accept, a positive order from Dom Nogues would have been necessary, and the order had not come. Besides, he was not the only possible candidate, as he well knew.[12] Without insisting further, Dom Dominique contented himself with congratulating the community for its good dispositions, since it had voted first

[11] Letter to a monk, November 7, 1945.

[12] The apparent contradiction in Dom Sortais' conduct, namely, unconditional acceptance before God vs. the refusal of the chapter's vote, is explained by the fact that he was under constraint by two different duties which were in opposition to each other, and whose respective rights he only perceived clearly at the last minute. It seemed to him at that time that he should prefer the duty that was certain (Bellefontaine) to the duty that was doubtful (La Grande Trappe); in fact no obvious light had been thrown in favor of the latter duty. In a letter already old, he established a hierarchy among his duties: "If it were a question of material interests, the answer would be easy. But it is a question of souls, and those of La Grande Trappe are just as dear to the Heart of Jesus as those of Bellefontaine, and that is what makes it hard. Towards Bellefontaine I have duties of justice, and towards La Grande Trappe I have duties of charity." Letter to a monk, December 22, 1943.

for the superior who had been imposed upon it for two years as administrator. He then proceeded to the second scrutiny in which Dom Étienne Chenevière was elected. Dom Sortais was going to remain abbot of Bellefontaine, but for how long?

At the general chapter of 1946, the first in a very long time, for the great cataclysm that had turned the planet upside-down had rendered the regular meetings of general chapters impossible, Father Abbot underwent a series of great emotions. His personality had imposed itself upon the order for many years, and many abbots already thought of him as Abbot General. This was, perhaps, the desire of Dom Dominique himself. Still, the fact remains that they had undertaken a great circuit of pastoral visitations together in July 1945, in Belgium and the north: Orval,[13] Clairefontaine,[14]

[13] Orval (or Golden Valley) is an ancient Cistercian foundation in the Belgian province of Luxembourg, commune of Villers-devant-Orval in the canton seat of Florenville and the arrondissement of Virton. St. Bernard of Clairvaux, at the appeal of Alberon, Bishop of Verdun, ordered the Abbot of Trois-Fontaines in Champagne to make the foundation. A small group of Cistercian monks installed themselves at Orval in 1132. They acquired a vineyard at Boyenville, between Metz and Nancy. The monastery was burned down in 1252. Afterwards the monks suffered in the war between France and Spain. Abbot Bernard de Montgaillard (1605–28) restored the buildings and temporal income. The monastery was again destroyed and pillaged during the Thirty Years War, but the buildings were restored and enlarged by Abbot Henri de Meurgen. Abbot Charles de Bentzeradt who succeeded him established the Strict Observance in 1683. Abbot Menne Effleur undertook a new reconstruction during his abbatial tenure. The French Revolution struck in 1793, and Orval was again destroyed. It remained in ruins and abandoned during the 19th century. Two monks of La Grande Trappe in Normandy went to Luxembourg in 1926 when new expulsions were feared. The owners of the property at the time, M. and Mme. de Harrene, offered them Orval. An entirely new monastery was built beside the old one which was in ruins. Today it is a tourist center subsidized by the State. *Catholicisme,* op. cit., t. 10, col. 303.

[14] Clairefontaine is a Trappistine monastery re-founded in 1935 in the diocese of Namur in Luxembourg, under the auspices of Queen Astrid, the Baron de Moffarts, and Dom M. Albert van der Cruyssen. The ancient Cistercian monastery was founded by Ermesinde, Countess of Luxembourg, near the city of Arlon, in 1247. In 1250 the same Countess requested the Cistercian General Chapter to admit the monastery into the order. The preliminary inspection was made by the Abbots of Himmerod and Orval, and the latter became the Father Immediate. Despite certain vicissitudes, the abbey seems to have been occupied more or less continuously by Cistercian nuns up to the Revolution. It was burned down in 1794. *Dictionnaire d'histoire,* op. cit., t. 12, col. 1040–41; *Clairefontaine,* 1954 (a brochure printed by A.S.A.R., Brussels, Belgium).

Saint-Sixte,[15] Scourmont, Notre-Dame de la Paix, and Mont-des-Cats. Dom Dominique had full confidence in Dom Gabriel. He was himself beginning to feel the weight of responsibility. He was 67 years old and had already governed Thymadeuc for 24 years. It had been in 1928 that the General Chapter had elected him vicar for Dom Hermann-Joseph Smets. In Dom Gabriel he saw youth allied with competence and dynamism. For him he was the Abbot General already designated for the near future; it seems that he would have liked to make this future immediate.

Dom Gabriel did not agree. The reasons that had made him refuse the election at La Grande Trappe were all the more valid for the generalate. His task at Bellefontaine would not be finished, as long as there was no one to take it up, and he did not yet see anyone among his monks.

Finally—and Dom Gabriel's influence counted for something here—the votes inclined toward Dom Dominique who was elected Abbot General on May 1, 1946. He did not try to escape the responsibility. But the abbot of Bellefontaine had to accept the functions of vicar. This was the ransom for the few years of respite that were left to him.

At the end of the year Father General gave him the responsibility of the regular visitation of Melleray in the diocese of Nantes. The community was governed by a very sick man, wasted by tuberculosis; it also counted a good proportion of aged monks, and its finances were far from brilliant. Everything indicated the beginning of a critical phase. Dom Gabriel made his report.

As might be expected, he soon received an S.O.S. from Father Prior. The abbot of Melleray had gotten worse. When he died on Christmas Day, Dom Dominique informed Dom Gabriel that he had appointed him superior of the house. Father Abbot of Bellefontaine again had two communities under his wing. He had a strong temptation to excuse himself and to raise a storm as he had done once before, but his duty was clear. He had no thought of escaping it.

[15] Saint-Sixte or Sint Sixtus-Abdij is a Belgian Abbey in the diocese of Brugge.

"Really," he said on another occasion, "I only wish things to be as God has ordered them. They have been fixed from all eternity, and you know that I love the old stones and the old things too much, not to love decisions which bear the patina of eternity."[16]

The abbey of Melleray had enough old stones to satisfy him. It was a beautiful monastery, as they knew how to build in the 18th century. But Dom Gabriel had fallen out with classical splendors from that moment in which they had been placed at the service of monastic architecture. All things considered, he preferred the great rustic edifices of masonry without style, built by the Trappists of the 19th century. His poverty was intransigent, and it did not accommodate certain adaptations that were too sumptuous for his taste. When he had come to Melleray for the first time in 1936, he had declared that it was the monastery whose buildings displeased him most! But he had begun to lay aside his prejudices; besides, the ancient Cistercian church, so lovely even underneath the remodeling that disfigured it, had revealed itself to him.

As soon as he arrived, he began listening to the monks. "You cannot imagine how busy I am here. I have to see all the novices privately. I have to look at everything, regulate everything. And I have plenty of work on my plate."[17]

When he had formed ideas, and the situation had appeared completely clear to him, he acted: "Here I impose drastic measures and I take a stand," he wrote on March 10. "I admire the spirit of faith of everybody here. They return to regularity with edifying fidelity."[18]

Two important measures seemed necessary to him: reduction of lay personnel working at the monastery, in order to return the monks to the silence and solitude they needed, and rejuvenation of the community by sending a group of younger monks from another monastery, who would be able to assume the regular observance. Operations of this kind are always difficult. Monasteries are like beehives; it is not enough to place two

[16] Letter to a monk, December 10, 1945.
[17] Letter to a monk, February 10, 1947.
[18] Letter to a monk, March 10, 1947.

swarms from different origins side by side to form one family. It is a work of long duration, which requires the cooperation of all and a firm desire to surmount the obstacles. The Father Abbot of Timadeuc agreed to send 12 monks to Melleray. They were on their way to their mission on February 20.

A month and a half later, on Easter Monday, April 7, Father Abbot proceeded to a new list of appointments. Several monks have testified favorably to the delicacy with which he acted in such cases. He tried hard to see that no change should appear as a dismissal; he chose his words carefully to express appreciation for services rendered, and he possessed the art of discovering new functions by indicating their usefulness for the common good of the monastery. No member of the family need feel put aside or segregated, unless he had given cause for it by some scandalous action. Even though acting in this way, Dom Gabriel could not always avoid wounding someone. The subsequent development of their minds, in any case, did not depend on him.

During the same period he attended to the environment. As a young monk at Bellefontaine, he had suffered terribly from poor hygiene and parasites. When he became abbot, he had immediately tried to bring in the necessary improvements. He did the same at Melleray. But his attention was turned especially to the church which the former abbot had intended to renovate. He had at Bellefontaine a talented architect in the person of Father Patrick Vannier. He brought him along in order to oversee the renovation. "Father Patrick works zealously. Our forward-looking projects will really make Melleray a beautiful monastery. Some windfall, however, will be needed, and it has not happened yet."[19]

Melleray's church could not, of course, be compared to those of Thoronet or Sénanque, but it is a lovely building in conformity with Cistercian traditions, simple, robust, and pure. The first stone was laid about the year 1145, and the consecration was celebrated on August 7, 1183. It is composed of a large nave flanked by two aisles, from which it is separated by massive pillars of rose-colored granite. The sanctuary and the transept crossing, less elevated than the nave, open onto it by three

[19] Letter to a monk, April 10, 1947.

large arcades of white stone, one of which, that of the sanctuary, is emphasized by a border of rose-colored granite.

The accretions of centuries had swallowed up this simple and powerful unit. An enormous screen had cut the nave in two. The south aisle served as the fourth side of the cloister. The north aisle had been partitioned off into independent chapels; the pillars had been quite covered over by wooden wainscoting and paneling; immense paintings decorated the upper portion of the walls, and apse and chapels were encumbered with retables of every description.

Dom Gabriel lovingly followed the work of restoration. He spoke of it to anyone who would listen. Little by little the church emerged from its former skin, rejuvenated, unrestricted view. It was opened in April 1949. A month later its altars were consecrated by the eight Cistercian abbots of the monasteries of western France. And in September, a gauge of Melleray's renaissance, an abbatial election placed Dom Louis de Gonzague Le Pennuen at the head of the monastery.

Now the abbot of Bellefontaine felt liberated from a heavy burden, for his task as vicar was hardly compatible with that of governing two monasteries. Since July 1946, in fact, Dom Dominique had made him responsible for several regular visitations: Rivet, Echourgnac,[20] where the community needed a less precarious industry to support themselves, and La Coudre at Laval. In July and August 1947 an immense tour had led him to the monasteries in the province of Quebec, Canada, to Manitoba, and to Gethsemani, Kentucky, in the United States. "You see that I am still, like St. Bernard, the chimera of my century, or at least the chimera of my order: neither religious, nor traveler, nor businessman, but a little bit of all three nevertheless."[21]

But neither his fatigue nor his desire for peace and quiet made him want a rest: "It seems to me that I am doing what God is asking of me, not making any bones about it or sparing myself,

[20] Echourgnac was founded in 1868 in the diocese of Perigueux in the department of Dordogne. It is about 75 miles east of Bordeaux. The abbot of Sept-Fons, Dom Jean de Durac, got Dom Henri Vandenbroucque, abbot of Port du Salut, to attempt the foundation. It was suppressed in 1910, but reopened in 1922 for Trappistines. *Dictionnaire d'histoire,* op. cit., t. 14, col. 1360.

[21] Letter to a monk, July 4, 1947.

wanting only to serve the divine Master. I am not deluded. If my homework is done well, it is the homework of a child of six. I would be incapable of succeeding at a more difficult homework. But I rejoice like a first-grader who brings home good marks at the end of the week. My soul is at peace."

Chapter 13

FATHER AND SHEPHERD

Between 1940 and 1947 the number of monks at Bellefontaine increased from less than 50 to almost 80. The vitality of the community is undeniable. Father Gabriel did nothing to attract novices. He scrupulously avoided letting his personal influence come into play. It was even rare for him to go to the guest house to see the postulants before they had made a firm decision to enter. He had full confidence in the confessor for the guests. But once the novices had become his sons, his "children," as he tenderly called them, they felt themselves surrounded by his attentive affection, which, to be frank, was maternal and encompassing as well.

Many have told of the unforgettable impression made on them by this first meeting: "You see, they hardly even know you yet, and already they love you; everyone loves you here." Afterwards Father Abbot could be firm and exacting, but one always sensed the presence of a heart full of tender affection, inclined to any indulgence, underneath the outward severity.

"You listen to a master," he said, "but you only follow him, if you love him . . . the abbot will only be followed and obeyed, if he is loved. In order to be loved, first of all, he must love."[1] He only wanted novices who had a solid attachment for God and had decided to lead the Cistercian life generously: "I would rather have less people in the novitiate, than accept mediocre vocations on one point or another. St. Teresa said, 'We ought to weigh the religious and not count them.'"[2] He was even careful

[1] *Notes on the Rule of St. Benedict,* ch. 2.

[2] Letter to a monk, May 15, 1944. We read in his *Notes sur la Règle:* "God is a connoisseur. . . . And that is why he prefers a small artifact of pure gold to

with regular oblates: "I do not want oblates with half-vocations, who are half-responsible."[3]

"You have done well to keep Brother X," he wrote one day, "since he amended himself. You must watch his stubbornness and not give in. If he had not corrected himself, especially if he did not seem to be responsible for his stubbornness, you would have to let him go. Anyone can correct a bad habit, but bad judgment or incomprehension can hardly ever be corrected."[4]

Despite all his principles, however, he was brokenhearted, when he had to decide to send a novice away. He had to do violence to himself: "(In regard to Brother X) I am still perplexed, and I think I am inclined to dismiss him, by making my heart be quiet, which asks me to be kind to the child. My heart is attached to Brother X, because he is trusting. He entrusted himself to us with abandonment. We feel a little of what our Savior must experience with regard to those who trust in him. We are seized, attached."[5]

If he was himself easily attached to those who trusted in him, what drew others to him at first was a kind of limpidity of soul, a transparency, a frankness which emanated from his person. He radiated life and joy. He was a good and tender giant, imposing, but one in whose presence one felt quickly at ease. Some, however, could not get rid of a certain sense of being overwhelmed, provoked by his nobility and natural power. He was a man in every sense of the term: strongly virile, handsome, great, distinguished. He looked at his interlocutor with the look of a laughing child who surrounds him with warmth and sympathy; sometimes people guessed he was a mocker or was cunning, for he was a tease though never cruel. His maturity was strongly allied to a spirit of infancy, to the unalterable youth of the soul.

He had very enchanting reactions. He told of all the pleasure he had had alone in his office, watching a little mouse dig with gusto into the *Dictionnaire des connaissances religieuses.*

---

a large imitation jewel. A little real love is dearer to him than the alloy, even a large quantity of it. In this order of things quantity will never compensate for a lack of quality." *Commentary,* ch. 58.

[3] Letter to a monk, March 9, 1944.

[4] Letter to a monk, May 21, 1944.

[5] Letter to a monk, September 26, 1948.

His natural dignity was intimidating, but his gaze, in which his heart could be seen, was captivating. Children were quickly at ease with him. In 1945, on his way to La Grande Trappe, he had a stopover at Le Mans; in order not to inconvenience the Capuchins with whom he ordinarily stayed, he settled himself comfortably on a park bench and took out a hunk of bread. It was spring, and a gang of children were amusing themselves by running in the sand near him. One of them had the idea of taking off his sandals and going barefoot, but what should he do with his footwear? Without hesitation he went to take them to Dom Sortais and ask him to watch them. Soon all the others imitated him: "Of course, dear children, don't worry; I will take good care of them." "I found it pleasant to watch them," he said afterwards, "and I was glad that I could render them this small service!"

What gained him universal sympathy was his directness, clarity and spontaneity. People sensed great integrity in him. He was very sensitive, sometimes hypersensitive. When he first became superior, certain contrarieties made him literally sick, to the point of forcing him to lie down with a fever. His imagination sometimes blew up minor difficulties into short dramas. He was emotional, and tears came easily to his eyes when he was confronted with distress. Several aspects of his sensitivity made him feminine. It was easy to touch his heart, from which tenderness overflowed. He was literally prodigal with it, so much so that anybody had a perfect right to consider himself privileged. His kindness was exquisite, his attention profoundly touching. His affection even surrounded the families of his monks; he went to see them and gave them the pleasant notion that he was in some way related to them. He knew how to assist them in their difficulties in a marvelous way. He was seen in the parlor embracing the children and holding them in his arms.

With the poor and humble he abolished all distance. His sensitivity to mentalities quite different from his own was surprising. It was impossible for him to pass anyone in misery, without making the misery his own. One day at Angers a priest friend took him in the bishop's car to the Bon-Pasteur[6] house,

[6] Bon-Pasteur house: the motherhouse of the Congregation of the Good Shepherd at Angers, an offshoot of the Order of Notre-Dame de Charité founded

where the monks of Bellefontaine were usually made welcome. At the turn at the bottom of Rue Brault he saw a drunk lying on the pavement, where he could be the victim of an accident at any time: "We cannot leave him there," he said to the chauffeur. "Let us lift him up." Between the two of them, Father Sortais and his companion hoisted the poor man into the automobile. They found out where he lived and brought him into his house. "It is a decent thing that you have done," concluded the man. "I promise you that when you are in the same predicament, I will render you the same service!" Dom Sortais was as though wounded by the suffering, even when it was apparently deserved, of the poor. It immediately became his own.

Together with that his sense of humor was invincible. He had an inexhaustible source of joy, even in the midst of the most crucifying trials. He had the reactions of a high school boy. He could find a humorous note in any situation. Outside of his monastery his monks seemed hardly to recognize him, so liberated for a few moments from his responsibilities did he feel, and close to them. There was no affectation, and this did not prevent him from sometimes recalling a play or doing a little acting with preference for the comic.

He did not take himself seriously. Although he had the highest respect for his charge, he remained simple, quick to act and quick to speak. His spontaneity and his direct and human attitudes were disarming and disconcerting. He had a ready and communicative laugh, without ever forgetting his responsibilities.

He did not think that humiliating himself publicly when he felt guilty entailed a loss of dignity. One Christmas Day, when he had not risen for Lauds, he simply went to take his dinner on the floor of the refectory, voluntarily assuming a penance then customary in the order.

Dom Gabriel had cultivated a kind of passion for beauty. He loved things that were well-made. They took him to God, whom he never found so effectively except in the midst of na-

---

in the 17th century by St. John Eudes. The latter congregation was a loose federation of autonomous houses, but on April 3, 1835, the house in Angers became the motherhouse of all those founded by it, and Mother Euphrasie Pelletier the foundress of a new congregation. The house in Angers is found at 3 Rue Brault. *Catholicisme,* op. cit., t. 2, col. 155–56.

ture. Bad taste and lack of harmony horrified him and provoked strong reactions on his part.

His monks well knew his great generosity. He kept going until he was exhausted. He was present at the night Office at 2:00 a.m. after returning from his trips. They had the worst trouble getting him to take care of himself, and he sincerely thought of himself as a model patient! "What pains and discourages me is to hear you repeat to me that I do not do what I can for my health. I think this reproach is undeserved and erroneous."[7]

He always gave duty precedence over indispensable precautions of health. In this regard he was without pity, almost inhuman towards himself. He neglected himself absolutely, crushing his body under an insupportable burden.

This responded to an aspect of his character: In love with the absolute, he was carried to extremes. It was necessary not always to take his teaching literally; since he was himself pulled between two extremes, his ideal and his extreme goodness, he sometimes ended up looking bizarre and ridiculous because of apparent contradictions or abrupt changes in attitude.

He was well aware of it: "Dom Jean-Baptiste told me that an abbot must be 'man' and 'woman' at the same time," he wrote one day. "I think this is very true. It means that he must be ready to act firmly like a man in the strict sense of the word, and with the sweetness and tenderness of a woman when there is need.

"I have, he told me, these two attitudes. I think he is right. My misery consists in having developed these two attitudes too much. I am too much 'man' and too much 'woman' . . . I have not succeeded in reconciling these two aspects of the soul of a superior. From time to time I am man, very much man, man to the very end, and I am then capable of doing great deeds of courage, of making energetic decisions possible, without caring about potential suffering or wounds. At other times I am capable of showing very maternal goodness and sweetness, motherly indulgence, motherly tenderness. . . . The difficult thing for me is to moderate and reconcile. . . . Instead of being man and mother at the same time, I am successively man and mother. . . . This is painful for others. They are given alternate

[7] Letter to a monk., November 16, 1945.

shower-baths: hot-cold, hot-cold. And that is how the qualities of my soul become occasions of suffering to others."[8]

Dom Gabriel knew, then, that he was sometimes a trial for his monks by his unforeseeable shifts. He willingly allowed himself to suffer because of others. His was a magnanimous soul that no ingratitude was capable of repulsing. He could ask much because he never did anything without practicing it first himself. That anyone could bear a grudge because of an offence did not enter his mind. It was beyond him. He would be disconcerted to learn that it was not the same for everybody. His ease in pardoning was almost unbelievable, as his intimates report.

He incarnated the ideal of an abbot in the eyes of his monks. He was a man made to command, to direct, and to decide. He imposed himself on all as Christ's representative. He loved to see everything for himself, visit the monks in their place of work, listen to them, and understand them. He kept himself informed on the different employments, but since he was not himself a manual worker, he happened not to take account of the exact nature of certain types of work. It was not important! His good will was all that mattered. He was really aware of the practical difficulties of each one.

His heart had its weaknesses, its inclinations that were in some way incoercible, but they usually did not create jealousy, such was the paternal tenderness each one felt himself surrounded with. Besides, he knew how to be firm, and he said forcefully what he had to say. In such cases it was useless to discuss it with him. He would never compromise. What he had said, he had said. He was sometimes very absolute, having then terrifying requirements.

It was indispensable, according to him, for the abbot to stick to his decisions, while being open to all sorts of counsel: "It is sometimes said (of the abbot), 'he sticks to his own ideas.' But that is not bad. In fact it is much better than to be a weathercock spinning at any wind. A person ought to stick to his own ideas, at least until they are shown to be wrong, or until someone brings in a new element."

[8] Letter to Mère Bernard, January 4, 1945.

"It would certainly be excessive to think that other people always perceive our own affairs better than we do, but that they know less about them than we do. Besides they are unaware of the difficulties of a problem they have not had to solve. But it can very well be that others less 'emotional' than we see what we do not see. It can also happen, and it does happen, that others are more competent than we in such or such a matter, for the abbatial charge does not bring universal competence with it. The abbot has a thousand things to occupy himself with."[9]

Every time it seemed to him that an important principle was at stake, he became irritable. He immediately discerned the possible consequences even of acts that were not very important in themselves and intervened energetically. There were sacred things that should not be discussed, and the principle of authority was one of them. Nevertheless, when he alone was the target, he often hesitated to intervene through humility and self-effacement.

Here is a characteristic story that dates from the generalate period: One day Dom Gabriel received complaints about a monastery, and they were justified. He immediately wrote of it to the abbot. Shortly afterward, a monk who knew of Dom Gabriel's letter wrote him an insolent harangue. Should he take punitive action? He showed the letter to an abbot to ask his advice, reflected a minute, and then said simply, "If the brother had said this in public, I would be obliged to intervene; I would have no right to tolerate such an attitude. But he and I are the only ones involved. I believe it is better to say nothing." So he contented himself with a few lines to the brother in reply, to thank him for his letter, to ask his prayers, and to assure him that he would think of him particularly during his Mass the next day.

But usually, when obedience, poverty, or the spirit of penance were in question, his abbatial conscience reacted immediately, alerting him perhaps erroneously and tending to go too far. One monk or another has sometimes been deceived by the fact that he was indulgent in respect of acts, but very severe as regards tendencies that were likely to end in deviations or deformations of the Cistercian spirit. And so, when the guilty

[9] *Notes on the Rule of St. Benedict,* ch. 61.

one immediately came to accuse himself, Father Abbot was as though disarmed by this honesty, and he was unable to punish.

"To hate vices without loving the brothers would involve abuses of severity detrimental to the good of souls. In that case we would lack indulgence and almost justice. . . . To love the brothers without hating their vices would involve the abbot in simple-mindedness and compliance, also detrimental to the good of souls."[10]

Dom Gabriel's temperament was authoritarian; his presence alone imposed his authority. It was difficult not to follow him. He himself admired the qualities of a commander in others very much. Giraud[11] had furnished him and his men with transportation during the war: "A person would throw himself out the window," he said, "to obey a man of such quality." Foch[12] represented an ideal for him. His conception of obedience was mystical before being ascetical. In fact he thought it was the way to give oneself entirely to God, to prove the love of a soul that, no longer belonging to itself, turns away from itself in order to be ruled by God. That is the source of the totality he claims, the exclusiveness and jealousy not to take anything away from his control.

"Continue to accept God's will for you completely," he wrote. "That is everything. When we refuse to submit, we are

[10] Ibid., chap. 64.

[11] This mention of Dom Gabriel's opinion of General Giraud is interesting; Giraud's military exploits are not inconsiderable. His differences with De Gaulle are well-known. He had escaped from the German prison at Königstein in April 1942 and been made head of all French armies in North Africa. He resigned from the Committee of National Liberation at the end of 1943. However, he presided over the rehabilitation of the French armies until April 1944, and he played a decisive role in the liberation of Corsica. *Larousse,* op. cit., t. 5, col. 490.

[12] Acclaimed Marshal by three governments (France, England, and Poland) in the aftermath of World War I, Ferdinand Foch will be a stranger to no one. When he heard in Metz of the annexation by Germany of Alsace-Lorraine, his life's career had been traced out. His life was lived in the service of France. He taught his doctrine of massive frontal attack at the War School for six years, later compiled in two famous books, *De la conduite de la guerre* and *Des principes de la guerre.* His principles were given full play in 1914, when he contributed to the victory at the Marne, through his vigorous action at Saint-Gond, where coordination of the French forces with the Belgian and English was essential. Finally, the battle for France in 1918, where again coordination was essential between French, English and American forces, gave him full scope. He had the joy of seeing Alsace-Lorraine returned to France. Ibid., t. 5, col. 82–83.

out of tune in the concert of our community, whose harmonies ascend to God. Perhaps it will be said that, if only one note is out of tune, that is nothing. It is nothing for those who are not musicians, but for those who have an ear, one note out of tune is enough to make a piece imperfect and keep it from conveying to the hearers what they expect."

"Dear daughter, try to omit nothing of what God asks from you, try to offer him in this way perfect melodies, even if they are modest. Say 'yes' to all that he wills, for he asks nothing but what is reasonable."[13]

"It is usually relatively easy to do God's will. What is difficult and meritorious, what presupposes a lot of love is to always do what God wants, to do all that he wills. However, that is the only wise conduct. God has arranged everything. Our own wisdom consists in conforming ourselves to that."[14]

At certain times Father Abbot had violent but brief fits of anger. He quite rapidly came to the boiling point. If he sometimes got angry for a small reason, it was because he was sincere. The first movement arose from its source and was immediately externalized. He could then seem harsh and abrupt. He did not control his tongue very well, and his words exceeded his thought. He was no longer himself. "There were times when it got hot!" declared a brother about these outbursts. The ready laugh, swift compassion, and sudden anger are so many indications of a character with a tendency toward action. He was temperamentally impatient and did not like delays. His impulsiveness kept him from full control of his reactions. He needed to go ahead. His propensity to anger, however, sometimes gave way before somebody who managed to get him to laugh. Then his indignation blew away as though by magic. But prudence was necessary, because he did not like to have his will thwarted.

When he noticed that he had allowed himself to be carried away once more by his irritability, aggravated by his fatigue and overwork, he was desolate. He did all he could to make reparation. Humiliations cost him nothing, such was his desire to heal the wounds that he had involuntarily caused. Thus he passed

[13] Letter to a nun, June 3, 1953.

[14] Letter to a nun, October 2, 1951.

from excessive severity to excessive kindness. At such moments he showed great sensitivity and attentive tenderness. How often he knelt down to ask pardon for an outburst! He suffered much from losing his temper, but perhaps he did not always consider the effect his outbursts had on certain people of a different character. After such an occurrence, he would remember only vaguely the disagreeable things he might have said. Nevertheless, he would guess he had wounded someone, without knowing the extent of the wound. This would make him desolate, and he would make new resolutions and punish himself, but his fatigue and nervous tension would cause him to fall again. This would always be one of his own crosses, as well as of his immediate collaborators. He tried to compensate by being extremely considerate and attentive, and by being as open as possible, for he had great respect for others and for their mystery.

He tried to love his brothers with the absolute love of Jesus who had given his life for those he loved. He knew no other ideal. His repentance made him enter each time more deeply into this gift of his heart to his sons. He also used these humiliations to go more boldly to God: "That is really a grace," he said, "to draw near to God by humiliation, to love more because one has been covered with confusion, interiorly through a better knowledge of self, exteriorly through admitting one's fault."[15]

They looked forward to his abbatial word with impatience. No doubt we need not see anything more than a caprice in this story that he enjoyed telling: "One day a monk came to my office to see me and said:

'Reverend Father, I would like to tell you something.'

'Well then, tell me.'

'You see, I am worried about my health.'

'You are right to tell me, but what is amiss?'

'Well Reverend Father, anymore I have unshakable insomnia in chapter.'

'What is this, Father X? There is no one to surpass you in sleeping in chapter!'

'But it is true, Reverend Father. With Dom Jean-Marie we used to be able to sleep peacefully, and I found it restful. But

[15] Letter to a nun, July 26, 1954.

now with you it is impossible; as soon as anyone starts to bow his head a little, you stamp your foot to wake us up!' "

In fact it was seldom that anyone slept when he spoke, except in cases of extreme fatigue. Besides, he did not like it. He knew how to hold his audience spellbound. His chapters made a strong impression on the young monks. His spiritual teaching was profound.

His teaching was direct, substantial, and extremely practical. There was always something new and passionate, adorned with exciting stories which he told in an admirable way. He possessed the art of self-renewal, of insisting upon a new aspect each time. They all understood him effortlessly. He was clear, concrete, never banal, and extremely simple. There was much to absorb in what he said, for he shared his personal experiences. The community was avid for his talks, even though they were sometimes a bit long. He would only begin to repeat himself toward the end of his tenure as abbot of Bellefontaine, when taken up by his duties as vicar, he would no longer have sufficient time to prepare his chapters. He read little, having little time for himself, yet he read very attentively and took notes. An admirable gift of prudence enabled him to find immediate concrete applications. He excelled in putting principles to work, remaining very close to life.

By force of circumstances his theological formation had remained superficial. He supplied for it by great surety of judgment which instinctively led him to safe, proven, and solid doctrines. A kind of pre-established harmony existed between him and the teaching of the church. Nevertheless he had suffered greatly from not having had good teachers.

His Sunday homilies awoke fervor more than they nourished the intelligence. He was especially excellent in his morning chapter talks, where he gave his monastic doctrine by commenting on the Rule. He prepared himself for them by recourse to ancient authors: meditations on the rule by Dom Symphorien Bernigaud;[16] an old anonymous printed commentary, composed

[16] Dom Symphorien Bernigaud of Sept-Fons was a Cistercian author who died in 1913. The work referred to is *La Règle de saînt Benoit méditée* (Nevers: Mazeron, 1909). *Dictionnaire de spiritualité* (Paris: Beauchesne, 1988) t. 13, col. 809.

in 1486 for the Célestins;[17] Dom Mège;[18] Dom Martène.[19] He

[17] Célestins: originally the Hermits of St. Damian. They began in Puglia, Italy, on Mt. Morrone in the mid-13th century. The founder, Peter of Morrone, became Pope Celestine V, so the name stuck. The congregation was united to the Order of St. Benedict in 1264 and approved by three popes: Urban IV, Gregory X, and Celestine V. At first they spread only in Italy, but Philip the Fair introduced them in France in 1300. Endowed with royal favor, they spread extensively. By the beginning of the 15th century there were ten houses, and six more were founded by its end. However, the religious wars brought the Celestines much suffering. Monasteries were plundered, churches and libraries ruined, and monks killed by the Huguenots. Despite some half-hearted attempts at reform, the Celestines never fully recovered. By 1768 there were only about 170 professed monks. Two years later they were forbidden to receive novices. The French Revolution dealt them the death blow. *Catholicisme,* op. cit, t. 2, cols. 751–52.

[18] Dom Antoine-Joseph Mège was a Maurist Benedictine. He was born at Clermont-Ferrand in 1625. This capital city of the department of Puy-de-Dôme in south central France is 88 miles east of Limoges. He entered the monastery in Vendôme, a town in north central France, department of Loir-et-Cher, about 50 miles southeast of Le Mans, in 1643. He became prior of Rethel in Champagne in 1681. Rethel is in the department of Ardennes in northeast France, on the Aisne River; it is about 30 miles northeast of Reims. On retiring from his charge, he withdrew to Saint-Germain-des-Prés, a famous and ancient Benedictine monastery in Paris, which was once the chief monastery of the Maurist congregation and center of its intellectual life. Today only the church and abbatial palace are left. Here Dom Mège lived a life of prayer and study. His *Commentaire de la règle de notre Bx Père, saint Benoit* is an attack upon the rigorist interpretation of De Rancé. A chapter of Maurist superiors forbade its publication in 1689 at the insistence of Bossuet. Although the chapter envisioned a revised edition to be undertaken by Dom Claude Martin, Dom Mège demurred. He died at Saint-Germain-des-Prés in 1691. "Mège," *Catholic Encyclopedia* (New York: Appleton, 1911) vol. 10, 146; *Dictionnaire de spiritualité,* op. cit., t. 10, cols. 935–37; *Webster's New Geographical Dictionary,* op. cit., 270, 1282, 240, 1007; *Larousse,* op. cit., t. 9, 513.

[19] Dom Edmond Martène was a learned monk of the Benedictine congregation of Saint Maur, born at Saint-Jean-de-Losne in the diocese of Dijon in 1654. His family was related to Sainte Jeanne de Chantal, to Madame Sévigny, and to Bossuet. He made profession at Saint-Remi in Reims in 1671. He studied philosophy and theology at Saint-Denis. The prior there was Dom Claude Martin, son of the Ursuline mystic, Marie de l'Incarnation. Martin encouraged his studies on the Rule of St. Benedict. In 1681 he joined the group forming around Dom Mabillon and d'Achery at Saint-Germain-des-Prés. His first book was indeed the *Commentarius in Regulam S.P.N. Benedicti litteralis, moralis, historicus* (Paris, 1690), printed in Migne, P.L. LXVI. He died at Saint-Germain-des-Prés in 1739. *Catholicisme,* op. cit., t. 8, cols. 727–28.

found Dom Delatte[20] and Dom Marmion[21] helpful also, especially Dom Delatte. An instinctive knowledge of the requirements of the monastic life permitted him to discern the essential and to lead souls to it untiringly. It is possible that his affirmation of the principles was not sufficiently nuanced. Practice was what inspired him with the indispensable flexibility. Whatever he said was marked by fundamental good sense, shrewdness, and great breadth of viewpoint. His vision, in fact, went far beyond the immediate future; it was open to the remote future, leaving behind the events near at hand.

Dom Sortais was the exact opposite of abstract and speculative. He aimed at what was useful. He had the sense of man and

[20] Dom Paul-Henri-Olis Delatte was Dom Gueranger's second successor as abbot of the famous abbey of Solesmes. He was born at Jeumont, a town in the department Nord, at the Belgian border, in 1848. He studied at the seminary in Cambrai in the same department and was ordained in 1872. He served as curate at N.-D. de Roubaix and later at St.-Étienne in Lille. The Catholic university in Lille chose him for the philosophy chair in 1879. He sought to implement the directives of Pope Leo XIII on Thomism. When he entered the novitiate at Solesmes in 1883, he abandoned a promising scholastic career. His teaching qualities were much appreciated, and after profession he taught dogmatic and moral theology and sacred scripture. He became abbot and superior of The Congregation of France in 1890, overseeing a sumptuous building program at Solesmes. The community of Solesmes was exiled to the Isle of Wight in 1901. It was here that he composed his commentaries on the Rule of St. Benedict, as well as those on the gospels and on St. Paul's epistles. Advanced age and illness forced him to resign from his abbatial charge in 1921, while still in exile. It was his successor, Dom Germain Cozlen, who returned his community to the shores of France in 1922. There he died in 1937. Ibid., t. 3, cols. 551–52.

[21] Joseph Marmion (in religion Dom Columba) was born in Dublin, Ireland, in 1858. His family was originally indigenous to Normandy in France but had moved to Ireland before the start of the Hundred Years War. His mother, Hermine, was descended from a family of Lorrraine. After his studies at Belvedere College and the seminary at Clonliffe, he went to the Irish College at Rome. He was ordained there in 1881. On his return to Ireland he passed through Belgium and visited Maredsous. He became curate at Dundrum, teacher of philosophy at Clonliffe and chaplain for the Redemptorist nuns and for the prisoners at Mt. Joy. He entered Maredsous, whose abbot and founder was Dom Placide Wolter, in 1886. His solemn profession took place in 1891. In 1909 he was elected abbot of Maredsous. He died in 1923 after an exemplary life. His major works are *Christ the Life of the Soul, Christ in His Mysteries,* and *Christ the Ideal of the Monk,* in which he exposed his famous doctrine of mystic assimilation to Christ, based on the *Rule of St. Benedict,* the epistles of St. Paul, and the monastic liturgy. Ibid., t. 8, cols. 697–98.

his real needs. The oratorical power of his teaching was rooted especially in his conviction and simplicity. He delivered himself in what he said. His ardor communicated itself.

By the mysticism of his love, he belonged—although without explicit dependence, at least at this date in his life—to the great Cistercian and Victorine spiritual writers of the 12th century, among whom he hardly knew any except St. Bernard. For William of St. Thierry, Cîteaux was the schola caritatis: In his modern tongue Dom Sortais never preached anything else.

That which he preferred to teach, then, was the primacy of love, the necessity of contemplation, and the conditions—individual as well as community—that favored its development. Nothing else, to sum up, than what he would say during his period as Abbot General in his circular letters, which would give birth to the collection *Les choses qui plaisent à Dieu.*

"If there are very few contemplatives in our monasteries," he said, "it is because we do not have enough renunciation. But if there is only one contemplative in a monastery, it is enough to justify its existence, so precious is the contemplative life in God's eyes."

Nevertheless, he was, by temperament and by formation, more father and shepherd than teacher, so great was his tendency to put into practice—his own as well as that of others—what he had learned! Furthermore, he had understood the very substance of the religious life in a way that is extremely rare. He had perfectly assimilated what he himself had received; he had then taught it to others, after having enriched it with his own experience. On listening to him, people sensed that he knew the country he was describing. In his commentaries on the Rule he made the pastoral and moral viewpoint predominate over the strictly doctrinal aspect. He had the knack of taking up the ideas of others and improving on them, after having made them his own.

Some monks and nuns benefited from his personal direction. He was a sure guide, judging and directing any concrete situation in terms of the primary values. His docility to the action of the Spirit, rather than rational study, led him to discern with disconcerting precision the necessary application of moral principles. He perceived the will of God in the action required, with all its nuances and its exigencies of entire submission to the image of Christ who became obedient unto death; he infallibly discovered what was in harmony with God's design on himself and on others.

In his relations with those who confided in him, perfect loyalty rendered easy the exchanges needed for any kind of direction. The quality of their souls was his highest preoccupation. It pleased him to imagine what the monastery would be like, where there was a Curé of Ars or a Thérèse of Lisieux. Those he directed sensed his effective help and guidance. He relaxed, aroused, and invited to climb. They had, in fact, to go on generously. Giving the Lord half-measures found no support in him. He was compliant and harsh at the same time, and he was not afraid to humiliate anyone, when it was necessary. His severity was extreme toward those he loved most.

"When you love, you do not let the one you love rest. Jesus does not let us rest when he loves us and we respond to his advances. We are slightly overwhelmed, sometimes a bit breathless, yet we love this state, because we know very well that it reveals a love that is never entirely satisfied; it is a predilection."[22]

Direct contact with God, intimacy with him, the interior life: that was the only thing that counted for him, and he spoke of how important it was to sacrifice everything to reach it. He proposed practical methods, little formulas to awaken fervor and perform all the gestures of adoration, which are numerous in the monastic life, conscious testimonies of love.

The reading he advised were the books that had helped him: First of all there was Thérèse of the Child Jesus. He was also attached to Père Grou, Father Faber and Mgr. Gay; without repudiating these, he would afterwards orient readers towards St. John of the Cross, St. Teresa of Avila and St. Francis de Sales.

He not only had compassion on the trials of his sons; they became his trial. Untiringly he preached confidence in God and abandonment to his will.

"Dear little one, Jesus is the sculptor of your soul. Leave yourself alone. Tell yourself that Jesus is the artist, and that he is such a good artist, that he makes no false blow. All his blows

[22] Letter to a nun, November 2, 1958.

reach their mark and beautify the soul which abandons itself. If the soul does not abandon itself, if it flinches, Jesus misses a blow, so to speak."[23]

In difficulties he tried to communicate his faith, a faith to move mountains: "Since you will thank the good God in eternity for granting you the grace of sending you this obedience through the intermediary of your superiors," he wrote to a nephew, "why not give Jesus the joy of having made you happy even now?"

It was impossible for him to speak of Christ's sufferings or of Mary's without tears coming to his eyes.

A formula describes him admirably: "When a monk comes to accuse himself for a fault against the Rule, he is reprimanded; if the omission is important, he is scolded; but if he comes to admit a grave fault, we embrace him and weep with him." In addition, it often happened that he transgressed the measure of indulgence before the third degree!

Despite everything, he taught with St. Benedict never to despair of God's mercy: "We want to present ourselves to the good God with our papers in order, but we will never make it!"

He also spoke much of the Virgin. His own interior journey had begun with her. This had marked him indelibly. "I love the Holy Virgin very much, and I am beginning to love Jesus more, but I am well aware that I will never go to him directly. It is better and surer to go to him through Mary, and then before finding Jesus we find Mary, and we sense her love in passing. I do not know how I could do without her. I know I can confess my heresy to you. Jesus would not be enough for me. But it was substantially Jesus himself who taught me this heresy, and that reassures me."[24]

The formula is abrupt, and he knew it. He would have been the first to nuance it in the light of theology. As it stands, it shows very well how he loved Mary. We could multiply citations showing the filial character of his devotion. He had remained a little child in Our Lady's presence in every sense of the term. Two extremely moving texts prove it better than

[23] Letter to a nun, February 19, 1947.
[24] Letter to a monk, March 6, 1944.

André Sortais (standing on the right) with his brother and two sisters

First Communion

All photographs courtesy of the Abbaye de Bellefontaine.

Student at the Academy of the Beaux-Arts

Novice at Bellefontaine

On the day of his abbatial installation, with Bishop Rumeau

Military chaplain returning from imprisonment

At Bellefontaine

1950, in front of the chapel at the convent of Bons-Secours

At the monastery of Phare in Japan

Pope John XXIII visits Monte Cistello, the students' residence

As Abbot General

The church of Monte Cistello

lengthy developments would. The first is about distractions in prayer, the second about insomnia, which tortured him often in the course of his life: "I too have distractions, but I do not think I have ever consented to them. I spend the time of prayer seated on the Holy Virgin's knees like a child, like a little baby. I ask her to teach me to go to Jesus, to rest near him and to love him. I remain curled up close to her heart the whole time. I stay like a very little one in the arms of its mother. . . . I never find the time too long close to her."

The second text is taken from an admission made to a priest around 1943: "I do not sleep, because I am so worn out, but I have had some delightful nights. Last night I thought I would sleep. I lay down, but sleep did not come. I started to write letters. Then it seemed to me that I would sleep. I lay down on the floor in my office, and I sang with the Virgin. I was happy to be with her. I remembered the songs I used to sing in my childhood. I sang *'Sur le pont d'Avignon, Nous n'irons plus au bois.'* I sang like that for an hour, and I felt that the Holy Virgin was very happy."

This, then, was the strong man from whom so great an impression of power emanated, an impression which was left on each one of his monks and nuns.

Before God he loved to make himself the soul of a poor man. He was not provided with intellectual qualities, he said. The Lord gave him whatever he needed for his sons. Unaware of how rich he was, he believed his hands were empty.

It could have been said of Dom Gabriel, as the disciples [illegible] St. John of God said of that saint, that he had a heart of stor[illegible] himself, a quasi-maternal heart for his neighbor and a [illegible] living fire for God.

Chapter 14

POSTWAR YEARS IN THE *MAUGES*

In order to provide shelter for a community which was growing more and more numerous, Dom Gabriel would have wished to undertake the construction at Bellefontaine that he had planned since before the war. But he lacked the resources. Although it was old, the east wing was still standing. By fixing it up a bit, it was possible to make room for newcomers. At the abbey of Les Gardes, however, the oldest part of the monastery (the ancient convent from before the Revolution) was in an extremely dilapidated condition. Parts of the buildings were in ruins and were no longer inhabited. Father Abbot, then, believed it was right to give priority to his daughters.

Nevertheless, he wanted to give his own monastery a nicer approach. The solemn portal, flanked by its granite columns was not without greatness in its austere simplicity, but for entertaining the monks' families there was only the choice between kind of humid guardhouse whose narrow window was fur- d with a bar and a tiny unheated room.

at 1944 the abbot's brother, M. Jean Sortais, came to live undes, having fled Nantes which had become an inferno he dre cessant bombing. In friendship for the community, and the ans in view of a transformation of the old stable spirit of a use garage: a fascinating arrangement in the and enhan nastic architecture, with discreet utilization structions. It interesting elements in the ancient con- project and br Abbot great joy to open this building had Father Patr cessful conclusion. Dom Sortais also of the enclosure harming rustic oratory at a corner the statue of St. John Nepomucene.[1] The Trappists of La Val-Sainte had brought the devotion to the saint from their travels in Central Europe at the time of the wars of the Revolution and Empire.

Opening onto the west wing of the cloister by a double archway, the oratory of St. Mary Magdalene is also the fruit of Dom Gabriel's devotion. Father Patrick Vannier was asked to draw up the plans, and it was completed during the winter of 1948. The quality of its construction is impressive. The altar was consecrated by Father Abbot on February 5, 1949.

As for the old chapel of Notre-Dame de Bon-Secours, restored by the Trappists in 1832, Dom Gabriel hardly found it pleasing. It is true he admired how the sections of the apse overlapped outside and thought it quaint; the two-storied bell tower of slate dominated the scene; nevertheless, he could not admire either the triangular pediment of the façade or the pilasters or stucco decorations in the style of Louis-Philippe,[2] which adorned the interior. And so, when an inhabitant of the *Mauges* came to confide to him that he had vowed to restore a chapel of the region in recognition of the protection he had received during the war, he joyfully guided his generosity towards the chapel of Bon-Secours. Here again his architect was Father Patrick. Despite the generous donation, the sum allotted could not suffice to finance all the work; a part of it, therefore, was done by the monks

[1] Unfortunately, the latest studies do not confirm the martyrdom of this saint. P. De Vooght (*Catholicisme,* op. cit., t. 6, col. 467) calls his martyrdom a "legend" that "is no longer trustworthy today": "St. John Nepomucene, martyr of the seal of confession, never existed." The person envisaged by Pope Benedict XIII in his bull of canonization of 1729 was John of Pomuk, vicar general for John of Jenstejn, bishop of Prague, whose date of death was not 1383, as given in the bull, but 1393. The legend owes its popularity partly to the credulity of the epoch and partly to the repercussions of the Counter-Reformation. The feast of St. John Nepomucene in the universal calendar was suppressed in 1961.

[2] Louis-Philippe (1773–1850) was king of the French from 1830 to 1848. He became a constitutional monarch after the July Revolution (1830). He favored the middle class, and his reign was characterized by economic prosperity. The February Revolution (1848) caused him to abdicate and flee to England where he died two years later. The year 1830 coincided with an important turning point in French art. A new idealism was being sought, and it was discovered in the past. Three influences became prominent: neo-Gothic, neo-Renaissance and neo-Baroque. It is the latter to which Dom Guy refers. *Larousse,* op. cit., 1962, t. 6, cols. 875–76.

themselves. The chapel emerged completely unrecognizable. The pilgrims of the old days would not have known it. Everything was new: the paneled framework, the surface of the walls, the altar, the paintings of M. Chapleau. The exterior was only modified by the addition of a beautiful open-raftered porch. The restoration was perhaps excessive. Such was Dom Sortais' preference.

As has been said, the north wing of the monastery of Les Gardes was the last vestige of the constructions that had surrounded the sanctuary before the Revolution, and it had been long abandoned. It was certainly a beautiful specimen of the conventional architecture of the 17th century, built around 1605 by the Augustinians with a stone staircase and large rustic chimneys. At every regular visitation for more than a quarter century, the urgency of its restoration had been mentioned. So dilapidated had its condition become that a reconstruction pure and simple was imperative. Dom Sortais asked Father Patrick to draw up the plans and studied the estimate. Neither Les Gardes nor Bellefontaine was prepared to finance a building project so extensive. But Father Abbot had an idea. One day in September 1948 he remarked to some American abbots who had come for the general chapter at Citeaux about the antiquity of the buildings; then he turned to the abbess of Les Gardes and said, "Well, Reverend Mother, it is decided! We will rebuild. The demolition will begin in January!"

He was as happy as a child rigging up a "surprise." To limit expenses he had arranged a program. Father Patrick was the architect; the young monks of Bellefontaine would make up the demolition teams and unskilled labor. In January the young priests studying theology and some brothers set off for the hill with Father Prior. The days were organized in such a way that the philosophical and theological studies would not suffer too much. Father Abbot came often to see the workers and, on occasion, to try a few strokes with the pickaxe. He sent supplies of food in order that all these hungry young mouths would not make too great a dent in the nuns' stocks. And then he himself held out his hand, a thing he abhorred doing. "At the end of each month, Reverend Father sends me the money to pay the contractor," wrote the Abbess. "I told him that he could just as well pay this money himself. But no! It was just another kindness on his part, of which there were so many." In addition, he profited from the work in progress to enlarge the sisters' enclosure. The work of demolition went ahead smoothly. By Paschal time the embankment was finished. The following year the monastery had a new wing whose architecture was worthy of the ancient structure; it contained the refectory, the novitiate, and the infirmary.

The popularity Dom Sortais had acquired in the *Mauges* and the seat he occupied on the Committee of Liberation obliged him almost despite himself to intervene in public affairs and in the religious and political controversies which arose after the war was over. He had joined the committee in order to represent the great Catholic majority of the region against an active minority that intended to profit from the circumstances in order to impose their own program.

In their first meeting after the liberation, the cardinals and archbishops had asked the new regime for a solution to the question of the schools; in their declaration of February 28, 1945, they had defined "the principles which govern the essential problem of the present hour": "We ask that freedom of education, inscribed in the laws of the Republic, be effectively assured, as it is already for the other democratic countries." The declaration had made the rights of the family and the inalienable responsibility of the parents uppermost; it had added, "but this liberty should not be the privilege of money; we do not understand, therefore, why the parents should be forced to pay a double contribution because they wish to fulfill their duty."

Beginning with the given facts (recognition of liberty of education by the laws of the country), the bishops had gone on to the principles upon which this liberty was based: the rights of the person, genuine functioning of the state, and the teaching mission of the church. Their request, then, had been presented as a strongly motivated demand.

The Consultative Assembly had responded to this appeal in its own way during its session of March 28, 1945, by abrogating the aid which had been granted for some years to private schools by the government. This measure had been taken under Marshal Pétain: That had been enough to make it "anti-democratic."

The religious and social conditions of the *Mauges* aggravated the injustice of the procedure. In fact, almost all the children of the region went to private schools. A significant number of villages did not even have a public school because it had never been possible to get together the minimum number of students required in order to justify opening one. So the Catholics had had to support their own schools, and they had also paid taxes for an institution from which they had derived no benefits.

Confident of his prestige as a former member of his department's Committee of Liberation, the pastor of Notre-Dame de Cholet, Canon Douillard, took advantage of the great festal procession of Corpus Christi to launch an appeal to the Christians of the *Mauges* in favor of private schools. "For months freedom [of education] has been under attack by tracts and posters. In our city where two thirds of the children go to private schools, peacefully because they only ask to work peacefully with others, in our region of the *Mauges* where more than four fifths of the children go to private schools, some intellectuals are proposing that they be strangled, or at least die of poverty and hunger, by refusing them subsidies. . . . These are the sinister practices of the Camps of Buchenwald and Dachau . . . We do not want them in France."[3]

A passionate controversy followed in the local press, which only revived the zeal of the pastor of Notre-Dame. Despite the efforts of the M.R.P.[4] to moderate his enthusiasm, Canon Douillard collected a vast crowd of Catholics at Cholet; the hindrances caused by the public authorities accomplished nothing, and on August 30, 1945, 30,000 of the faithful invaded the center of the city to protest in favor of their schools. This was the point of departure for a vast popular movement that Father Sortais would support with all his strength.

Msgr. Douillard was made bishop of Soissons in 1947, and

[3] L'Avenir de Cholet, June 9, 1945.

[4] The M.R.P. *(Mouvement Républicain Populaire)* was "a liberal and Catholic party in France. Its antecedents can be found . . . in two small groups of the period before World War II, *La Jeune Republique* and the *Partie Démocrate Populaire*. . . . The M.R.P. was the product of the French resistance movement during World War II. . . . The party program is based upon Catholic principles of ethics and social justice. . . . as a Catholic party, it has always espoused the cause of government subsidies for Catholic schools." *New Catholic Encyclopedia*, op. cit., vol. 10, 55.

the associations of parents from the Western provinces continued the fight.[5] Gathered around Mgr. Cazeaux, bishop of Luçon, they made up action committees for the freedom of the schools. On Sunday, April 23, 1950, large crowds were gathered; there were 120,000 people at Saint-Laurent-sur-Sèvre,[6] 100,000 at Folgoët,[7] 70,000 at Pontmain,[8] and 10,000 at Château-la-Vallière.[9] An extreme measure was decided by a show of hands: that of refusing to pay the tax until justice had been obtained in the scholastic domain:

"Become in large measure creditors of the state, you can, without violating the moral law," said the Bishop of Luçon, "postpone payment of the tax until your debtor agrees to pay his own debts. . . . There could be no question here of a pure and simple refusal to pay but only of a time limit."

There was one episode in this struggle in which Father Sortais got involved in a very personal way: It concerned the school of Saint-André-de-la Marche, not far from Bellelfontaine.

In the canton of Montfaucon-sur-Moine[10] a controversy had

[5] For the events about to be recounted, it is well to take note of the administrative structure of France which is divided into "departments." Both local and federal governments are very different from our own. Thus it would be misleading to speak of "towns" in our sense. "Commune" is the lowest level of administrative structure. *Arrondissement* is a gathering of communes and cantons around a larger town. The text mentions "communes" mainly (although the interesting case has to do with a "canton" and its "municipalities"). On the level of the department, the "prefect" is assisted by a "general council" made up of a delegate from each canton. The number of cantons can vary from 11 to 70. Each arrondissement has its sub-prefect who assists the prefect of the department. Perhaps the canton is best thought of as the departmental representative at the commune level. *Encyclopaedia Britannica. Macropaedia* (Chicago: Benton, 1974) vol. 7, 604–05.

[6] Saint-Laurent-sur-Sèvre is a commune in the arrondissement of La-Roche-sur-Yon, capital city of the *Vendée* department. *Larousse,* op. cit., t. 9, 522.

[7] Folgoët is a commune in the *arrondissement* of Brest, in the department of Finistère on the Atlantic coast. Ibid., t. 5, 90.

[8] Pontmain is a commune in the *arrondissement* of Mayenne on the Mayenne River, in the department of Mayenne. It is about 20 miles northwest of Le Mans. Ibid., t. 8, 668.

[9] Château-La-Vallière in the *arrondissement* of Tours, in the department of Indre-et-Loire. Ibid., t. 2, 919.

[10] Montfaucon-sur-Moine is in the *arrondissement* of Cholet, in the department of Maine-et-Loire, in the *Mauges* region. Ibid., t. 7, 492.

begun over the maintenance of the public school of Longeron,[11] which was attended by only one student, and all the municipalities except one had voted to close it. In order to break the resistance of the mayors and councilmen, the administration decided to reopen a public school in the canton in a commune which no longer had one. Saint-André-de-la-Marche was chosen. The school had been closed in 1940, at which time it had had no more than three students; the building was used as a post office and a place for celebrations.

The mayor of Saint-André, M. Paul Nerrière, was made of tough fiber. He refused to be intimidated. *Mauges* inhabitants were amused, as they witnessed a short administrative war with many diverse episodes, waged according to the law, including forced authoritative closures and reopenings. It was no secret to anyone that the mayor asked Dom Sortais' advice in order to avoid any false steps; the latter consulted Paris lawyers and various professionals and returned to direct his client how to act.

The administration was disarmed and resigned itself to less pompous measures. The bishop of Angers was approached, but he refused to intervene. And so one day Father Abbot saw the prefect of Maine-et-Loire arrive at Bellefontaine, escorted by the sub-prefect of Cholet. The two dignitaries had come to tell him of the annoyance the whole affair had caused them. One word from the clergy was all that was needed to stop all resistance! He, the abbot of Bellefontaine, would obviously be more listened to than any other.

For Dom Sortais the only solution resided in the restoration of things to the way they had been before the mistaken intervention of the government. He affirmed this forcefully.

"But really, Reverend Father, what do these manifestations at Saint-André accomplish, when the government will always have the upper hand?"

"Would the prefect tell me if, after the problems you have had at Saint-André, you would be disposed to try the same thing elsewhere, at Bégrolles, for example?"

[11] Longeron is a commune in the *arrondissement* of Cholet, in the department of Maine-et-Loire, in the *Mauges* region, on the river Sèvre Nantaise. Ibid., t. 6, 836.

"Certainly not."

"Well then, your honor, what has happened at Saint-André will suffice for the purpose."

As a matter of fact, the resistance stopped as soon as the certitude that similar maneuvers would not be repeated had been acquired. The affair had become famous well beyond the confines of the *Mauges*.

Another affair in which Father Sortais' role was evidently prominent would have still broader range. It was his intervention in favor of General Weygand.[12]

On November 12, 1942, the day following the invasion of the free zone by the German army of occupation, General Weygand had left Vichy for Guéret,[13] where Marshal Pétain had invited him to stay temporarily; he had, however, been arrested near Saint-Pourçain[14] by the German police. He had been guilty of reorganizing the African army after the armistice, which had started again to fight the Germans as soon as the Allies succeeded in their landing at North Africa. The general had been freed on April 29, 1945, at Itter by the advancing American troops, but he had been almost immediately conducted to

[12] General Maxime Weygand was born at Brussels in 1867. He graduated from Saint-Cyr military academy in 1887 as a cavalryman. He is said to have preferred the service to teaching, although he did his share of both. In 1914 he became Foch's chief of staff. The two were not separated until 1923. He was sent to Poland in 1920 to help combat the Red Army. Between 1923 and 1935 he served successively as high commissioner in Syria and Lebanon, director of the Center for Advanced Military Studies, member of the Supreme War Council, chief of staff for the army and supreme commander of the army. He retired from active duty in 1935 and was recalled in 1939. Foch had said, "Call Weygand in time of trouble." He was called too late. He could not save Belgium, and he had not enough units to form up a defensive front on the Somme and the Aisne. Hoping to save French territories in Africa and reorganize needed forces there, he recommended an armistice. He became Pétain's defense minister. Later he became commander in chief of French forces in Africa. Hitler demanded his recall at the end of 1941. He was held prisoner until 1945. On his release by the Americans, he was again detained by the French provisional government. In 1948 all the charges against him were withdrawn, and all his rights restored. *Larousse,* op. cit., t. 10, 940–41.

[13] Guéret is the capital of Creuse department. It is a relatively small city, about 557 miles south of Paris and about 100 miles west of Vichy. *Larousse,* op. cit., t. 5, 681.

[14] Saint-Pourçain-sur-Sioule is a canton-seat in Allier, the same department as Vichy, quite near that city. Ibid., t. 9, 535.

Lindau,[15] where a greatly upset General de Lattre[16] had had to inform him of the order of General de Gaulle, which obliged him to send him to Paris under official guard, in order to place him in the custody of the Ministry of the Interior. Before his departure De Lattre had confided to him that a few days earlier De Gaulle had told him that it would have been better if neither Pétain nor Weygand had returned to France!

On May 9 at the Ministry of the Interior a warrant was served on the former general, specifying that "the one named Weygand, former Minister of National Defense, had plotted against the internal security of the state."

People were so confused in mind, and the "liberated" press was so irresponsible, that no one had dared to raise a voice publicly in his defense. "In July 1945 only the Cholet newspaper *(L'Avenir de Cholet)* defended my father in a courageous article," wrote Jacques Weygand. "The author was Dom Sortais, superior of the Cistercian abbey of Notre-Dame de Bellefontaine, and member of the local Committee of Liberation."[17]

In fact the first article had already appeared on June 23, 1945. It would be followed by others of the same kind: "Rest assured that feeling ran high in Belgium, England, and the United States, where there was nothing but admiration and friendship for the general," wrote the abbot. "For my part, I think feeling ran still higher in the hearts of many Frenchmen who felt deeply hurt and humiliated at the news of this injustice, this mistake.

"Let us speak frankly. Neither the prestigious lieutenant of

[15] Lindau is a city in Bavaria, on an island in Lake Constance, in West Germany. It is a picturesque tourist center. It is not far from the Austrian border. Ibid., t. 6, 769.

[16] Jean-Marie Gabriel de Lattre de Tassigny was made a general in May 1940, and his command was the 14th Infantry Division, which distinguished itself at Rethel. He commanded the 17th Division of the French Army of the Armistice when the Germans crossed into the free zone in 1942, and he was taken prisoner for his action on that occasion. He escaped and reached Algeria. He participated in the Allied landing at Provence at the head of the First French Army. He crossed the Rhine and reached Constance. On May 8, 1945, on behalf of France he received the German surrender. He died at Paris in 1952 and was posthumously made a Marshal of France. *Le Petit Robert dictionnarire universel des noms propres,* ed. Alain Rey (Paris: Dictionnaires le Robert, 1995) 1182.

[17] Jacques Weygand, *Weygand mon père* (Paris: Flammarion, 1970) 414, note (he wrote "Prior" by mistake).

Marshal Foch, nor he who was unable to work a miracle to save us in June 1940, nor he who agreed to take charge of our army at the armistice, in order thereby to maintain patriotism, was imprisoned. It was the leader who was sent to aid Poland during the summer of 1920, when she was threatened by the Red Army, who was imprisoned; he destroyed the invading Bolsheviks before the very walls of Warsaw. Weygand committed an unforgivable sin there, in the eyes of some.

"On behalf of a non-commissioned officer and deserter whose return to France was acclaimed by a political party (Thorez[18]), a kind of amnesty was granted, which, however, did not wash away his crime; in addition it was thought possible to reserve honorific posts for the former mutineers at the Black Sea. Yet we remain inflexible toward General Weygand because he was the Marshal's minister for a short time."

Weygand greatly appreciated this chivalrous intervention. It was the beginning of a loyal, intimate and warm friendship which lasted until Father Abbot's death. The general would defend Dom Gabriel in 1950, when he in his turn would be mistreated by a review appearing in *Ecrits de Paris,* in regard to his participation in Cholet's Committee of Liberation.

This review was particularly ill-advised. If Dom Gabriel had not been stingy with his assistance for Frenchmen wanted by the Gestapo, neither was he stingy toward Frenchmen wanted by Frenchmen and guilty only of having understood their patriotic duty in a different way than other Frenchmen did. The abbey of Bellefontaine had never been searched by the German police, but it was searched on March 24, 1947, by the French police, and they found nothing, since no suspect had turned up there for several months. The abbot was absent at the time. A police inspector went to Melleray in search of him and questioned him

[18] Maurice Thorez (1900–64) was a French communist. He was employed by a mining company when he became a member of the party. He was made secretary general in 1930. He was elected a deputy in 1932 and 1936 and worked at forming a coalition with the Socialists at the heart of the *Front Populaire.* Shortly after the signing of the pact of Germany with Russia, he was mobilized and left his regiment to go to Russia. Though condemned to death for desertion, he was awarded an amnesty after the liberation of France and given a place in De Gaulle's provisional government. *Le Petit Robert,* op. cit., 2051.

at length. In the end, in order to get rid of him, he made some admissions. Yes, he had an important declaration to make. Yes, he knew of a very guilty person who was still at large: He was a non-commissioned officer of the French army, who had deserted during the mobilization of 1940! The inspector did not insist.

The *Vendée militaire* was Dom Sortais' adopted country, the true land of his choice. He felt himself at home there in accordance with the famous episodes of the insurrection of 1793. He felt the necessity of maintaining a living memory of them among the rising generations. That is why he gave his full support to the work of *Souvenir Vendéen.* For him the *Vendéen* war had been above all a war in defense of religious liberties, and he thought with good reason that its result had been positive, because Bonaparte had acquired the conviction that no pacification of the country was possible without a negotiated concordat.

In fact the mind of the first consul was complex, but whatever his personal convictions may have been, however essentially pragmatic and changeable at the whim of the requirements of his political career, he did recognize as an indisputable fact that the Revolution had suffered a loss on the terrain of religion. This had proven that it was impossible "to reduce everything to political unity," even by appealing to bloody coercion. The state had been just as powerless to eliminate the Catholic religion, that of the majority, as it had been to found a new one.

On the very eve of his Italian campaign, the *Vendéen* pledge influenced Bonaparte's decisions. If the problem of the West had not been solved at the time when he was waging a dangerous war against Austria, it would have been impossible to have all his military forces at his command. At that time he had neither the desire, nor, he believed, the ability to wage a war on two fronts, one internal and the other external. After his lightning victory over Austria, which assured him of external peace, he sensed the necessity in addition of internal pacification, and in order to make sure of it, he wished to reestablish the exercise of religion in the fashion desired by the people, that is solemn and public and in communion with Rome. In this regard Dom Sortais' judgment and that of the men of *Souvenir Vendéen* was justified: "The *Vendée* was defeated on the battlefield but victorious on the field of religion."

During the winter of 1793–94, the forest of Vezins had served as general headquarters for Stofflet.[19] He had installed his storehouses, printing press, and hospital in the most remote part, about a league from the edge. From January to May 1794, at the time of the Columns of Hell, and also later, women, old men and children had been massacred in the forest by Republican soldiers next to the real combatants. It is known, for example, that between March 16 and 18 Grignon's column pursued a band of 4,000 to 5,000 *Vendéens* in flight in the forest, "men poorly armed and women." Crouzat, for his part, entered the forest at the end of March; later the sack of Stofflet's hospital took place, possibly in May, finding new victims in wounded soldiers, nurses, and the personnel in charge of the storehouses. The collecting of many families hidden in the forest had made these attacks very murderous, and the tradition, losing historical perspective, had lumped all these events together in one immense massacre perpetrated in March, in which great numbers of victims would have died: one said 1,200, others even 3,000. The location of Stofflet's camp had been called "Cemetery of Martyrs"; a cross was planted there in 1821. Finally, in 1863, a lovely funeral chapel was raised, and next to the apse there was a kind of oratory where pilgrims could go.

In 1949 this memorial was in a state of great dilapidation. Dom Sortais asked Father Patrick to draw up plans for its restoration. The monks of Bellefontaine took charge of the woodwork, and Father Abbot lent his aid to the members of Souvenir *Vendéen* for the collection of funds.

The oratory was finished in autumn 1950. The opening ceremony took place during the day on June 10, 1951. Vespers was chanted in the evening, outdoors in the forest; Father Sortais spoke for the occasion, reminding his audience of the contemporary persecutions in Russia, the Ukraine, Poland, Czechoslovakia, Rumania and Hungary. "With us," he said, "the best

[19] Jean Nicolas Stofflet was a leader in the *Vendéen* war. He was a game keeper in the employ of the count of Maulévrier and one of the first insurgents in the *Mauges*. With Cathelineau he took Cholet. He was a chief of staff under D'Elbée, a commander in Anjou, and he also fought under La Rochejaquelein, whom he replaced. Having once surrendered and taken up arms again, he was apprehended and executed at Angers. *Larousse,* op. cit., t. 9, 1012.

parishes were those that remained faithful at the moment of their greatest trial. Wherever the soil was drenched with precious blood, the land kept producing rich harvests."[20]

Among the numerous exploits of the Columns of Hell, there is remembered, not far from Bellefontaine, near Chemillé, the Melay massacre. On January 25, 1794, Crouzat's column had captured 57 women and children there. Before their victims' eyes, the Blues had desecrated the church and its altar, profaned the sacred vessels and burnt the edifice, before burning the village's houses. When it was no longer anything but fire, they shot the prisoners. Young Marie Boulestreau held the hand of her little sister who was crying; "What is this, Louise! You are crying, and we are going to heaven!"

On July 22, 1951, Dom Sortais blessed a commemorative plaque in remembrance of the slaughter, after having sung the pontifical Mass in the church. "I love this land chosen by the Lord at a terrible time to rescue the honor of Catholic France," he wrote two years later. ". . . Sometimes I am embarrassed when I think that our land of the *Mauges* has not yet seen the cross lifted up over all its battlefields, or even over all its fields of martyrs."[21]

Dom Sortais' heart certainly belonged to this land where he had not been born, where his ancestors had not lived, and from which he would soon be uprooted; he had lived there for 27 years in peace and in the search for God.

[20] *L'Avenir de Cholet*, June 17, 1951; *Revue du Souvenir vendéen*, no. 16, August 1951, 9–11.

[21] Letter to Dr. Coubard, featured in *Revue du Souvenir vendéen*, Christmas, 1953, 1–2.

Chapter 15

ELECTION OF THE ABBOT GENERAL

The general chapter of 1948 took away Dom Sortais' last illusions, if he still had any: "Our Most Reverend Father is very old," he wrote, "and he fulfilled his task at the chapter with difficulty. I have hardly any hope left. This year I was reelected vicar almost unanimously. And now, if our Most Reverend Father were to die or offer his resignation, the result of the chapter would hardly be in doubt. When I think of it, I can only look straight into the eyes of the good God."[1]

During his last years as abbot of Bellefontaine, Father Abbot was forced to be absent frequently. Dom Dominique Nogues entrusted many missions concerning monasteries of the order to him or had him take his own place. One long circuit in May 1949 allowed Dom Gabriel to visit the monasteries of the central plateau: Notre-Dame des Neiges,[2] Notre-Dame du Desert,[3] Bonnecombe[4] and Bonneval.[5] Another in April and May 1951 led

[1] Letter to Mère Bernard, September 20, 1948.

[2] Notre-Dame des Neiges was founded by Aiguebelle in 1850 in the diocese of Viviers (department: Ardèche; *arrondissement:* Largentière; canton seat: Saint-Étienne-de-Lugdarès; commune: Saint-Laurent-les-Bains) in southeastern France, about 80 miles north of the Mediterranean coast. *Catholicisme,* op. cit., t. 9, col. 1150.

[3] Notre-Dame or Sainte-Marie du Desert, also founded by Aiguebelle in 1852, is in the diocese of Toulouse (department: Haute-Garonne; canton seat: Cadours; commune: Bellegarde); it is about 22 miles northwest of Toulouse. *Dictionnaire d'histoire,* op. cit., t. 14, col. 336.

[4] It was again Aiguebelle, at the instance of Bishop Bourret of Rodez, that acquired the ruins of the ancient abbey of Bonnecombe and refounded it, sending there some of its monks in 1876. It is about nine miles south of Rodez, in the department of Aveyron, about 78 miles northeast of Toulouse. *Catholicisme,* op. cit., t. 2, col. 147–48.

[5] Bonneval was an ancient foundation of Cîteaux. It was restored for Trappistines in 1875. It was again Bishop Bourret of Rodez who acquired the ruins.

him to the province of Quebec and New Brunswick. The abbey of Echourgnac continued to require all his care. He had to make the regular visitation there every year. In addition, since he had the gift of saving souls *in extremis,* appeals to him were frequent: "I am always busy with poor little lost sheep," he wrote in November 1950. "The nuncio sent for me and told me of his satisfaction with me and that he was entrusting some difficult assignments to me for the welfare and return of certain priests. It is because there are two praying monasteries behind me. No doubt that is why Jesus chose me, because my misery allows me to have compassion more easily."[6]

Of his own accord he added assignments that were not asked of him. His relationship to the milieus of the fine arts had allowed him to discover many miseries. Many were the times when he clambered up the sordid staircases of Montmartre[7] to find the dismal hole where some artist was in agony, and to help him bring off his return to God or defeat his prejudices against priests.

The community of Bellefontaine was not without suffering, on account of his frequent absences. If its hardships were great, its affection for its abbot was equally great, but those who complained did not always do so in the most becoming manner. A certain monk cites absences due to his speeches at Paris on behalf of the prisoners. This was no longer a concern

---

The 12 Trappistines (six choir nuns and six lay sisters) came from Maubec in the diocese of Valence. Bonneval is situated in the Boralde valley (department: Aveyron; *arrondissement:* Espalion; commune: Cayrol) in the diocese of Rodez. It is a mile north of Espalion, which is about 100 miles northeast of the Mediterranean coast. Ibid., col. 152–53.

[6] Letter to Mère Bernard, November 15, 1950. In his notes on the Rule we read, "This poor little one, now an apostate, about whom I spoke last time, was once one of my sons. Yet, not once, because once a father you remain so always. He told me, 'You love me differently than you did before'; 'You love me more than before.' It was true. You know very well, when a religious commits a slight fault, his abbot punishes him; when the fault is more serious, his abbot's punishment is more severe; but when the fault is very grave, his abbot embraces him." *Commentary on the Rule of St. Benedict,* ch. 64. He liked to repeat the last phrase which has been transcribed in various ways.

[7] "Montmartre, Butte, a northern district of Paris on the right bank of the Seine River, occupying the highest point in Paris, long a favorite residential area for artists." *Encyclopaedia Britannica,* op. cit., vol. 6, 1025.

after the liberation, and Father Abbot had stopped them since 1943. Sometimes Dom Gabriel's exhaustion was alarming, but he was stimulated by every appeal, and he created the illusion of regaining his strength at the moment of departure: "My time has never been my own: trips, general chapter, two trips to Les Gardes, two trips during which I lay down for a very short rest, feverish and tired as I could possibly be. I was told that this is God's will for me. I believe this also, but sometimes it is a bit overwhelming all the same."[8]

The greatest hardship of the monks of Bellefontaine was that of finding him less available. Certain manifestations of the soul could not wait. When Father Abbot returned, it was too late to make them. In addition, Dom Gabriel sometimes gave the impression that Bellefontaine was too limited a field of action for him. In reality he was incapable of pulling up stakes, if he thought there was question of the salvation of a soul. Any distress, especially spiritual distress, took away sleep from his eyes. He was in a way constrained to do all that was humanly possible, in order to relieve it. This sometimes involved him ahead of time in new obligations which overburdened him. Besides, he was a man of obedience, and the wishes of Dom Dominique were virtually taken as orders. And then, he thought that by backing him up as best he could in the exercise of his responsibility, he could help him to fulfill it a while longer and thus avoid his own feared election. In a way he played the part of the fire for the very good of his own abbey.

And so by fulfilling the duties of a commercial traveler for the Father General, he ended up knowing half of a good hundred monasteries of the order personally on the eve of the general chapter of 1951.

The chapter opened at the abbey of Cîteaux on September 12. Not long before, Dom Nogues had made the regular visitation of the abbey of Rivet, and feeling very tired, had wanted Dom Gabriel to assist him. He suffered from lapses of memory and was often absent-minded. At the end of the visitation, eyeball to eyeball, he asked his companion in confidence:

[8] Letter to a monk, September 25, 1947.

"Dom Gabriel, tell me the truth: It is time for me to retire, is it not?"

"Yes, Most Reverend Father!"

Dom Dominique presented his resignation shortly after the chapter opened. "It is I who will preside at the end of the general chapter," wrote Dom Gabriel. "And we will then have to fix a date for the election. There is a clear tendency to make it as soon as possible. They are talking about November 1." There was hardly any doubt about the outcome of the election, and Dom Gabriel was desolate over this. He had known perfectly well what was waiting for him, when he had answered Dom Dominique so clearly. "Rumors have reached me already," he had written in July. "Such propaganda *against* me! The dear Father! If he only knew how joyfully I would hug him, if it were to happen as he predicted!"[9]

Between September and November Father Abbot kept a promise he had made to preach the retreat for the nuns at Notre-Dame de la Paix at Chimay;[10] then he went to Spain for the dedication of the church at the abbey of Viaceli. He took advantage of the opportunity to stop at the Abadia San Isidro.[11] At the beginning of November he was at Citeaux to join the abbots gathered there.

Before this moment he had confided to a beloved spiritual daughter: "Knowing your absolute discretion, I will tell you that the outcome of the abbatial election set for November 7 is not doubted by anyone now. My poor heart is broken, and I know very well that my wound will never be healed on this earth. However, after a conversation with the Reverend Father of La Grande Trappe, my superior, I have decided not to try to do anything to escape the blows that the good God in his mercy

[9] Letter to Mère Bernard, July 12, 1951.

[10] There is both a Trappist and a Trappistine monastery at Chimay in Belgium. The Trappistine abbey of N.-D. de la Paix is at 6260 Chimay in the diocese of Tournai; its Father Immediate is located at the Trappist monastery of Scourmont, also in the diocese of Tournai. Its address is 6464 Forges. Tournai is located in the department of Hainault in southeastern Belgium *Elenchus monasteriorum O.C.S.O.* (Trappist Generalate: Rome 1997) 9, 41.

[11] Viaceli is in the diocese of Santander, and San Isidro in the diocese of Palencia, both in northern Spain; Santander is on the coast, and Palencia about 125 miles south of it. Ibid., 18, 16.

will give me. I will accept everything, and I will do so with a smile. I will all that he wills. I will the ability to accept it as he does, and possibly even more than he does."[12]

In an analogous situation, in the year 1946, he had said, "Would God make me conspicuous, in order to make me humbler? Nothing humbles a person more, well do I know it, than to be obviously unequal to a task voluntarily accepted. This public embarrassment will perhaps be salutary for my soul."[13] He was elected on November 7.

It was the Father Abbot of La Grande Trappe, as Father Immediate, who should have assumed the government of Bellefontaine, pending a new abbatial election. But Dom Gabriel wished to conclude several affairs that required attention concerning his monastery, so the abbot of La Grande Trappe proposed that he keep the government of the community until the installation of his successor.

Father Sortais' vocation was to be a father. To be an abbot without monks, simply to direct a large group, surpassed his comprehension: it was literally impossible for him to form this idea. In principle the Abbot General remained abbot of Citeaux, and through the intermediary of an auxiliary abbot exercised a certain paternity over a real community. But this juridical fiction could not satisfy his heart. However attached he might be to his new title with its rich history of eight and a half centuries, the monks of Citeaux were not "his sons" in the same way as those of Bellefontaine. And so he envisaged his role as Abbot General from this moment on from a very particular angle. He understood his personal contacts with the abbots and monks of his order to be multiplied, and the order counted at that time more than 4,100 monks and more than 1,600 nuns, and it was expanding rapidly, especially in the U.S. In the year 1952 alone it would increase by 210 members.

For his own part, then, the Abbot General could not be an intermediary between the Roman congregations and the order, a kind of procurator general armed with more extensive powers. His function was much more important and effective:

[12] Letter to Mère Bernard, September 17, 1951.

[13] Letter to Mère Bernard, March 9, 1946.

"Exempt from the occupations and extra duties of a Superior *de regimine,* (the Abbot General) has much more time for reflection and meditation than the others. In his solitude at Rome to which he returns several times a year, after having visited a certain number of monasteries, he will have the duty and the leisure to think over the great monastic problems and to weigh the difficulties encountered by the superiors and religious who have written to him. . . . Trying never to forget the objective to be attained, which is that of making available to the members of the order the best possible conditions for the development of their contemplative life, he will be careful not to confuse the essential with the accidental or the spirit of the Rule with the various observances, and he will avoid hastily calling legitimate needs caprices and seeing indications of laxity in reasonable desires necessitated by one's state of health or adapted to what real good there is in the mentality of the century we live in."[14]

The Roman aspect of his charge did not attract him at all. His unlimited devotion to the sovereign pontiff, his love for the church and his sense of the hierarchy did not manage to overcome his instinctive repugnance for the ministerial life he thought he would lead if he stayed for any length of time at Rome. His imagination took pleasure in blackening the picture, without giving him time to glimpse the lovely aspects, or to guess at the solid friendships that would be formed. The day after Christmas he was invaded by immense sadness: "These days I have had great temptations to discouragement. . . . I have felt so powerless before the task that awaits me. I have found my life here so insipid, because it is partly worldly, that I had only one wish: to get out."[15]

Memories of his abbeys in Anjou sharpened his regrets; he suffered because a page in his life had been turned, and that the past was gone. Life had cast him onto another beach: "The day will come when the name of Les Gardes or Bellefontaine will not bring back a single face or memory, and that day I do believe a tear will form in my eye. It is true that I have deserved to be crossed out by the personnel of these monasteries, beloved as

[14] Discourse at the general chapter before the election, November 7, 1951.
[15] Letter to Mère Bernard, December 6, 1951.

they are, whom I have not cared for as I should have!"[16] A tear! To speak truly, since the day he knew he would have to leave Bellefontaine, he had shed many. The deacon who served his Mass on the day when he was to leave the abbey, never again to return except for the event of the election of his successor, was impressed by the long quiet sobs which shook him during the canon and the *Pater; fiat voluntas tua.*

Complaints would return frequently to his pen. But he was already completely engrossed in the demands of his charge: Action kept him from thinking too much of his suffering which brought him tangible proof of his love for his own, and he would not wish to be deprived of that at any price: "I do not belong to myself in any way. I lead a life of overwork in every kind of way. I no longer have time to think of anything, to do anything, to pray or to rest. I listen, I speak, I write, I make twenty important decisions a day. In order not to err, it will be necessary to be united to God to the point of being stuck to him, as Holy Scripture says. And I feel myself to be nothing, nothing at all."[17]

However, a transformation was imperceptibly brought about in him, the miracle of his new duties. Attached by each fiber of his being to his country, its traditions and its greatness, he sensed nonetheless that his heart was expanding to the dimensions of the Cistercian family, to the point that he could make the sentiments of each one of his sons his own: "I love all my children with the same heart, and I can surely say, with the same love. I no longer separate those of Bellefontaine or those of Citeaux, those of Germany or those of Spain; they are all my sons, and I feel that God has given me a father's heart for all my sons and daughters."[18]

"I love all my children, white and black, yellow, and red, good and not so good."[19]

He would take stock again, even better, a few months later, after his first voyage to the monasteries of the Far East. His nationalism had burst asunder, or better, had allowed him to

[16] Letter to Mère Bernard, May 14, 1952.
[17] Letter to Mère Bernard, February 18, 1952.
[18] Letter to Mère Bernard, April 1, 1952.
[19] Letter to Mère Bernard, May 3, 1952.

discover and enter into the soul of each country: "I have the strong feeling that this sojourn in Japan has changed me; I feel more and more that I am no longer from any nation. I declare (for God has done the work without me), that I am just as much Japanese as French, just as much American, just as much Spanish, just as much Chinese as French. I am from all the nations where I have children, and this I am without effort."[20]

The true universalism, that of the heart, grows spontaneously in soil of this quality. Stateless persons do not have what it takes to understand and respect, as he would do, the intimate riches of each people. This would not keep him, however, from thinking in French or from remaining very much a member of that nation by his reactions.

At the entreaty of the Father Abbot of La Grande Trappe, Dom Gabriel had returned to Anjou immediately after the election, in order to take leave of his two communities. He had been deeply moved. In chapter at Bellefontaine he had humbly asked pardon of his sons for his negligence and for the shortcomings of his government. He had prayed them to excuse him for his many long absences. And in reparation, as though he had been the one principally responsible for this state of affairs, he had assured them that he would not confide missions to his successor that would deprive the monks of his presence: "I promise you this!"

The election for the abbatial office at Bellefontaine was set for January 26. The Abbot General arrived on the 20th, in order to counsel his monks on the dispositions they should have, but he did not wish to give advice on persons, unless he were asked particularly. He did not wish to influence the community's choice.[21] The abbot of La Grande Trappe had advised him not to preside over the scrutiny, in order not to betray his intimate sentiments. But it was to him that the abbot-elect came to ask his final advice, before accepting the election.

[20] Letter to X, winter 1952–53.

[21] This is found among the counsels he gave at the time of the election: "The most desirable thing is not so much that the abbot should excel in this or that but that he should be whole, lacking nothing. Choose the one you would choose, if you were to leave the monastery the day after the election." Notes for his conferences.

"My dear child," Dom Gabriel would write to him tenderly after his departure, "let me say again, that it is a great consolation for me, to have left you my inheritance in leaving my beloved Bellefontaine for good. . . . I pray for you, asking God to give you what you need. I would wish that you do more good than I. Ground has been lost that must be regained."[22]

"The abbot's fatherhood does not seem to me to be spiritual only. A father is not father only when he begets. He is father as long as he has a son, and as long as he cares for his son, educating him and passing on to him something of his soul. That is why I believe that an abbot, if he is really abbot and father, should love his sons with his whole human heart. I hardly believe that a man can be a father, or that a man can be an abbot, without loving with his whole heart. Oh my dear child! It seems that I have really been your abbot, I have been abbot to all of you, despite my faults, because I have loved you with my whole heart. My poor heart is broken, because I am no longer your abbot, and that is the proof of my love."[23]

"May God excuse the faults I have committed as abbot! They have been many, and I weep for them from time to time, when it pleases God to enlighten me. But I think that I do not have too many things to reproach myself with on the love that I owed my sons, or on my duty to give them all, to devote all my time and all my powers to them. Despite my misery, I have given all."[24]

Dom Gabriel decided to confer the abbatial blessing on his successor himself, in virtue of a privilege enjoyed by the abbot of Citeaux, even though an act of this kind ran the risk of offending Msgr. Chappoulie, bishop of Angers. He would return on March 21, the feast of St. Benedict, for that occasion, after his first visit as Abbot General to the monasteries of Alsace, Austria, Germany, Holland, and Belgium. He had wished to visit first those of his sons who had been most tried by the war.

The celebration of the abbatial blessing had a profound effect on the community of Bellefontaine. Dom Gabriel was

[22] Letter to the abbot of Bellefontaine, February 16, 1952.
[23] Letter to the abbot of Bellefontaine, February 29, 1952.
[24] Ibid.

moved and serious. He fulfilled his function with extreme dignity, he who had always been a bit ill at ease, when he had had to pontificate. Father Abbot celebrated his exodus; he lived the ultimate uprooting which preceded every divine vocation; this uprooting is all the more cruel, when it separates us from goods that are more elevated, and snaps bonds which the Lord himself has fashioned. Like Abraham, Dom Gabriel accepted the sacrifice of what was most dear to him, in order to become the father of a multitude of men of faith. His confidence was complete, assured as he was of God's fidelity, but his heart bled, and in personal intimacy it was impossible for him to hold back his tears.

"When you offer God a sacrifice, when you tell him, 'Lord, I am yours, I belong to you,' do you have the right to be surprised afterwards, if God takes you at your word and uses you?"[25]

"I regret nothing," he said again, "for God's will is lovable through thick and thin, and . . . I experience great satisfaction in offering the good God what I hold most dear. How sweet it is, then, to love so good a God, that, not only does he fill us without counting, but knowing that there is more joy in giving than in receiving, he furnishes us with the occasion and the grace of giving him something!"[26] Such a phrase is characteristic of Dom Gabriel's spirituality: "Let us try," he said, "to be always satisfied with the good God without restriction. This satisfaction does not relieve suffering, but it brings peace. And this peace begets joy, a joy compatible with suffering."[27]

[25] Sermon for a profession at Les Gardes, December 2, 1951.
[26] Circular letter of December 8, 1951.
[27] Letter to a nun, February 19, 1953.

Chapter 16

PILGRIM ALL OVER THE WORLD

In the Cistercian order the general chapter holds supreme authority, and it usually meets once a year. The Abbot General gives an account of his administration to the general chapter. Between general chapters the Abbot General's essential mission is to maintain a constant vigilance over the observance in the houses of the order. He also confirms the elections of abbots and other superiors. Each member of the order can have recourse to him. The Abbot General can also visit any monastery of the order or delegate someone else to do it for him, without prejudice to the regular visitations that the Fathers Immediate would make to their own daughter houses.

When the congregations sprung from La Trappe had been unified under Leo XIII in 1892, the order of Cistercians of the Strict Observance had been essentially composed of houses located in France, Belgium, and the British Isles. Only certain monasteries had been implanted outside of this perimeter (Nova Scotia, U.S.A., and Spain). In 1951 the map of the order looked very different. The Reformed Cistercians had spread liberally in Holland, the Iberian Peninsula, Canada, and the Far East. Immediately after the war a new expansion began in the monasteries of the U.S.A., the profusion of which was in proportion to that of the continent, a kind of rush towards the contemplative and penitential life, an invasion of the centers of silence and solitude. In a few years there was a flood of novices submerging by their youthful ardor and enthusiasm the older religious living in the three oldest monasteries: Gethsemani, New Melleray, and Our Lady of the Valley (moved to Spencer in 1950). Seven foundations followed one another between the years 1944 and 1951, without any perceptible decrease in the numbers of the religious in the founding abbeys. This did not come about without posing serious problems. Monastic formation is a work which requires time and attentive and constant care. The functions of abbot, prior and novice master are not functions that can be improvised. To be a monk, a few months of intensive training like that in the army are not enough. When Dom Sortais became Abbot General, Gethsemani counted 110 monks and 124 novices, Spencer 91 monks and 45 novices, and New Melleray 102 monks and 37 novices.

Nuns' monasteries formed a more homogeneous group, with 13 French abbeys and four Belgian. But Japan was the theater of a movement that, proportionate to the number of Catholics, surpassed that of America in abundance. Besides this, there were 45 monasteries of Cistercian nuns in Spain, a certain number of which expressed the desire of incorporation into the order.

This is a rough sketch of the situation of the order of Reformed Cistercians at the moment of the election of Dom Sortais as Abbot General. He bore the title of abbot of Citeaux himself and performed some functions of that office, while being substituted for in the effective direction of his community by an auxiliary abbot.

His predecessors in the responsibility had had the role of coordination and assistance above all. The Abbot General is not the superior of a centralized order over which he exercises direct government. But Dom Gabriel's vigorous personality and the particular circumstances of the milieu in which the order had to evolve at that time would stamp his generalate with a very personal style. He had, as it were, an incoercible need inside him to act, from the moment that he felt that a situation could become detrimental to souls. Considerations regarding places and persons did not stop him when a difficulty arose, and the solution was not obvious. He was afire to find it himself, in order that souls could again serve the Lord freely in conditions favorable to their life.

Besides, it was impossible for him to get interested in generalities, in large wholes, independently of concrete situations. He did not know abstractions. Everywhere he saw living men thinking, working, suffering, and loving. It was in contact with monks and their daily difficulties that he formed judgments. He wanted to know each monastery with its individual physiognomy, its particular problems, its own beauty and its weaknesses. Every soul of the monks and nuns of the order seemed to him to be a priceless treasure. In fact he had the ability to discover the interesting side of each person; he loved to get them to speak, to listen to them expose their difficulties themselves. Life had taken nothing away from his original sensitivity, only refined and supernaturalized it.

It cost him, no doubt, the sacrifice of his tranquility, silence, and peace, as well as his intimate solitude with God, which had attracted him to the Cistercian life. But he had less awareness than ever of belonging to himself, because God's call was more powerful than all these interior attractions:

"Basically, we did not come to the monastery to find there a certain kind of life. We did not become monks in order to find quiet hours for choral or private prayer, for *lectio divina,* or for familiarity with God, but in order to answer God's call, in order to obey. What good would it do a monk to assure himself of quiet hours and a perfectly regular life? The objective is not to get something for oneself or to find happiness, but to do God's will. And if he wills that I seek him without finding him here below, then I will it too."[1]

"Your life," he wrote to an abbot, "is a squandered life. Who wanted it that way, you or God? If it was God, tell him quickly that you also want it, and that you wish no other life."[2]

Perhaps his heart was too closely attached to his sons and to his own monastery. His need for spiritual fatherhood was so great! In exercising the responsibility of abbot of Bellefontaine with such extreme generosity, he had unconsciously mixed sentiments that were too human with it. He declared that friendship led him more effectively to God than certain kinds of detachment and interior solitude. No doubt! But perhaps he had not yet succeeded in pacifying his own heart completely. He remained attached to persons, to manifestations of affection and even to tenderness in the highest sense of the word. The

[1] Letter to an abbot, March 5, 1955.
[2] Ibid.

role of Abbot General came to break the dearest bonds and set him up in interior solitude.

Dom Gabriel, then, keenly felt the change imposed on his life: "Where is the quiet of Bellefontaine, my monks united in spirit, the warm affection of my sons? . . . Here there are whole hours of council with fathers of different languages and various mentalities, whose reactions are sometimes quite contrary."[3] His dwelling place was no longer, properly speaking, a monastery of the classic type, built in the peace of the countryside, in the midst of nature which he loved and used in his contemplation. It was the general's house in Rome on the Aventine, near St. Prisca, where the members of the definitory lived with him, and also the procurator general and some young monks who came to study in the Roman universities.

"Now I am a monk without a monastery, whom the dignity bestowed upon him renders somewhat embarrassing everywhere he goes in the order, who must devote himself unceasingly to peacemaking, to reconciliation, to arranging things. Happily for me, this situation which causes me to break with all that is not God or for God, is by that very fact sanctifying."[4]

Dom Sortais was too much a cultist of God's will to waste time on useless regrets: "The duties of my state have removed me from the common life and the observances which I loved, which took me to God, and from the Divine Office as I knew it since 1924. But I have found everything in adhesion to God's will: the praise of God and the road towards God, and the delightful security which I once enjoyed in the regular life has been exchanged for a greater security, because it is not based and no longer depends on anything but my Father's goodness. He has taken everything away from me. But is it not he who has given me everything? He was free."[5]

The certitude of doing God's will brought him profound peace: "We do not always sense," he wrote to a friend who had received heavy responsibilities, "this help from God consciously, when we are asked to accept responsibilities which seem very

[3] Letter to Abbot X, December 27, 1951.
[4] Letter to friends, Holy Saturday, 1953.
[5] Letter to a nun, April 2, 1955.

heavy to us. Nevertheless, God is present in this call and decision of those who represent him for us, and faith gives us the certitude, that his paternal goodness and wisdom will not deprive us of the grace we stand in need of. I find strength and consolation in the thought that it is not only in order to obtain our obedience that God speaks to us through our superiors, but also to assure us that the mission they invest us with is his will, and that it is the best way for us to be united with him."[6]

And so Dom Gabriel meant to give himself to his new task. He applied himself to it immediately with the ardor and "wholeness" that characterized him. "Our order is my constant solicitude. I think of it like a fool thinks of his fixed idea and keeps coming back to it. I really feel that I am carrying the weight of the order. I suffer from all the weaknesses of its members. I am slightly crushed by them. I am well aware that my health is undermined by it, but I prefer to have it that way, because otherwise I would love less."[7]

For the good of souls, then, he agreed to be without family, without a fixed abode, an eternal vagabond. He preferred to go about the world in search of his monks, in order to understand them and help them in their vocation, instead of staying very long in this general's house, which was not, for all that, without some charm.

He did not minimize the difficulties of the work he had to do: "My role is to animate a body, and this task has been rendered, humanly speaking, more delicate and difficult by the fact that I must influence people from different countries, with different temperaments. It is not easy to forge unity, the unity necessary to a body."[8]

[6] Letter to Msgr. X, January 20, 1960.

[7] Letter to Mère Bernard, June 8, 1953.

[8] Letter to a monk, March 22, 1954. He was extremely attached to the system of affiliation in the order, as a factor of unity: "It is because we are not organized into provinces, that we remain uniquely Cistercian. Thanks to our system of filiations, the order propagates itself without reference to nationality and demonstrates the beautiful and rare spectacle of charity without territorial limitations, in a century in which nationalism is everywhere exacerbated. Let us guard our ancient organization as a precious treasure, our traditional filiations, and let us continue to give the example of our fraternal unity and of our catholicity." Discourse at the general chapter of 1958.

His good will was limitless. His ambition was to become all things for everybody: "I would like to do much for the order, for the good of the souls Jesus has called to it. . . . I have a hundred projects in mind, but will I be able to complete them? Certainly not alone."

His intention was to give priority to the deprived monasteries, those without intellectual or material resources or even without great spiritual resources. "Last time I told you that I wanted to see the new Father General favor the little communities. Since it is I who have received this charge, I will do my best to fulfill what, as vicar, I regarded as one of the duties of the Abbot General."[9] That is why from the beginning of his generalate he decided to undertake a vast circuit which, after having allowed him to meet his sons in Germany and Holland, tried by the war, and those of the New World, would lead him to the most isolated monasteries in the order, those of the Far East.

The Communist persecution had destroyed the two monasteries the order possessed in China; Notre-Dame de Consolation founded by Tamié in 1883, which had 100 monks, and the monastery it founded in 1928, Notre-Dame de Liesse in the apostolic vicariate of Cheng-Ting-Fu.

The monks of Consolation had been arrested and condemned by a popular tribunal. The abbot, a Frenchman, had remained with his wrists tied behind his back with steel wire for 59 days and nights, eating and sleeping like a beast. Many of his monks had had their heads crushed between two pieces of wood. The procedure was simple and fast: two planks joined at one end by a hinge and at the other by a cranking device. The patient's head was placed between the two planks, and they were pressed together until the head burst. Other monks had been beaten to death with a lash. All kinds of torture had been used. More than 30 religious had perished in this way, among them those with any responsibility. Finally the Communist troops had dynamited the monastery, in order that no memory of it would remain. When the survivors had been released, they had tried to meet together and continue their monastic life. The community had survived secretly in this way for some time in

[9] Letter to an abbess, December 16, 1951.

the suburbs of Peking under the direction of a Belgian, Père Jean-Marie. The monks said the Office at night and sang the Mass very early in the morning in low tones, before going out to work. Consolation had changed in this way into a harmless cheese factory whose workers tried to maintain an integral common life. But it did not take the police long to discover the real nature of the enterprise. Several religious were sent to prison, and Père Jean-Marie deported as a foreigner. As his successor he appointed a young religious, Père Benoit Wang. A new attempt at monastic life was made, followed by new imprisonments.

The fate of Liesse had been slightly less severe, for it had not, to begin with, been in a zone controlled by the Red armies. When the Nationalists retreated, the monastery was surrounded, but the religious could be evacuated by American planes. The community was re-founded further south. The new monastery was again surrounded in the same way. Only a few religious were taken away by airplanes; seven or eight went off to seek asylum in Manitoba, in the Canadian Midwest, in the monastery of Prairies. Father Paulinus, the Chinese superior, designated the city of Hong-Kong as a meeting place for the others. Eleven reached it. Thirty or 35 others remained in communist China. Five of them paid for their attachment to their church and order with their lives. Father Vincent, the second superior, died of blows received in prison, proclaiming his faith in God the Creator. "You will be set free, if you affirm that God did not create man, and that man descended from apes!" Three times he had refused.

One by one, then, the survivors presented themselves at the Hong-Kong border: first a young choir monk, then a lay brother, then others, then Father Paulinus. When they were positive that no others would arrive, they counted themselves: three priests and eight brothers. The English governor could not grant them any land in Hong-Kong, which was overpopulated; he offered them the rocky uninhabited portion of Lantao Island. A makeshift monastery was built among the rocks battered by the waves. It was the monks who brought in some arable earth in baskets. They lived in extreme poverty.

Dom Sortais had a great desire to visit this community, the poorest of all, as soon as possible, and to study close at hand how he could render some assistance. Before that, as has been said, he wanted to go to see the monasteries of Austria and Germany, passing through Switzerland and returning through Holland.

Afterwards he devoted the months of April to July to the monasteries in the United States: "I dread this journey from the health standpoint. Eight visitations, one after the other, many voyages, responsibilities to accept, no confidence, an enormous amount of mail . . . and all that to be done in America's hot climate."[10] The abbot spoke no English and had to use an interpreter constantly. This increased his difficulties in understanding the mentality of his sons in America.

Dom Gabriel began with Spencer, not far from Boston; then he contacted the first monastery of Cistercian nuns in the U.S., Wrentham, founded three years before: "The monastery farm has 40 cows, and a great many calves; the nuns are young American girls, fresh from the comforts of their civilization, and they take care of all the cows, milk them, take out the manure, bring in the fodder, choir sisters and lay sisters together, dressed in grey robes, every one with patches, wearing rubber boots, with joyful faces and ready step."[11]

At Genesee, some distance from Niagara Falls, the poverty of the 30 young founders pleased him very much: "Arranged like the prisoners' barracks in Germany. It is extremely congenial and capable of developing a spirit of brotherliness and simplicity, which is beneficial, even if it does not last forever. . . . I am settled in a small room with a window that does not open, and so the door is left open onto the large cloister where the religious do their reading, hang up their cowls and hold their chapters. . . . In the refectory not an inch is wasted. When all are seated, it is full. They pass the plates as well as they can."[12]

Father Abbot said he had been won over by his American sons, "so simple, so spontaneous, so generous."[13] His admiration, however, was not blind: "No doubt there is misery, just like everywhere else, and some American monks are more Americans than monks, lovers of noise and speed and mixing

[10] Letter to a monk, April 15, 1952.

[11] Letter to Mère Bernard, May 3, 1952.

[12] Letter to an abbot, May 8, 1952.

[13] Ibid., June 11, 1952.

all that up with fervor and generosity in God's service. But aside from these errors of certain ones, what freshness and youth in the self-gift of these young people raised in comfort who now live in greater poverty than in Europe and have unlimited good will, who humbly ask to be told how things are done elsewhere in the order, because they themselves certainly do not know how to do things well!"[14]

The American journey continued, harassing in the heat of early summer. The monastic wave submerging the monasteries preoccupied the order's head. How would all these young people attracted by the monastic ideal be formed? Long ago among the Desert Fathers, the candidate for the monastic life had placed himself under the direction of an old man and had remained with him for many years. In the monastery conceived by St. Benedict, the novice master and the abbot had not taken care of an army of monks, but a more or less restricted group: "I must direct young superiors, young pilots who hardly know the high seas. Mine is a difficult role. At certain times I will need to hold a council. I will need light from the definitory."[15]

In his log book for the journey, Dom Gabriel had noted down his causes of concern opposite the positive elements he had discovered in the American monasteries. He insisted on the necessity of effecting a rigid selection among the novices: How many of them had followed an authentic contemplative vocation? Monasteries had no right to monopolize the spiritual resources of a diocese by accepting without distinction all those who asked to be admitted. There were young men among them whom God was calling to other forms of life. It was important for the future good of the monasteries themselves to find out for what these youths were made: the life of a secular priest or religious life in other spiritual families.

Dom Gabriel meditated on making the admission of novices the subject of conversation at the general chapter. Until he was able to launch this project, he contented himself with composing a letter to the novices of the order: "At the moment you have largely exceeded the number of 750, thus representing a

[14] Ibid.

[15] Letter to a monk, May 8, 1952.

notable portion of the order's effectiveness. And do you bear in mind that in a few years you will be professed monks of mature age, and it will be you who will give your respective monasteries their tone? What you learn today you will teach tomorrow to the younger monks by your example, and the order of Citeaux will be tomorrow what you make it, that is to say, for all practical purposes, what you yourselves are."[16]

In his letter Dom Sortais tackled the principal problem of the relation between observances and spontaneity, and of the value of observances as "expressions of love."

If the abbot deplored the agitation of some American monks and their love of noise ("When someone is noisy with a tractor or a large motor, he is as noisy as 10 or 50. *Noli aemulari in malignantibus.*"[17]), he also admired the heroism of these youths who conformed themselves to the lifestyle of Citeaux, where the number of local adaptations was still so small: "Poor little monks," he wrote to a confidant, "who have to lie down dressed in clothes drenched with sweat, in a dormitory which smells of oil, a kind of odor of rancid perspiration which is frightful! . . . Postulants are the most fortunate from this point of view. They go to choir in short-sleeved shirts open at the neck. They will do penance for it when they take the habit!"[18]

After this a dangerous accident occurred that almost prevented America from ever seeing the abbot of Citeaux again. He had wandered from one end of the continent to the other in search of his monasteries lost in its deserts: from New England to the Great Lakes; from the Midwest to the Rocky Mountains; from New Mexico to the Carolinas, Virginia and New York. Now Dom Gabriel wished to make one last trip with the abbot of Spencer to Virginia to visit a property proposed for a future foundation. Mr. Grace, Spencer's benefactor, took them in a chartered plane. All went well on the way there, but on the return flight the runway was too short for the large two-engine plane carrying eleven people. It was the feast of SS. Peter and Paul. The passengers were the two abbots, Mr. Grace, his wife

[16] Circular letter to the novices of the order, July 16, 1952.
[17] "Be not envious of evildoers," Ps 36:1; letter to an abbot, June 11, 1952.
[18] Letter to an abbot, June 20, 1952.

and three sons, a priest-monk and a lay brother from Spencer.[19] They were reciting the rosary together. The plane rose from the ground, but it had not reached the necessary speed for a successful takeoff. It seemed to hesitate, then made a nosedive into the trees. Hitting the ground at over 90 miles per hour, it crashed and the cockpit literally split in two. Luckily no one was hurt: "The abbot of Spencer, after having fled with all the passengers, in order to escape a possible explosion," related Dom Sortais, "fell to the ground, and for a few minutes which seemed like a few hours we thought he had died, but swift first aid revived him; we had to take him to a clinic. I was told that he still had some fever, but was not in a serious condition."

"It had a strange effect at the time," he added by way of conclusion. "We expected to be burnt up from one minute to the next. I hope to be united with Joan of Arc whom I love very much."[20]

The next day he boarded the plane for Rome, but it was in order to prepare the general chapter and especially the important trip to the monasteries of China and Japan. He flew to the Holy Land with the abbot of Bricquebec at the beginning of October; he wished to visit the abbey of Latroun in Palestine, a monastery founded by Sept-Fons in 1890, under the title of Notre-Dame des Sept-Douleurs. Dom Gabriel made his pilgrimage to Jerusalem with intense emotion: "My first letter will be for you, dated from Jesus' homeland, from the place where he saved the world, from the city where he was sacrificed, which also saw Mary's acceptance. I knelt down in the place where it is thought that Jesus died, where he was buried after his death, where also he rose to life. Tomorrow morning I will celebrate Mass in the Holy Sepulcher, the altar, no doubt, having been prepared immediately beforehand, over the stone where, it is believed, Jesus was laid."[21]

[19] The priest-monk was Father Laurence Bourget, and the lay brother was Brother Leo Gregory. The accident occurred in the early afternoon. Dom Edmund Futterer, abbot of Spencer, was crushed by the crumpled fuselage and was hospitalized at Hot Springs, Virginia. Margie Grace, her three sons, and Brother Leo stayed with him, while the others, Peter Grace, Dom Gabriel, and Father Laurence, went on to Washington, D.C., by taxi and then by train to New York. The source of this information is Father Laurence Bourget himself.

[20] Letter to an abbot, June 30, 1952.

[21] Letter to Mere Bernard, October 3, 1952.

The few days spent at Latroun were followed by a pilgrimage to the place of Jesus' infancy: "I had not been scheduled to go to Galilee, but at the last minute I was able to visit Mount Carmel and Nazareth, where I spent the night and celebrated Mass in the Basilica built over the Blessed Virgin's house, Lake Tiberias, Capernaum, Magdala and Mount Tabor. I also saw the place of the visitation of Elizabeth by Mary, Magnificat."[22]

From Beyrouth Dom Gabriel set out for Hong-Kong by way of Saigon. His first care was to study with the bishop and missionaries the future chances of the little monastery of escapees from communist China. Then he took the boat for Lantao Island. The crossing was not without risk, because the previous ship had been stopped by corsairs from Red China; but this time a small man-of-war of the British Navy escorted the crossing.

From the inhabited part of the island to the monastery they again had to take to the sea. A junk managed by two brothers came to get the Abbot General. There was no landing place. They got as near as possible to the rocks and jumped overboard. Dom Sortais' suitcase was dropped into the sea. It was retrieved. "Then the bark again approached the bank, and I jumped onto the rocks and held on to them: this was slightly precarious. . . . When we were all settled, a small Chinese stayed in the bark; he drew away and stowed the anchor, because it had not been thrown to the rocks and returned to the water. In order to get the bark back again, he went into the water to take the boat and bring it close to the rocks again. . . . We had climbed the rocks as best we could, one helping the other, and then further along we had arrived at what they called the monastery. There were some wooden barracks, a small building they had already roughly built. . . . They lived there. . . . We spent a week with them. . . . I was dressed like them in sailcloth with a large hat."[23]

[22] Letter to an abbot, October 17, 1952. In a talk at the abbey of Igny on December 31, 1953, he said, "I will always remember that night and the closeness I had with Mary. I told her, 'I went to you all the same. I have seen . . . that it is good! . . . I thought that your room was there next to my room. Doesn't that tell you anything? It is necessary to have been at Nazareth and to have awakened there.'"

[23] Talk given at the abbey of St. Romuald in Canada.

There were only three priests at Lantao. The largest number of choir religious who escaped from Notre-Dame de Liesse were in Canada, at Our Lady of the Prairies; after his visit to Japan, Dom Gabriel went there: "I saw them at Prairies. They had obviously kept painful memories of the communists, and were from afar a bit panic-stricken at the thought of returning. They thought the island was too exposed. In fact it was not exposed directly, but it is a fact that at Lantao there are islands at the side occupied by communists. I explained this situation to each one, not hiding from them the possible danger, but telling them also that it would be better to be faithful to their community. And all the Chinese privately asked to go, without consulting one another."[24]

After having reconstituted the community of Lantao, Dom Gabriel's chief concern was to assure them of living quarters that were less precarious. Some years later he returned to bless the church. From that time on a monastic presence at the very gates of Red China continued to be assured.

On October 21 Dom Gabriel flew from Hong-Kong to Japan where he was to stay for almost two whole months, contacting a miniature Christianity in a country that was completely pagan. "There is cause for tears in seeing these people who do not even know Jesus' name, who live and suffer without recourse to Mary, who do not even know that God exists. Just yesterday there was an official ceremony of reparation with respect to cats at Tokyo, in one of the city's temples. It was a public petition for pardon from cats, for having been so egotistical as to kill them, in order to use their insides to make strings for musical instruments and their skins as furs."[25]

"I had no idea of the pagan way of life in the strict sense of the word. I have had a glimpse of it here, and it is profoundly sad. Also in this Japan, closed for so long to everything non-Japanese, there is to be seen that frightful battle of the evil challenging God. Saints would be needed among God's combatants. It is always they who are missing."[26]

[24] Ibid.

[25] Letter to a monk, October 25, 1952.

[26] Letter to an abbot, December 3, 1952.

"This is a country where one has a clear impression and sometimes a strong feeling that one is not with the good God! To see the troops of children (it is extraordinary that they are found in Japan) and look at them with love, for one really knows that they do not belong to the good God. . . . To see old people and say to oneself that they will perhaps die without anyone invoking Jesus' presence or Mary's countenance over them!"[27]

Confronted with the mass of unbelievers, Christianity was almost nothing. What are two or three hundred thousand Catholics against 80 or 85 million pagans? But the power and vitality of the Christian yeast impressed the Abbot General of Citeaux. A church that counted one nun for every 37 Catholic women gave him every reason to hope in its future.

The Cistercian order was implanted in Japan in 1896. The bishop of Hakodaté, Msgr. Berlioz, had sensed the necessity of creating an island of contemplative life in the middle "of this people . . . inclined to meditation and prayer." Dom Lehodey, abbot of Bricquebec, giving up the idea of rebuilding his own monastery anew, devoted the resources collected by his predecessor to the Japanese foundation. Our Lady of Phare or Tobetsu in the northern island, Hokkaido, counted 65 religious in 1952, almost all of whom were Japanese, governed by a Japanese superior. A monastery of nuns at Tenshien, "Palace of Angels," had been founded in 1899 on the other bank of the bay of Hakodaté. In 1935 a swarm had left it to establish itself at Yawata-Mura in the center of Japan. It had taken the name of Seiboen, "The Virgin's Garden"; the nuns had not remained at this place, and Seiboen had been transferred in 1947 to the vicinity of the town of Nishinomiya. Both of these monasteries contained a hundred religious, and numerous postulants were waiting their turn to enter.

"Our nuns' houses are both too small to hold the hundred religious in each one. More than 60 persons are enrolled in one, 30 in the other, awaiting admission, all or almost all of whom had been pagans until the age of 20 or 25."[28]

Father Sortais took notice of the unbelievable attraction exerted by Our Lady of the Angels. Tourists came by the thou-

[27] Letter to Mère Bernard, December 3, 1952.
[28] Letter to Abbot X, December 23, 1953.

sands to this place where there was only a mediocre chapel and garden, the guest house with its statue of St. Thérèse of the Child Jesus and the enclosure. As for Seiboen, the lack of everything was hardly credible. Dom Gabriel allowed his heart to be touched: The poverty and heroism of the sisters, many of whom had broken with their families in order to follow their vocation, the kindness of the most courteous people on earth wove close bonds between him and his Japanese sons and daughters. "I have the impression that part of my ability to love has stayed there in our communities. I have not experienced anything like it in any other country in which I have traveled until the present."[29]

It is a fact that, from the very first, in winning over the Japanese soul, he was won over himself: "This country is full of charm for the tourist and very captivating for the one who, like me, is able to enter into direct contact with souls and understand something of the truth. I have the impression that part of my heart is still there in that little country with richly colored costumes outlined against charming landscapes, as though dim with sadness by the fog up high with the fir trees, and so romantic at night when the moon, particularly beautiful in these countries, shines clearly on the mountains, the rocks, the gardens and the trees, all of which resemble Christmas Trees."[30]

Giving himself with his whole heart, Dom Gabriel had become exhausted. After the Midnight Mass, sung at Our Lady of the Prairies in Manitoba on his return from Japan, he had to go to bed. On the Feast of the Holy Innocents he entered St. Boniface Hospital for a stay of 15 days with a bronchitis so bad it threatened to turn into pneumonia. He came out as sick as when he went in and made the regular visitation at the monastery, suffering from renal colic which he concealed under the reassuring name of "lumbago." He went to Our Lady of the Lake to open the visitation. On the second day the doctor, on his own authority, had him transported to Montreal, to the hospital of Our Lady of Hope. His weakness was extreme. At the age of 50 he felt as tired as a man of 70. The first operation was the removal of a stone from the left urethra, and it left him so exhausted that the

[29] Letter to a prioress, January 15, 1953.
[30] Letter to friends, December 21, 1952.

surgeon asked himself whether he could possibly survive the second which was much more important, the removal of one kidney, which was obstructed by stones: "Father, it is very possible that I may miscalculate." But the operation was absolutely indispensable. In four months it would be too late. Besides, the extraction of the kidney would not be enough; in the near future it would be necessary to envisage other interventions, when the sick man would be better able to endure them.

"The operation still seems risky," he wrote on February 10, "and the surgeon told me he would only attempt it if another doctor wrote a specific request, so exhausted did I seem to him. The good God seems to want me to make some slight reparation for my past offenses at this time, and that I may not remain inactive while awaiting the second surgical intervention, He sent me shingles on my right chest, and on the left I had a bad fall which caused much swelling on my hip and a lot of pain which I still suffer from. All this still unites me to God."[31]

"If I am operated on, the following days will be very difficult, because there will be a needle every four hours. I spoke to the sisters about it to try to space out these alleviations, but I will have difficulty in obtaining this, for I am told that I will not be able to endure the pain. You well know how weak I am before suffering, but I have so much to obtain from God, that I would have loved to unite myself to Jesus crucified. If I am declared incapable of doing it, I will be humiliated by my weakness, and I will try to make up for it some other way."[32]

So great was his joy in thinking that he had almost reached the end of his life, Father Gabriel told the surgeon, "Thank you, Doctor, and if I do not awaken, I will thank you still more." A few days before, when he thought the time had come for him to return to God's house, he had written, "I have so often turned my back on this house of the Lord in my poor life, that it fills me with joy to think that the divine hunter has finally caught up with me, and that he is holding me to let me go no more."[33]

He had been rescued from a close call. Whatever he may

[31] Letter to Mère Bernard, February 10, 1953.

[32] Letter to Mère Bernard, February 15, 1953.

[33] Letter to an abbot, February 17, 1953.

have thought at the time, his life had really not been in danger; however, even though provisionally cured, Dom Sortais could have no more illusions. The perspective of death was now outlined upon the horizon of his life: "If I recover from this, I remain seriously affected. In this condition I will continue my life as Father General prudently, but without laxity, however long I have left. In wartime we risk our life from morning to night for our fatherland; I must do this again for Jesus' sake in the order, and I have nothing to complain of on this account. I am satisfied with all that the good God decides."[34]

Since God had granted him a reprieve, Dom Gabriel determined to take advantage of it, in order to complete the projects he had at heart as soon as possible. In one year he had acquired a global view of the order and personally felt its needs. He had observed, noted and tried to understand the different mentalities and the requirements of each concrete situation; he now felt he was ready to respond to the necessities he had verified, even if he had to knock down apparently insurmountable obstacles.

[34] Ibid.

Chapter 17

FOUNDATIONS IN MISSION LANDS

Dom Sortais' experience of great suffering gave him the idea of writing a letter on infirm religious to the members of the order. He finished and signed it on the feast of the Sacred Heart, June 12, 1953. Tasks of another kind awaited him.

The surprising, almost unbelievable, growth of monasteries in Japan made him grasp in a tangible way, in the course of his voyage, the role of contemplative orders in the new Christianity and the mission countries. Dom Sortais would be misunderstood if it were thought that his sudden affection for the Japanese people were of a purely sentimental or artistic order. He had certainly enjoyed his reception and the courtesy and rich delicacy of this artistic people, and he had liked the landscapes and discreet, subtle monuments of the archipelago. Above all, he had sensed a spiritual malaise in the Japanese people, otherwise so full of life; they had gone through a spiritual desert, and immediately after the war souls were confused. Just when the national ideals had failed, the emperor had simply become a man again in the eyes of his people.

Since God had placed him at the head of an order devoted to prayer and penance, Dom Gabriel deepened his own vocation to the Cistercian contemplative life in the light of the missionary vocation of the whole church.

Another circumstance led him to reflect: while he was still in Japan, in November 1952, he had received a request from the rector of the Gregorian University in Rome. Would he agree to give a conference on "The Function of the Contemplative Orders in Mission Lands" for the fourth centenary of the Roman College in October 1953?

"At first I meant to refuse," he said, "then I agreed: 1) for myself, in order to examine a question which is related to a part of my responsibility, since the order exists in mission lands; 2) to stimulate generosity in favor of these monasteries which often lack gifted individuals."[1] When he speaks of generosity, he is thinking especially of Cistercian houses and of that form of generosity which agrees to let the best religious go to the overseas monasteries, if they feel called to do so.

"In fact it is obvious that, if I am convinced of the utility of these distant monasteries, I will be more eloquent in their favor. I immediately planned my work."[2] He was still in Japan, at Our Lady of Phare, when the first outlines of the work were sketched out, a canvas that was still incomplete and for which he humbly and simply solicited suggestions, as he always did.

The expansion of monasticism in Asia, Africa, and South America in the course of the last forty years should not mislead us. In 1953 this had only begun. The Cistercian order had, under Leo XIII, at the end of the 19th century, successfully made several foundations; many had also failed: Staouëli in Algeria; Akbès in Syria; Notre-Dame des Iles in New Caledonia; Notre-Dame de St.-Joseph in N'Dembu in the Congo. Since then the order had been content to send certain religious to assist monasteries in China, Japan, Algeria, and Palestine in their development. There had been no new initiatives.

Certain branches of the monastic order even seemed to give up the contemplative life to devote themselves directly to missionary work: the Benedictine Congregation of St. Odilo and the Cistercian Congregation of Marianhill; the abbey of Saint-André-les-Bruges, for its part, took responsibility for an Apostolic vicariate in the Congo. Marianhill's evolution toward a life of direct missionary work had even led the Cistercian order to give up foundations in mission lands for a time. A fundamental incompatibility between contemplative monastic life and presence in mission lands was feared. But however beneficial it may be, the work of monastic missionary congregations does not make the contemplative life present in mission lands; missionary monks are sent there, because evangelization is the first task.

[1] Letter to a monk, November 7, 1952.
[2] Ibid.

The appeal launched by Pius XI in 1924 in favor of the implantation of centers for prayer[3] had aroused an immediate response in the Benedictine and Carmelite orders. The Cistercians had been content to develop what they had started. Afterwards the war had broken out, and this had prevented any new initiatives. But in 1951 the monks of Aiguebelle had begun a foundation at Cameroun in Minlaba, deep in the tropical forest.

"The church counts on the monks and nuns just as much as on the missionaries to advance the reign of Jesus on earth," wrote Father Sortais.[4] "The objective is not a kind of compromise between the monastic life and the apostolic life, but the monastic life pure and simple, which should be animated by an apostolic spirit."[5]

"Our apostolic vocation consists in revealing the contemplative face of the church, since that aspect of the church is just as essential as the aspect of charity. In the measure that we stop being contemplative, we cease to fulfill our role as apostles."[6]

In fact monks are in a position to bear a witness to those without faith, a witness which they are the only ones able to bear, but on the condition of coming in person to live in the midst of pagans. They, like all the faithful, have to participate in the church's mission, by working for the salvation of the world by prayer and penance. Besides that their duty is to aid the messengers of the gospel in an effective way, in case of need, by their presence, but above all by completing their work: "It is possible to say that a church is only really founded when it is complete, and it is only complete when contemplative vocations begin to bud."[7]

In response to this need which he had deeply felt, the first task Dom Gabriel proposed to complete was the foundation of two new Cistercian houses in Japan. The monasteries of Tenshien and Seiboen, as has been said, were overcrowded with their hundred nuns; the many requests for admission multiplied, without the possibility of granting them. "It seems impossible to remain

[3] The bull, *Umbratilem*, July 8, 1924 (A.A.S. 16:385–90); the encyclical, *Rerum ecclesiae*, February 28, 1926 (A.A.S. 18:65–83).

[4] Circular letter, December 8, 1953.

[5] Talk given at Cîteaux, December 1954.

[6] Ibid.

[7] Project for the conference.

unmoved by this conduit of grace which leads so many young Japanese to our life. We cannot dream for a moment of constructing new buildings at Anges and Lourdes, because these communities both have more than 100 people, and that number is too many for the poor overworked Superiors, with so many special interviews to grant. . . . The only solution is to found."[8]

The customs of Japanese courtesy made the prioress's task overwhelming. Father Sortais explained jokingly in a talk on the Japanese monasteries: "In Japan there is a polite code called 'Guiri,' which should never be transgressed. It is certainly the strictest country in this regard. You cannot visit anyone and stay less than 20 minutes. To do so would be an unpardonable insult; it cannot be done. Consequently, when anyone goes to see Reverend Mother or Mother Mistress, she must stay at least 20 minutes, even if she has only a word to say."[9]

Tenshien's poverty and Seiboen's extreme misery kept these monasteries from finding a solution themselves. How do you found a monastery without buying land, without buildings, without assuring for a certain time at least the existence of new monasteries? Dom Sortais therefore decided to take on himself the majority of the expenses. He had no reserve fund, but he counted on Providence: The Lord would send what was necessary for each day. Father Abbot had his own brand of wisdom, composed of confidence and detachment: "Abbot X wrote me to request a sum for the construction of a church," he wrote one day. "Draw 20,000 F. from my account and send it in my name. I am broke, but in need of the mercy of Providence, and I think it wise to be generous."[10]

A letter to a missionary reveals his customary way of conceiving alms: "I regret that I am no millionaire who could assist you more effectively. But I don't think it is necessary to wait for riches in order to think of others. The poor ought to help one another."[11]

As soon as Father Abbot's decision was known, gifts miraculously poured in: "The good God is rich. Without my asking for

[8] Letter to a prioress, May 23, 1953.
[9] Talk given at the abbey of Saint Romuald in Canada.
[10] Letter to a monk, January 31, 1956.
[11] Letter to a missionary, October 14, 1961.

anything the money comes, and I hope to have the necessary sum when the moment arrives. . . . I already have a good part of the money. A visitor unknown to me before came to Citeaux and gave me 150,000 F. Another forced me to accept 100,000 F. etc. After only one month I have 450,000 F., and others are promised. But I will need millions! I would like so much to help Jesus spread in Japan, where our monasteries have already done so much good!"[12]

That was how both of the Japanese nuns' monasteries were able to make a foundation, one after the other: Our Lady of the Angels founded Our Lady of the Holy Family in Shindenbaru, in the Kiûshû, the most important island to the south of the Japanese archipelago, in 1953; the following year Seiboen founded Our Lady of Nasu between Tokyo and Sendai, on a plot of land donated by the Emperor to Père Flaujac, a missionary who was very popular for his social work.

"Sire," the old priest had told the emperor, "I wish to found a new working center north of Tokyo."

"Do you have any property?"

"No, Sire, I have no property. I will look for some."

"No, you will not. I have a country house there with lots of woods: You will settle in the woods."

Père Flaujac told the emperor that he wished to have a center for prayer at the heart of his works, so that they might prosper. That was how the foundation was decided. Before the religious were settled in, the emperor and empress had come to contemplate Father's first barracks.

Dom Sortais was in a hurry to see the Far East again. Someone wrote from Japan that they waited for him "with a stork's neck." He returned to spend two months there at Christmas 1955. Not satisfied with the construction of two new monasteries and the equipment necessary for maintenance, he decided on the construction of the church at Seiboen and of an extremely large wing to replace bad or unsuitable buildings. "It seems to me that it is necessary to have a firm intention never to seek anything except what pleases God, an intention to arrange things for a regularity that is easier, but at the same time to refuse anything that would be a concession to well being and

[12] Letter to a prioress, October 22, 1953.

vanity." He knew how to be intransigent on the point of monastic poverty, excessively so even, in the eyes of certain monks. This imposes sacrifices, even in what concerns the structure of the life. A poor house will very often be an ugly house, because they are identified.

His virtual cult of the beauty of creation and his love for old stones and masterpieces of ancient Cistercian architecture did not keep him from having a start at the sight of some contemporary monasteries whose construction did not respect the requirements of poverty: "Here and there, almost everywhere, I suffer when I see the lack of poverty, especially in buildings. I do not know where the Lord wishes to lead me, but for some years now I have felt attracted more and more to a poverty that is real poverty. I can say with all truth that I suffer when I see monks without poverty. This seems to me to be a misunderstanding of their vocation, to make it meaningless."[13]

"You know what a poor house is," he once wrote to a nun. "Practically, most of the time, it is a house that is not lovely. . . . In itself poverty is not pretty and is only charming when it is confused with something else. By itself poverty adds nothing. It frees, it detaches, it leaves God freer and gives him more room in the soul. . . . A few weeks ago, I took a postulant to Z. . . . She desired true poverty, but the true poverty of which she had no inkling had no attraction for her. The poverty she wanted, which would reveal God to her, was this lovely poverty that talented artists marvelously present with a few simple, pure, black, thin lines against the background of a white wall. My postulant has gone elsewhere to seek that which Z . . . could not give her!"[14]

[13] Letter to a monk, Palm Sunday, 1957. Regarding an article which had questioned the poverty of the monasteries of the order, he had taken some notes for his own benefit: "It seems to me that the important thing for us is the half truth it contains. That serious-minded people should have thought and written such things that are extremely painful for us to read, that they should have felt duty-bound to say them in public in order to remove abuses ought to make us reflect. We take a certain number of accusations made against monks. We say that some of them are false or exaggerated. Then we examine ourselves humbly, to see if these serious charges have any truth in them. If so, we would try to eliminate the abuses from our lives, for if our neighbor is shocked, it is possible that God, too, is displeased at them."

[14] Letter to a nun, undated.

It was this poverty that really was poverty that attracted Dom Gabriel so much to Japan, Lantao and Cameroun, Aiguebelle's foundation.

When he went to Africa in 1954, he saw the priests at work there, leading a primitive life in a severe climate, far from everything, "full of scorpions, snakes, and nasty ants."[15]

"There are many problems to be solved for our monastery here, and the abbot of Aiguebelle is not here to discuss them. . . . It is touching to notice how much the missionaries want us and count on us. All the bishops would like to have us, but the conditions for life in these tropical countries are even hard for the missionaries, but for monks bound to a regular life, they are incontestably more difficult."[16]

He wanted to take charge of the construction at Cameroon also: "Besides the two Japanese foundations which took a great deal of my money, and the partial construction at Seiboen, I have agreed to take upon myself the construction at Cameroun. I admire the finances of the good God, which are always in good condition, despite the deliveries he has made to his contractors. When Seiboen and Cameroon are taken care of, the heavenly treasury will have granted me more than 200 million French francs in four years. When I think of this, I instinctively look around me to see if I have failed in poverty, for I am convinced that, if I had failed, the finances of the good God would dry up, as far as I am concerned."[17] He knew how to link wisdom and a prudence highly conformed to the thought of St. Benedict to an immense spirit of faith.

The Cistercian life with its uniform observances in the order as a whole and its rigorous regimentation made adaptation to countries whose climate and way of life was different from that of Europe far from easy. This was felt particularly in Africa and in the tropical regions. His trip to Cameroon allowed

[15] Letter to a monk, February 14, 1954.

[16] Letter to an abbot, February 19, 1954.

[17] Letter to a nun, November 26, 1956. These 200 million French francs are only a part of what Dom Sortais received. In 1961 or 1962 he confided to a monk, "I have just balanced the budget of the good God. It is wonderful how rich he is, and how right we are to trust in him." At the end of ten years he had received gifts totaling about 350 million francs.

Father Abbot to take note of this first-hand. But this life among Africans, stripped of elementary comforts, represented an ideal for him: "I began to dream of forced retirement, and I saw myself going there . . . deep in the forest, where the monastery is going to move. It is because in Cameroon we are in the truth."[18]

After 1953 Cistercian foundations in mission lands multiplied. The monks of Tilburg made a foundation in Indonesia, in Java (1953) and another in Kenya (1956). Scourmont made a foundation at Kivu (1954), Mount Melleray at Takipau in New Zealand (1954), Mt. St. Joseph in Australia in the diocese of Melbourne (1954). Achel established a colony in the Congo (1958), Mont-des-Cats sent monks to Madagascar (Notre-Dame de Maromby, 1958), San-Isidro to Angola (Our Lady of Bela Vista, 1960), and Mt. St. Bernard to western Cameroon (Bamenda, 1963), while the monks of North America kept South America for themselves: Spencer made a foundation in Argentina (1958) and another in Chile (1960).

For the nuns the movement assumed less impetus, for their monasteries were less numerous, and the problems of adaptation more difficult to resolve: however, Igny founded Notre-Dame de la Clarté-Dieu at Bukavu (Zaire, 1955), and Les Gardes founded Étoile Notre-Dame at Parakou in Dahomey (1960).

The spring of 1956 was taken up with a trip to the monasteries in Africa. Dom Sortais found nature there in its primitive state. "The site in the Mokotos is extraordinary. We are next to a lake at an altitude of 5577 feet. The lake is elemental. A few cabins of blacks, and that is all. The large clouds which bring the daily storm in this rainy season are reflected every day at noon in this lake, which is two and a half miles long. Further away, hippopotamuses sun themselves. We cannot see them from here. . . . About 12 and a half miles from here is the end of inhabited country. There are nothing but forests inhabited by tigers, gorillas, and elephants"[19] And comparing the tusks of elephants with the magnificent horns that adorn the head of the humble cows: "Two immense horns with a little animal at the

[18] Letter to a monk, March 7, 1954.

[19] Letter to Mère Bernard, May 6, 1956.

end," as the natives say. "I will have them measured," wrote Dom Sortais, "to put the cows of Maine-Anjou to shame."[20]

The Abbot General was one of those principally responsible for this effort by the order. He supported, encouraged, and stimulated it. But he wisely discouraged requests, when it was no longer possible to satisfy them to the extent required: "We must surely remember on the one hand that requests are much too numerous for us to be able to satisfy all of them," he wrote to a bishop in Latin America, "and on the other that the order has made a considerable effort in these last years to establish foundations in different countries, and that this effort cannot be sustained indefinitely without mishap."

"I must, therefore, be honest with Your Excellency, in order not to raise hopes that the future will not confirm. Independently of the financial question, although that is also important, for a poverty that is too extreme is generally unfavorable to the establishment of a serious regular life, the personnel problem is the one that gives us most pause on the path of expansion in Latin America or anywhere else. It is one thing to be a monk in a long established community, and something else to create a monastic community from all the pieces. The latter enterprise requires not only tried virtue but also special qualities of judgment, flexibility, intelligence, etc., which are not easy to find together. To undertake a foundation with mediocre personnel is almost surely to doom it from the start. In a word, it is the abbot of each monastery who must judge if his community is ready or not to undertake a foundation. . . . What good will it do us to increase the numbers of our houses, if each one of them is not a real hearth of prayer and sacrifice?"[21]

He was all the more wary of encouraging proposals concerning foundations in France: "Your offer touches me very much," he told a friend of the monks. "It is a sign of Christian sentiments and a testimony of sympathy, to which I cannot remain insensitive. But there can be no question of our making another foundation of our order in France. As far as I am concerned, our country has, by and large, her quota of monaster-

[20] Letter to an abbot, May 4, 1956.

[21] Letter to a Latin-American bishop, September 10, 1962.

ies, nuns as well as monks. Another house could no longer be founded without hurting the others. The effort of founding is rightly being carried today to the countries which are developing, where no monastic life, or hardly any, yet exists."[22]

In his eyes it is absolutely necessary that the monastic life be present wherever the church is implanted. The conversion of the world is not, first and foremost, the work of missionaries and specialists in preaching; it is the fruit of the presence of the church. In fact Dom Sortais loved to recall that the church is the real missionary, really the only one, because that is her nature. "It is not by the action of certain members of the church, specialists in the apostolate, however generous they may be, that she will extend (Christ's kingdom) in the new nations; it is by going there herself, with all her essential elements."[23]

Since the monastic life is not developed on the margin of the church, but is nothing else but the church looking deeply into God's mystery, effecting his great design of purity by *ascesis,* and raising the ardent cry "Come, Lord Jesus" to the Bridegroom by prayer, it follows that contemplative monks and nuns are a necessary part of each particular church. By his whole being and his whole activity, the monk is, in fact, before God and men, the organ of the pilgrim church's desire and the witness to the hope that carries her to the heavenly Jerusalem.

Objections should, then, recede before this essential consideration which infinitely outweighs every other. The founding of centers for prayer in Christian communities that are still young is a "normal" enterprise in the sense that it conforms to the principal norms of monastic life, even if it presents special dangers and demands the taking of certain precautions. The specific activity of the monk is, no doubt, not limited to his place of residence. His prayer and penance have a universal efficacy in space and time, but if the contemplative is a depository of the church's riches which, properly speaking, do not belong to him, he must, in order to be true to the deposit he has received, allow all the local churches to benefit from it concretely, as far as possible.

[22] Letter to Mr. X., August 13, 1963.

[23] Conference read at the abbey of Ligugé, July 9, 1961: "De l'implantation de la vie monastique en pays de mission," 8.

In some countries the Holy Spirit has raised up forms of life spontaneously, which were afterwards grafted onto the old trunk of Latin monasticism. This was the case in Vietnam, for example, where Cistercian monasteries were started at the initiative of a missionary. But this does not dispense monks from their duty to spread the monastic life. Ancient history of East and West illustrate the double process: spontaneous blooming of a bud brought in from somewhere else, often from outside, and a systematic foundation in places deprived of monastic institutions. Perhaps this will happen in the present epoch as well.

To limit ourselves to the level of testimony and of apostolic efficiency, monasteries are often better collective preachers than the laborers of the gospel themselves: "To see how God loves his sons and may be loved by them, to the point that some do not hesitate to consecrate their whole life to the sole study and development of that love, is (for the pagan nations) a teaching more penetrating and efficacious than a great deal of preaching."[24] In some cases it will be the only one heard and the only one understood.

The final objective remains that of transmitting the monastic patrimony to the new churches. The first stage is the presence of monks, but it will be necessary, at the cost of indispensable adaptations, to reach the point of implanting monasticism in a definitive way; at a more or less distant time, the native monks are called to replace the founders. It is important to do it quickly when that moment arrives, under pain of allowing the moment chosen by God to pass. Political structures evolve rapidly. The church should be sufficiently rooted that she might not seem like an importation from abroad. Great difficulties are caused by uncertainty about the future and the social instability of countries recently opened up to the Gospel, but monks should have confidence in God: "We must rid ourselves of defeatism. The net has been cast in Africa at the pope's word. We are not in the wrong boat. Will we succeed?

"Success," declared the abbot, "consists in satisfying God. This success and this joy are ours. The rest depends on God more than on us. It is certainly necessary to live the time remaining to

[24] Ibid., 11.

us, without worrying too much about the future which is not worried about itself."[25] Such were his thoughts. His invincible optimism rested on his faith, and his faith was unshakable.

[25] Letter to a nun, August 23, 1963.

Chapter 18

ADAPTING THE OBSERVANCES

"A Trappist is a man who gets up at two o'clock and awakes at four," said a former abbot of Aiguebelle.[1] Cistercian life is harsh, and it requires strong men, in order to be led in its integral observance. The mitigations imposed by Leo XIII in 1892 had remained timid. Later, in 1925, a general chapter had authorized a slight repast in the morning called *frustulum.*

Dom Sortais himself had only mediocre health. He did not take care of himself, and he felt keenly how severe the Cistercian life could be to certain temperaments, and what heroism it required to remain faithful to this program of austerity. There was, no doubt, a radical way to mitigate the inconveniences: It was to resolutely turn every candidate with deficient or average health away from the monastic life. But didn't this amount to practically ending recruitment? Above all, was it in conformity with the thought and desire of St. Benedict who had wished to open up access to the monastic life to those whom God had really called to it, by proposing a reasonable observance?

The hours of sleep and the diet were felt to be insufficient for the general health of the rising generations. But to prolong the hours of sleep amounted to a rupture of the equilibrium of the monastic day, and the delicate balance bequeathed by the ancients between prayer, work, and *lectio divina.* Seeing that the Cistercians, far from being content, like their fathers of the 12th century, with the canonical Office of the Rule of Benedict,

[1] "Despite all our small industries and despite habit, the brevity of our repose will always be our great mortification; Dom Chouteau was still not used to it at the age of 87." *Notes on the Rule,* ch. 4, instrument 37.

had added to it in the course of centuries various other offices in addition: the hours of the Little Office of the Blessed Virgin, and on certain days, those of the Office of the Dead. With this avalanche of vocal prayer, some souls could not find free converse with God. Finally, the spirit of prayer suffered from this. In this regard the lay brothers' life had more equilibrium and was often more expansive for souls. Father Sortais had always been strongly attracted to it.

For 150 years the uniformity of observances had been an unchangeable dogma in the monasteries of La Trappe. The heroism of the monks of Dom Augustin de Lestrange is well-known, and how faithful they had been to this observance in their unbelievable wanderings in the Revolution and in the Empire. In Switzerland, Central Europe, Russia, England, Spain, later in the New World, in the region of Baltimore, in Louisiana, on the banks of the Ohio, in New Brunswick, they had tried to maintain the daily schedule, fasts, observances, and habit, without the least notice of exterior circumstances or of practical difficulties. At times we begin to think of the English of the Victorian epoch, who carried all over the world, as an unchangeable deposit, the sacrosanct customs of the old country and would not agree to modify them in the slightest way.

After the Second World War, the pendulum swung back. The danger at this time resided in the more or less anarchic attempts at adaptation and in the anticipation of measures which seemed necessary. The common good of the order was at risk. In any case it did not seem reasonable to maintain the former status quo at all costs. Diverse tendencies were awaking in the order. There were those who were irreducibly attached to the old observances, the ideal of their youth and the support of their whole monastic life, and there were those who could see nothing but the general weakening of health. Dom Sortais himself knew the problems of each monastery sufficiently well to resolutely take an attitude of renovation, especially with regard to the shortening of the Office.

"Our young monks have a real attraction for the interior life, but it seems that this develops in them following slightly different paths than those taken by their immediate predecessors. They understand the Office in choir very well, but the accumulation of vocal prayers disgusts them. We did not think it was right to allow them to obediently recite an Office as a duty, without deriving any profit from it, besides which its maintenance did not seem to be in accord with the ethics adopted by our first fathers."[2]

Father Abbot knew the value of observances and insisted that they should never be trivialized in practice, but he was also convinced that their value was relative. Observances must always be kept in their place as "means" and understood as such.

"The essence of the monastic life does not consist in observances, nor in the habit, nor even in the fulfillment of the Divine Office. It is deeper, more interior, more intimate than all that. The essence of our life is the search for God. The monastic life is above all an attitude of the soul in the presence of God, an attitude whose analysis would reveal adoration, compunction, filial love and joy. Some think humility includes all these other virtues."[3]

Dom Gabriel also distrusted a certain kind of monastic fidelity which ran the risk of covering up a real lack of love, and which only resulted in justifying the monk in his own eyes: "If an action or a habit which passes for a mortification in men's eyes does not force us to a personal renunciation, this action or habit is not a real mortification for us. It causes nothing in us to die."[4]

"I have a hundred ideas in mind for the good of the order, or rather for God's glory through the order,"[5] wrote Dom Gabriel on All Saints in 1952. But it was important to proceed gradually, for minds had not been prepared to accept the collection of changes that had become necessary.

At the chapter of 1953 the abbot suddenly sensed the need to recall the unity of observance which had been the order's strength at the beginning of Citeaux, and the guarantee of its cohesion at the same time. This unity had been reaffirmed by the Reform of La Trappe in a way that was perhaps too unilateral, and it had come under serious attack since the war.

The necessity of adaptation was not questioned, but Dom Sortais could not accept the way in which it had been intro-

[2] Letter of January 3, 1957, to an abbot of the Common Observance.

[3] Letter to a young monk, May 3, 1947.

[4] Letter to a nun, January 26, 1957.

[5] Letter to an abbot, November 1, 1952.

duced. His sense of authority and of the respect due to law rose against the initiatives of certain monasteries. As Abbot General with the responsibility, by his office, for the good of the whole order, he felt that his duty was to oppose a movement which could have troublesome consequences in the long run. It was the concept of obedience which was in question here. If an abbot did not respect the laws of the order and claimed the right to take an initiative every time a real or apparent need made itself felt, where did he get the authority to oppose the exceptions that any of his monks might think were indicated to be applied to the observance in his own monastery?

"We admit that certain adaptations were desirable, even that many were necessary; nevertheless, it remains true that no one was authorized to make them *motu proprio*. The general chapter had the right and power to evaluate the necessities which were presented. . . . Are you certain that the power of the general chapter was not complete, which must be inspired by the Rule of St. Benedict, so discreet, and the Charter of Charity, far from being an inhuman code? . . . At the general chapter we must spend less time in the study of history and archaeology, and more in examining carefully the traditions and observances of the order, to see if they are still profitable for souls."[6]

After this chapter in 1953 the abbot formulated three core questions: on the time given to sleep, on the Office for devotion, and on the adaptation of the status of the lay brothers to the requirements of contemporary life. Immobility was no solution. Although it might reassure us for the moment with a superficial peace, the resurgence of the problems denied in a more critical form was on the way. Besides, it was a kind of infidelity perpetrated in the name of material fidelity, because, since circumstances had changed considerably, the order really was not what it had been in the thought of the founders.

"A religious institute is set up for the sanctification of its members. . . . It would not be reasonable, merely for the sake of a time-honored tradition, to preserve usages which have become

[6] Opening discourse at the general chapter of 1953. "Saint Benedict," he said in his notes on the Rule, "did not want a mitigated Rule, but a Rule adapted to the human condition." *Notes on the Rule*, Prologue, no. 30.

a burden for religious who no longer derive benefit from them for their souls. . . . Much renovation is necessary, if we wish to avoid novelties."[7] In this way he adopted a thought of Father De Lubac for his own purposes.

The chapter of 1953 decided a certain number of points. But the abbot encountered resistance on the part of the Congregation of Religious, a resistance he had not anticipated. He was asked not to modify the constitutions; derogations would be granted for any special cases. In other words, the law would remain unchanged, but it would no longer be applied literally. The abbot did not want that at any price. Two conceptions of the law had clashed. For the Congregation the law was a fundamental norm which should not be changed too easily, but which lent itself to diverse interpretations, as time and place differed; for the abbot the Rule represented an ideal to which each religious must conform himself, under pain of falling away; it is better to modify the Rule than to expose it to practical indifference. For monks law is a norm of perfection, and it is dangerous to interpret it after the manner of canonists. Father Gabriel kept an extremely distasteful memory of this first encounter:

"We have been extremely vexed these days about the decisions of the general chapter, which have received a serious setback at the hands of the Congregation of Religious," he wrote to an abbot. "They will finally be signed tomorrow by the cardinal prefect, and I will have them by midday, so I hope at any rate. Not all the requests have been granted, but we can rest satisfied, because there was a moment when I had almost felt that all was lost, except what concerns the lay brothers, which has won general consent by the consultors."[8]

Modifications had been accepted as usual *ad experimentum.* Dom Sortais had shown all the strength he was capable of showing. A principle was at stake, and the good of souls was the prize. In such cases he did not hesitate at violent words, allowing his ardent temperament full scope, without obliging himself to further acts of kindness and gentleness afterwards. At certain times, in fact, he was really fierce. Many found him so.

[7] Opening discourse at the general chapter of 1954.

[8] Letter to an abbot, November 13, 1953.

He found the resistance within the order very painful. In requesting a revision of the observances, he had acted under conscience, and not according to his natural tendency. By personal generosity he would have willingly been a strong supporter of austerity, but his duty was to make the monastic life accessible to many souls in its most intimate and essential experience, by sacrificing elements that were accidental and time-bound.

His personal position was far from comfortable: "It seems to me sometimes, that I am like a tightrope-walker high above the ground! One false step, and all is lost. If you only knew how difficult is the responsibility that I hold!"[9]

In fact he had to wage war on several fronts at once: make recalcitrants admit the necessity of adaptations, moderate the zeal of those who adopted them too soon, work on the incorporation into the order of new monasteries of nuns in the Iberian Peninsula, etc.

It was in this context of the battle for unity, that he prepared the general chapter of 1955. It would have to take a definite stand on the adaptations: "I am open to criticism and reproach, extremely painful to listen to. . . . I have done my best. It is now for the abbots to choose and decide, but to my way of thinking, not to admit that there are problems, and problems that are vocalized, is to lack prudence and wisdom. Of that I am firmly convinced."[10]

In his opening discourse he gave an account of the difficulties experienced by a large number of candidates for the monastic life, arising from the lack of equilibrium in the observances and from the physical and psychic consequences that often resulted from it: "Would it be reasonable for mortifications to be of such a kind as to ruin a person of normal health, exhausting his physical strength prematurely and considerably reducing in this way his chances of becoming a saint? For it requires a virtue that is already perfect for a soul to continue advancing towards perfection in a wasted body."[11] Nevertheless, penance and austerity are still the essential Cistercian way of life. All

[9] Letter to an abbot, June 6, 1954.

[10] Letter to an abbot, April 17, 1955.

[11] Opening discourse at the general chapter of 1955.

that is necessary is to find the right measure. "If this measure is now beyond the capacity of a large number, we have the right to ask the Holy See as obedient sons to reduce it to proportions which seem to us more reasonable at the present time, within which a person of ordinary strength might still devote himself to real penance without jeopardizing his health which he needs in order to make progress in the spiritual life."[12]

Father Sortais' guiding notion was to compensate for the mitigation of certain observances by greater fidelity to the two essential components of the spirit of the Cistercian Fathers: poverty of spirit and solitude. On this last point there is much testimony.

"The spirit of Citeaux," he wrote, "is above all a spirit of separation from the world, for service to God accomplished rigorously inside the enclosure. Without judging in any way the monastic institutions that have introduced an element of apostolic activity into the lives of their members, we have been placed in an entirely different context by our very fidelity to our founders; we must perform a different service, bear a different witness.

"Our monks give glory to God and serve the church by a life exclusively consecrated to the praise of God, to meditation and to recollection. The witness they are called upon to bear in this way to the one thing necessary is only valuable insofar as they remain strictly faithful to that one thing which is the only one necessary. That is why the general chapters have many times, as well as just recently, insisted on the exclusion of all exterior works.

"Would it be logical for a monk dedicated to God in silence and retirement to return again to men, unless it be in order to explain to them the meaning of this silence and retirement? Such a gift of self is impossible and incomprehensible, unless it be irrevocable."[13]

He only accepted exceptions with extreme circumspection: "Abbots owe their monks the example of a spirit of solitude rigorously kept and lived. Furthermore, the good they might do for people outside who petition them comes in large measure from this separation from the world, accepted by them on their

[12] Ibid.
[13] Letter to a friend of the order, July 3, 1959.

profession day, in order to live more constantly and intimately in God's presence."[14]

Dom Sortais was strict with himself, despite insistent invitations: "The monastic vocation, especially in its Carthusian or Cistercian form, cannot be likened to others from the point of view of its relation to the world. I would certainly be far from doing God's will for me, if I were to appear on television, when my life should remain hidden."[15]

Dom Gabriel felt comforted by the spirit of faith which he found among the capitulants, and by their mutual charity: "I hope the unity of the order will not suffer from the changes proposed to the Holy See. But a similar effort towards understanding must be made in each monastery, where opinions among the religious will be strong and will diverge. Charity is certainly the strongest bond which could be found."[16]

The chapter's requests concerning repose and devotional Offices again aroused many difficulties with the Congregation of Religious, such that Father Abbot asked himself if it would not be better for him to give in: "Providence came to my aid in an unexpected way through Msgr. Dell'Acqua himself. He has shown me wonderful kindness. He asked me to write a brief report which he would personally present to His Holiness, Pope Pius XII, who has become interested in our case."[17] It was the pope, in fact, who caused the matter to proceed in a decisive way.

Dom Sortais thought he should express himself strongly, aware that he had reflected upon the problem more than anyone else: He thought he was qualified as being the principal person in a position of responsibility. This would leave him free afterwards "to place myself in the spirit of obedience which would

[14] Letter to a bishop, March 28, 1962.

[15] Letter to a publisher, December 27, 1954. He wrote to the committee for preparation of a *Dictionnaire* on February 21, 1958: "As abbot general of a monastic order whose principal obligation is separation from the world, I can hardly consent to the least publicity, even if it be of the highest quality, being attached to my name. That is my answer declining your offer. It would be considerate of you not to insist."

[16] Letter to a monk, September 18, 1955.

[17] Ibid., November 24, 1955.

dispose me to accept everything as coming from God's hand, even that which seemed to be the lesser good."[18]

After ten months of laborious and sometimes noisy negotiations, he ended up gaining his purpose: "The Roman decree has finally been published this evening, not without inconvenience. An American reading it would say, 'Okay, it is a long document, its phrases are unending, but actually everything has been agreed to.' Here we are working at high speed to send you a document as soon as possible, which may be adopted at the next general chapter. You need not wait, in order to guess at its contents. What has been granted is definitive. There is no need to go over it again. . . . Health will improve because of it, and hopefully the interior life will benefit from it. Without the Holy Father we would have nothing or almost nothing."[19]

This was not the first time that Dom Gabriel had tried to establish direct communication with Pius XII. In 1946 Dom Nogues had been strongly opposed to any idea of mitigating the Rule or any change in the Trappist austerities. But Pius XII had in 1950 and again in 1951 given all religious congregations a different counsel.[20] Therefore, in the audience granted him at the beginning of his generalate on January 1, 1952, Dom Sortais put the burning question clearly to the Holy Father, after having explained how and why the problem of adaptation had come up in the order of Citeaux; he had asked if, yes or no, his predecessor's position ought to be maintained (let us not forget that Dom Nogues was still alive!). The Holy Father's answer was "No."

Father Abbot reported, "I can still hear the Holy Father add that the superiors of the Order should meet in *congresso*, examine and discuss the advisability of the measures to be taken and present their wishes to the Holy See whose place it was to make decisions."[21] Afterwards, whenever a new question came up, Dom Sortais would make it his business as far as possible to explain its terms briefly, clearly and objectively to the pope

[18] Letter to a nun, October 9, 1956.

[19] Letter to an abbot, September 6, 1956.

[20] Speech at the Congress of the States of Perfection, December 8, 1950 (A.A.S. 43:265) and apostolic constitution *Sponsa Christi,* November 21, 1950 (A.A.S. 43:5 ff).

[21] Speech at the general chapter, September 12, 1955.

himself and to ask his approval for the action to follow. He did this for the last time in the first audience granted him by Pope Paul VI on September 18, 1963. Some monk-priests of the order had abandoned the celebration of private Mass and contented themselves with communicating at the conventual Mass. Father Abbot did not think it allowable that a priest should put the celebration of Mass on the same level with a simple communion in the manner of laymen, especially that he should prefer the latter to the former. Paul VI fully confirmed him in his opinion and promised him a forthcoming document on the question.

This was how Dom Gabriel conceived the obedience of the order's leader who was left with the burden of initiative and responsibility. His express intention, many times repeated, was, by reforming certain points of observance, to promote the true search for God, thanks to an authentic interior life. He wished to assure all his monks whom he loved as his sons, together with their faults, their limitations or their mediocrity, easier access to a deep and true interior life and to a heart to heart talk with God in effective solitude and real poverty.

Chapter 19

STUDIES IN THE CISTERCIAN ORDER

"Regular and special studies were only imposed on the Cistercians around the year 1340 by Benedict XII, himself a Cistercian, we find in an old book on the Trappists. And why is this? Because the religious had forsaken manual work and fallen into idleness. Studies were only a remedy. Remedies are only prescribed for those who are sick. When manual work is held in esteem, there is no time wasted, and there is no need for remedies."[1]

The logic is precise without any doubt, but it is based on a premise that needs to be demonstrated. It is really a sophism. Since De Rancé, himself just as cultured as any of his adversaries, had taken issue against studies with a wealth of erudition enough to make any apologist of intellectual work turn green with envy, a great distrust of every kind of intellectual activity has reigned in many Trappist monasteries. The real issue of the controversy has often been lost in the scuffle. There is nothing in the Rule of St. Benedict about systematic, scientific studies, and with good reason. The Rule does speak of *lectio divina*. First of all, St. Benedict does not see it as a remedy against "idleness, the enemy of the soul"; for him it is an essential activity of the monk, ordained towards contemplation and continual prayer. By *lectio* the monk familiarizes himself with all that God has made known through his Word and that spiritual masters and teachers of the church have written.

[1] *La Trappe, origines, esprit, organisation actuelle de la Réforme de l'Abbé De Rancé* by a Trappist of Sept-Fons (Paris, 1870).

Dom Sortais himself felt no attraction for studies as such. He was neither intellectual nor bookish. He had neither taste nor aptitude for the work of scholarship, although he did not contest its validity. He even understood well enough that studies are necessary for the church as a whole. He himself had entered the anti-intellectual tradition of the Trappists without any second thoughts. It was only after personal experience and mature reflection that he realized it was insufficient to fulfill the deep purpose St. Benedict had in mind. *Lectio divina* had been neglected, and manual labor and penance had gained ground. What was left of *lectio divina* was too often wasted on banal pursuits. "Many" (monks or nuns), he reminded the general chapter of 1955, "devote their intervals to childish reading or to making holy pictures for the next visit of their grandniece."[2] Such waste of time and questionable use of intelligence, that faculty which enables us to know God, seemed wretched to him. But he also had an extreme distrust of unbridled intellectual activity, a kind of mental activism which is just as hurtful for contemplation as material activism.[3] Above all, he hated to break the equilibrium of Cistercian life.

Dom Sortais encouraged his monks and nuns to acquire a solid formation in basic theology and to work seriously at the project of knowing God better, but he did not like pretensions, nor did he want the self-sufficiency of the "knowing" man introduced at Citeaux. "Get a deep grounding in dogma, while remaining small in God's eyes. Never become a teacher in Israel. Never think of teaching the things of God as science is taught. The things of God must be taught humbly; they are only learned in a kneeling position. Only God teaches the things of God, and they are only understood by those who are little in his eyes. I am glad you are studying St. Thomas. He was a saint who was little while being an intellectual. His writings are lessons in humility for his readers."

[2] Conference on infantilism, given at the general chapter on September 13, 1955.

[3] Conference on activism, given at the general chapter on September 15, 1955.

Dom Gabriel also wanted the monks and nuns to remember in God's presence those who, by their dedicated lives, enabled them to apply themselves freely to the task of doctrinal research: "One of the advantages of the monastic life is the ability to apply oneself to study without anxiety, but we monks should not forget to pray to God for those who allow them to devote themselves completely to God, because of the responsibilities which they have undertaken."[4]

For that is exactly what monastic studies were in his mind: an activity with God as its sole object, and not merely its final object. That is why the monk must know all of theology well. Dom Gabriel did not want to see a student do research on one aspect to the detriment of his general formation. Such lack of equilibrium seemed to him to be at the root of many speculative and practical errors.[5] In addition, he wanted theology to be spiritually nourishing, and he urged the students to make use of the tractates of St. Alphonsus Liguori, Anselme Le Bail, de Lahitton and other similar writers.[6]

In any case excess seemed to him to be a serious abuse, because the monk in such a case strayed from the real purpose of his life, and his soul lost its freedom thereby. Here his thought was firm and immovable: "Contemplation only takes root and blooms in *otium* (repose). That is why monks who apply themselves to study with excess, even if it be holy study, do not have the leisure necessary for contemplation. A mind that is always busy, always distracted, even if it be over a problem of sacred scripture, theology or spirituality, is not entirely free. It is not that extremely sensitive lyre which resounds at the smallest breathing of God, at the least word which evokes the presence, action and love of God for it."[7]

An attitude of availability is needed to reach contemplation, to which everything else in the monastic life is subordinate.

[4] Letter to a young monk, December 2, 1947.

[5] Undated letter to a monk, Advent 1952.

[6] St. Alphonsus de Liguori, *Theologia moralis*, ed. I. Ninzatti (Turin, 1899); Le Bail, *La théologie affective ou St. Thomas d'Aquin médité* (Paris, 1845); new edition by Abbé Bougal (Montréjeau, 1903); J. Lahitton, *Theologiae dogmaticae theses juxta sinceram D. Thomae doctrinam* (Paris, 1932); cf. Letter to an abbot, June 3, 1952.

[7] Letter to an abbot, February 15, 1953.

It has sometimes been thought that the Abbot General did not understand intellectuals very well, and that he tended to discourage them. This is certainly not true. Like all masters of the spiritual life, he warned his monks against *curiositas* that closes the soul to God and opens it up to a thousand useless pursuits. In addition, he was involved in maintaining the equilibrium of Cistercian life that he loved and admired, with its long hours of manual labor and its simple occupations which simplified the soul. He was responsible for a tried and proven monastic tradition, and he could not, without infidelity, remake the economy as he saw fit. But it was his anxiety to favor contemplation which explained his choices in the last analysis. The soul of the monk suffers no division. There are many legitimate monastic occupations which are sometimes demanding, but there is only one end. A monk for whom any occupation, intellectual or material, becomes the end, loses his vocation. The danger is twice as great, if the work that so obsesses his soul takes him habitually or for a prolonged period outside the normal conditions of monastic life and outside the enclosure.

It is possible that Dom Sortais was by temperament and formation better at showing the dangers to which studies might expose the monks when they are badly organized than at pointing out their positive aspects. Or rather, he expressed his thoughts on studies while speaking of *lectio divina,* a subject which was dear to him above all others. Is it not, in fact, when study makes *lectio* more fruitful, and *lectio* opens out into *contemplatio,* that its riches are discovered? Any science which is not transformed into love is vain and empty. That is why the dispositions we bring to it are so important. The fruit of study is dependent on our purity of heart.

"We did not enter the monastery in order to be mechanics or farmers or to specialize in one of the branches, even the most spiritual, of intellectual work, but to be monks who 'search for God,' as St. Benedict says, and who, St. Bernard adds, 'search for God alone and for his own sake.' "[8]

"Let our reading be pure! We don't have to acquire knowledge, so we can boast about it afterwards, nor do we have to learn in order to teach. Preparing courses or conferences is one

[8] Circular Letter, July 16, 1961.

thing, and *lectio divina* is another. What we have to do, as we will always repeat, is to take care of our soul, to seek God. We must seek him for love of him, not for the sake of our self-love. We would run the risk of not finding him whom we seek, worse still, of forgetting him."[9]

"By giving himself to study diligently and with a pure heart, the monk deepens and clarifies his understanding of God and of the divine mysteries which furnish him in a way with the raw material for his contemplation."[10]

There was no problem of "intellectuals" in the Cistercian order in a general way. The problem was one of isolated individuals. Nevertheless, Dom Gabriel noted that there were to be found even in his religious family "some liturgists who no longer had any taste for the choral office, canonists who had trouble with obedience, historians very knowledgeable on Cistercian origins, who left their enclosures to visit libraries, musicians who knew all the chants, but did not know that song is essentially the expression of love in the heart."[11]

The question of the course of studies preparatory to the priesthood was much more important in a religious family where choir religious were usually destined to be ordained. Obviously there was a radical way out of the difficulty, and some were already proclaiming it then: give up the idea of ordaining monks and maintain even the choir religious in the lay state, because the monastic vocation in itself has no necessary link with the clerical state. Dom Gabriel did not favor this approach. His awareness of the grandeur of the eucharistic sacrifice was too great for him to envisage with gladness of heart a solution which would rob the church of a significant portion of her priesthood, which was uniquely dedicated to contemplation. He warned the monks more than once against the "new ideas," and he was not afraid to take steps on occasion to prevent their extension.[12] His basic position seems to have been that the monk who refuses the priesthood deprives the church where he has

[9] Circular Letter, December 8, 1952.

[10] First conference at the general chapter of 1957.

[11] Second conference at the general chapter of 1956.

[12] *Letter to the Abbots,* Christmas 1961 (Abbey of Westmalle, 1961) 52.

been baptized of the best spiritual alms he could give it: the offering of the body and blood of Christ by the celebration of the Eucharist. He even consulted Pope John XXIII on the matter during the audience granted him on November 11, 1959.

Since he had opted in favor of the priesthood, he had next to solve the difficult problem of theological studies. In a seminary of the classical type they did not present major difficulties at the time, but in Cistercian monasteries it was a different story. They could not be pursued there in the same way, without one of the essential elements of the monastic life being temporarily sacrificed: either the divine office, or *lectio divina,* or manual work, or monastic stability in the cases where monks had to be sent to a seminary or a theological faculty to pursue their studies. The equilibrium of the monastic life, the delicate balance among the various daily occupations, would be threatened, at a time when young monks had not been adequately formed.

An apostolic constitution on the reform of studies in seminaries and religious orders, on the creation of a *ratio studiorum,* and on the formation of professors appeared in 1956.[13] Such a document, destined for the universal church, could not, of course, take the special case of the contemplative orders into account. It was necessary for these latter to try to solve their problems by reference to what the law was intended to accomplish and to the special needs of the monastic life. This task was especially difficult for the Cistercians and Carthusians, more so than for the Black Monks.

The general chapter of 1956 gave a commission the responsibility of studying all the questions relating to the introduction of new legislation in the order, according to the norms of the Roman document. The question would be studied more thoroughly at the general chapter of 1957. As a preliminary to this, it was necessary to clarify the material: "Here at Rome on the 26th of this month, we will have a meeting of a good number of abbots and professors to study the statute on studies in our order," wrote Dom Gabriel at the beginning of January, "and it will probably last about 15 days."[14]

[13] Apostolic constitution *Sedes Sapientiae,* A.A.S. 48:354 ff.

[14] Letter to a monk, January 4, 1957.

One of the most difficult problems was that of the requirements at Rome for the qualification of professors: "Those monasteries which do not have the desired professors will have their right to a scholasticate revoked for as long as the dearth of persons able to teach lasts. And I was told at the sacred congregation that they will be very strict on this point. Any monastery which does not have the necessary teachers will have to send its students to another house of the order. This will be very annoying from a monastic point of view: no contact with one's own Abbot for years; few contacts with the community where one will have to make profession afterwards; lack of young monks in the monastery; reputation of the monastery in the outside world diminished."[15]

The problem of studies in the Cistercian order, thought Dom Gabriel, would not be solved by being evasive with the intentions of the Roman document, or by contenting oneself with a kind of minimum for monk-priests; it would only be solved by integrating serious clerical studies into the package of monastic formation, and by giving them a specific orientation.

"The real purpose (of the Roman document) is not to promote a more intense intellectual formation in the various institutes but to help the religious by means of a better intellectual formation to develop the qualities with which the Lord has enriched their soul and mind, and bring them to fruition."[16]

This was the fruit of his reflections at this stage in his life. The contemplative monk who does clerical studies certainly does not have the same purpose in mind as the usual student in the church. He is not preparing himself directly for the ministry of souls. Nevertheless, he must be ready when the time comes to exercise a ministry inside the monastery, for a good number of monks have the actual responsibility for souls: the abbot, the prior, the novicemaster, the confessors for the community, and the fathers in charge of the guesthouse: "It is not, in fact, at the actual moment when he finds the care of souls entrusted to him in one way or another, that the monk-priest will be able to acquire the knowledge that he needs for this task."[17]

[15] Letter to an abbot, October 9, 1956.

[16] Project for the Statute on Studies, rough draft.

[17] Second conference at the general chapter of 1957.

The wisest course, then, seemed to the Abbot General to prolong the time of preparation for the priesthood on the one hand, in order that the young monk might have the time to do his studies without being constrained to abandon the normal rhythm of community life, and to prevent, on the other hand, any premature specialization.

"It is rare," he said, "for a religious who keeps working at all the sacred sciences—theology, sacred scripture, philosophy and history—to become so attached to this study that he forgets his other duties. But the person who delivers himself and devotes himself exclusively to one well-determined discipline is easily possessed and as though fascinated by it, such that this specialization becomes, if not the cause, at least the occasion of deviation for him."[18]

Another crucial question remained: the formation of a satisfactory group of professors for the monasteries of the order. "This is not easy to arrange," he wrote in April 1958. "We spend seven hours a day discussing the texts. We do not yet see clearly, because the *ratio studiorum,* at least of the quality desired by the Holy See, is not viable in 75 percent of our houses. What should we do? I have an idea which most of the members of the commission seem to share, but I may be wrong. Please pray for us. Our task is extremely delicate and difficult."[19]

For a long time the Abbot General's house on the Aventine, near the Church of St. Prisca, had played host to the members of the order who came to Rome to take courses in the universities and get degrees in theology. Why not develop this embryonic monastery? This would allow a certain number of young priests of the order to do their higher studies without being uprooted from the environment of their Cistercian life.

Dom Sortais would not himself have gotten the idea to create a house of studies and encourage the young monks of the order to acquire degrees at the universities. It really was not his nature to encourage studies. The new Roman legislation had in a way forced him to it. But he thought it possible to derive some advantage for the order from it. He found prolonged stays of monks in national theological institutes repugnant. For one

[18] Fourth conference at the general chapter of 1957.

[19] Letter to an abbot, April 18, 1958.

or two years or even longer young monks would be in an atmosphere similar to that of students in the world, outside their monastery and in a way uprooted. Except for some exceptional individuals, this situation is ruinous for monks. "It should not be necessary for monks to go outside, for this is no good for their souls," as St. Benedict says in the Rule.[20]

If, on the other hand, all the future graduates of the order were to be gathered in a monastery for studies, this would establish a profitable exchange. Those monks more gifted than their brothers would probably fulfill important functions in the order later on, as abbots, definitors, novicemasters and professors. Their years of study together at Rome would have allowed them to get to know and understand one another, for the greater good of the order. They would also understand the governing organ of their religious family better. Young monks from across the Atlantic could visit European monasteries on their vacation and see their spirit for themselves. This way the Roman monastery would be a uniting influence for all the reformed Cistercians.

Since the order was then in rapid expansion, it was to be expected that those actually residing in the house of studies would continue, in the same proportion as young monks already formed were put in charge, and that it would be necessary to form other teachers. It was necessary also to reckon on foundations in mission lands.

We might ask ourselves also whether another factor had not played a more or less conscious role in the elaboration of the project. Dom Gabriel had suffered much from having become an abbot without a monastery. His paternal charism had grown to the point where it was a component of his spiritual personality. Wasn't it stronger than he was? He needed a community of young monks around him, to whom he could give himself. As a father he felt anguish at the absence of a family that was his. These considerations, or rather these spontaneous reactions (for he did not envisage the Roman project from this angle), almost certainly influenced the final decision.

In 1935, when the work of planning Rome necessitated the transfer of the general's house from the Via San-Giovanni in

[20] Rule of St. Benedict, ch. 66.

Laterano near Saint-Clement to another place, the abbot of Tre Fontane had proposed a plot of ground adjoining his monastery enclosure to build a new place. The place was far from the center of Rome and had no means of rapid communication. The offer had not been accepted at the time. Dom Smets had had a house built on the Aventine, in a peaceful neighborhood with many gardens, not far from Sant' Anselmo and the Dominican monastery of Santa Sabina.

When Dom Sortais had convinced the general chapter that the creation of a monastery for studies was a good idea, the new abbot of Tre Fontane renewed the proposal of 1935. Dom Gabriel was far from letting the opportunity escape. He chose a high hill overlooking the ancient monastery and gave it the name of Monte Cistello.

It would be difficult to write about the care he took with the building of "his" house. He wanted it to be beautiful, sober, poor and adapted to its purpose. He asked Père Nivard of Port-du-Salut, to whom he gave the guiding notion, to draw up the plans. Dom Sortais was very glad to see the project established, which seemed to him to embody the requirements of the monastic life, of poverty, and of true beauty, all at the same time. The work excited him. His artist soul was given free rein. And his love of beautiful gardens! To get away from the noise of Rome! To get back a little of his dear Cistercian solitude! There was no greater joy.

"This morning we arrived and even entered our new house, and we heard the birds and grasshoppers sing. What joy after living in a noisy city like Rome for so long!"[21] "You are one of the first to whom I am writing about our new home. This house is almost perfect, and I am ashamed to live here. Still, it is simple, but I think it has been so long in the planning stage and so carefully executed, that it is too good for us."[22] Dom Sortais was glad that the commission of town planning of Rome had of its own volition classified the project in the last category of real estate: that of workers' houses. However, it is possible that the material he had chosen was too poor, because after 15 years the outermost coat fell to pieces, necessitating further repairs each year.

[21] Letter to a nun, September 27, 1959.

[22] Letter to Mère Bernard, July 27, 1958.

The monastery at Monte Cistello was not finished when the monks began to live there. They were settled in a spacious wing which had reached completion. Some parts were livable, others still without doors. There were workers and dust everywhere! It had become necessary to proceed with dismantling the house on the Aventine. "You do not know what it is like to dismantle a monastery. Divine Providence tries to detach his children from all passing things, and he ordinarily arranges a fire from time to time, in the course of centuries, in all religious houses. It is annoying and sometimes distressing, but I think that when a house is dismantled, the trial undergone should be less painful."[23]

If Dom Gabriel had secretly desired to rediscover a monastery, he was partly disappointed. He did not take sufficiently into account the requirements for the life of these young monks who lived at Monte Cistello and had to go to their courses in different universities during the day. For his part he was demanding and sometimes very austere, and this caused tensions. Besides, his long absences from Rome kept him from getting to know his young monks very well, sent there from every part of the world. His ignorance of languages other than his own did not help matters. In the course of regular visitations he had to use the services of an interpreter. At Monte Cistello the language barrier became a real impediment for the monks with whom he lived in more continuous contact. Exchanges were necessarily in French. Dom Sortais attracted the young, but he also intimidated those who did not know him very well. He was the Abbot General! And so the students came to see him less often than he wished. For his part, he tried to increase the contacts. One of his most painful sufferings was his inability to inspire as much confidence as he had anticipated. There were also those fits of anger, those unforeseeable storms, caused as much by fatigue and insomnia as by his violent temper. Some of the students were afraid of him. He took this into account.

Nevertheless, Dom Sortais was not discouraged. Did he ever let himself be turned away by a problem? He often got the students together to speak to them, to give them spiritual teaching, to emphasize the great objectives of Cistercian life, to tell

[23] Letter to a monk, July 12, 1957.

them about the monasteries he had visited all over the world. Whenever he returned from a trip, he took time to say a few words to them, like a father. He worried about their health and went to see them when they were sick. With admirable humility he could realize his mistakes and beg forgiveness.

His solicitude to keep his young monks in a monastic environment led him to prefer the Benedictine College of Sant' Anselmo to the other Roman faculties, but the choice was not his to make. The abbots who sent their monks to Rome chose the college or institute where they were to enroll for their courses.

"His Holiness, Pope John XXIII has raised the Lateran Pontifical Institute, the Angelicum and Propaganda College to university rank, one after the other," he wrote to the Abbot Primate of the Order of St. Benedict. It followed that Sant' Anselmo was now in a position of inferiority.

"I am afraid this situation will have an unfavorable influence on the future enrollment in classes at Sant' Anselmo. In fact, to speak only of the order for which I bear responsibility, I think our abbots will certainly be impressed by this difference which now exists between Sant' Anselmo and the other institutes of sacred teaching. They will seem to them better fitted to give their sons superior instruction, and they will make them enroll in the Gregorianum and the Angelicum for their studies, instead of at your place on the Aventine. And this will be a great loss.

"The students themselves will think that the courses offered at Sant' Anselmo are not as good as those in the universities, and that the teachers there are inferior to the Jesuits and Dominicans. This will be a gratuitous judgment, but the students will still have a tendency to discount Sant' Anselmo and go elsewhere.

"Nevertheless, as I said at the beginning, your teaching is excellent, just as good as that given elsewhere. Besides, there is a monastic institute and a liturgical institute at Sant' Anselmo, and this is unique for Rome."[24]

At Monte Cistello the Father General's ill health (after 1956 he had again experienced severe trials accompanied by great

[24] Letter to the Most Reverend Dom Benno Gut, Abbot Primate of the Order of St. Benedict, June 11, 1963.

physical pain, as we shall mention later) did not keep him from being the first at the night office. He insisted on participating in all the exercises and giving a good example. He wore himself out. He was well-liked for his kind reception. Even though head over heels in work, he was open, cordial, good-humored and tender, always ready to tell stories to make people laugh and put them at ease, then quickly getting serious again to speak about God and Our Lady. He took advantage of every opportunity to teach the monastic doctrine of Citeaux, which he prized so highly, to the young monks: silence, solitude and poverty in view of ever greater intimacy with the Lord and his mother in continuous contemplation.

"If a sojourn at Rome includes great advantages, giving the soul with good will a stronger attachment to holy church and a more Catholic character to their minds," he told the young monks in 1960, "it also includes serious dangers . . .

"My experience of living at the side of students for nine years has taught me that those who showed self-reliance or who—a minority, thank God—spoke without charity, allowed themselves to fall into these faults more through human respect than for any other reason.

"We want to show others that we are not children, that we notice and understand things. We insist on letting people know that we have a mind, that we have a strong personality, and we are not going to be deceived; we know how to judge people and things, and we are not afraid to say it out loud."[25]

"It would not be wise for you to apply yourselves to study unreservedly, without setting aside the time necessary for your spiritual life," he said in greeting the students for the year 1963–64. "The spiritual life needs nourishment. . . .

"It is advantageous for a monk to have contact with the church in Rome and to listen to its teaching. . . .

"The monk does not belong to the avant-garde. He is a man of tradition, well-understood. A man of the church, he loves dogma and especially well-established dogma, defined dogma. He has no taste for controversy. . . .

[25] First conference to the students at Monte Cistello in 1960.

"What profit would it be for a monk to get a license or a doctorate, if he left Rome less simple, less humble and less recollected?"[26]

Monte Cistello celebrated its big day in the beautiful Roman fall, at the end of October, 1960. In order to show the whole Catholic world his great esteem for the monastic life, good Pope John decided to be present in person to pronounce an allocution on the contemplative life in the church of the new monastery. But, since he wished to have only monks around him, the day was only mentioned to a few privileged persons. The pope arrived during the afternoon of Thursday, October 20, at 5 o'clock: Eighty Cistercian students were there, joined by the community of Tre-Fontane.

"To mention St. Bernard's name," said the pope, "is to make the ardent piety and joyful austerity of your first fathers live again. It is to invoke after him an immense procession of holy religious through the centuries—*turbam magnam quam dinumerare nemo poterat* (Rev 7:9)—who have let the pervasive perfume of a life completely withdrawn from the world and entirely consecrated to God spread throughout the Christian world from within their cloisters. . . . The contemplative life! Oh how precious it is in the eyes of God, precious to the church! . . . It constitutes one of the fundamental structures of holy church; it has been present in every phase of its history of 2,000 years, always fruitful with solid virtue, always rich in mysterious and powerful attraction for the highest and noblest souls."[27]

A week later, on October 27, Cardinal Cento came to consecrate the church whose sanctuary was later decorated by the monumental Virgin of Roland Coignard, surrounded by angel musicians.

Was all this too beautiful to last? Ten years passed over the gardens and cloisters. Monte Cistello only shelters the Curia of the General's House now and a few of the Order's students, like the house on the Aventine before 1958.

[26] First conference to the students at Monte Cistello in 1963.

[27] Allocution of John XXIII, October 20, 1960, cf. *Les derniers jours d'Octobre 1960 à Monte Cistello* (Westmalle, 1960) 13, and A.A.S. 52:896ff.

Chapter 20

THE FATHER'S TEACHING

"When I am weak, then I am strong" (2 Cor. 12:10). St. Paul suffered from the constraints imposed on his apostolic zeal by his health. Dom Sortais' pilgrimages all over the world were also marked by severe trials which left traces in his body. He conveyed the impression of being a well-built person with a strong constitution. His death at 61 years of age within a few hours astounded many of those who had met him. His vitality could deceive. Nevertheless, since 1953, his life had been a long way of the cross. He was exhausted.

"The Lord needs our activity, as long as it is part of his plan, but he can do without it, and it is good for us to experience that. . . ."[1] "Those who are crucified are the ones who get people to behave almost perfectly; without them we would all go from bad to worse."[2]

Would he have understood the sick so well, if he had not been one of them himself? The forcefulness of his nature did not predispose him to this: "Love, however intuitive it may be, is not enough; it is necessary to experience suffering. . . . St. Ignatius attributed the tenderness he felt for the sick to his continual infirmities, and he thanked God. . . ."[3] "Suffering is something we cannot understand, without having experienced it."[4]

The solemn warning given him by the Canadian doctors after his two operations in 1953 did not succeed in convincing

[1] Letter to a relative, January 12, 1959.

[2] Letter to a nun, July 27, 1959.

[3] *Notes sur la Règle,* commentary on ch. 36.

[4] *Retraite au Bon Pasteur d'Angers,* January 13, 1934.

him to curtail his activity very much. He could even delude himself that he had recovered his resistance. He had, in fact, been informed that further surgery would be necessary in the near future, but months had passed, and it had not been strictly indispensable. In summer 1956 he returned to the way of prudence.

"After having left Chambarand for Aiguebelle on July 26, I went back there for a week, ordered by the doctor to have complete rest. They are worried about my eyes. One doctor feared complete blindness within a short time. But everything turned out well. It was only general fatigue and insomnia. I am better already, although I do not say the breviary yet. You can well imagine that having blindness in view, outside of the obvious trial, there was also hope of rest from temporal activity and of life in silence, an opportunity to take up my interior novitiate life again. It seems to me that with God's help I will profit from it."[5]

Then the long journeys began again, without respite. Arriving in Canada at the end of 1957, he was worn out and had to go to the hospital. "I am very tired, really exhausted to tell the truth. I am dragged from one laboratory to another, from one examination to another; every morning a sample of my blood is taken, and I receive transfusions. Soon I will be half Canadian. If that makes it easier for me to learn English, I will be all right."[6]

He joked, but he went through terrible physical and moral suffering. "A veteran O.M.I. missionary was in the hospital subjected to the same regime as I was: that is, having one X-ray after another, head elevated, head lowered, swallowing completely indigestible white liquids, giving blood samples every morning, undergoing numerous injections throughout the day, swallowing pills and capsules as much as food." One day which he spent in X-ray, his sister wanted news of him: "My sister," he replied, "I am afraid I do not have enough strength to stay in the hospital any longer. That is honestly how I feel."[7]

He seemed so weakened to the doctor, that the latter feared he would watch him die if he were forced to undergo an operation. The prostate was completely infected. It was a very difficult

[5] Letter to Mère Bernard, August 9, 1956.

[6] Letter to an abbot, January 4, 1958.

[7] Letter to a monk, January 28, 1958.

time, the most painful of his life. He left the hospital after a month and a half, poorly recovered. He spent a month convalescing at Notre-Dame du Lac at Oka; then he returned to Rome.

Dom Sortais was so made that, the moment he felt better, nothing could hold him back any longer. He said he was reasonable! And so the following year everything had to be done over: "On the 26th," he wrote in January 1959, "I will go to the clinic, and two days later I will be operated on. I know what is waiting for me, because it is the same problem as last year in Canada. I know the pain which they leave the sick person in ignorance of, until he actually feels it. This will bring me close to Jesus, who knew in advance what the chalice contained, which his Father presented to him during his agony."[8]

In Paris, just as in Canada, the surgeon gave up on the complete operation: "Finally it is exactly the same reaction as the surgeon in Montreal. Essentially they are afraid I will play a dirty trick on them."[9]

What good would it do to list his never-ending visits to the clinic? On May 20, 1963, Dom Gabriel wrote a friend, "Yes, I was operated on again for the seventh time."[10] Already the year before he had said, "I feel like a wounded person whose wounds have closed up, but who is still wounded." Everything had become painful for him. He hoped that it would pass in time, without harboring many illusions: "The Lord could make us live long, but I think it is reasonable to put my affairs in order."[11]

Since his allotted years were numbered, Dom Gabriel was going to get full use of them, without losing a minute. His solicitude for all the houses of the order left him no rest. Sick on his hospital bed, lacking the strength to compose a single prayer, he had his secretary slowly read the list of monasteries aloud, with long pauses. In one flashing thought he saw each of them in its own individuality, and he presented it to God with a gesture of offering, imploring and abandonment.

[8] Letter to a nun, January 17, 1959.
[9] Letter to a monk, January 17, 1959.
[10] Letter to a priest, May 20, 1963.
[11] Letter to a priest, June 7, 1962.

He humbly accepted his responsibility, knowing himself more humbled in being superior of a great order in the church, yet quite inadequate to the task, than in being a brother swineherd: "I occupy a conspicuous position," he said, "but that will serve especially to reveal my mediocrity."

He performed his duties generously, with no illusions about his own abilities, accepting agreeable and disagreeable tasks together: "For my part, I go about from one house to another. I impart advice. I understand many things, and I say many things. I need grace in order not to make mistakes, and in order to recognize a mistake, when I have made one. . . ."[12] "Life is not easy," he admitted to a confidant. "We spend our time fixing broken flower pots. We sometimes break them. We must restore the balance."[13]

Sometimes he had to wait for light to come to resolve a difficult situation. At such times the abbot celebrated Mass for that intention, submitting it to God after exhausting every human means: "There are times when God only waits for an act of abandonment to arrange something which we thought had no viable solution," he declared.[14] What he needed most often was energy, a vigor which would keep him from listening to the protestations of his own heart or his sensitivity: "Please ask Jesus to give me the gift of strength which I often need, in order to fulfill my role as Abbot General manfully, without laxity, and without allowing myself to appeal to those weaknesses which are often baptized so quickly and conveniently as discretion, wisdom and comprehension."[15] "I am not without trials. Some we can get used to, but not all!"[16]

Dom Sortais' strong personality had imposed itself on the order. He had not taken fully into account his tendency to flex the responsibility of the Abbot General in the sense of greater personal authority and centrality. Circumstances had brought this about. It does not seem to have been the result of a personal choice on his part. He even had to resist the tendency of the

[12] Letter to Mère Bernard, December 25, 1960.

[13] Letter to an abbot, May 6, 1955.

[14] Letter to an abbess, August 9, 1956.

[15] Letter to a nun, May 7, 1958.

[16] Letter to a nun, January 29, 1961.

Roman congregations to consider him the superior general of a centralized order. It seemed to him that the authority he had received was principally of the moral order, and he intended to use it to remind the monks of that which seemed to him to be most important in monastic doctrine. It remains true, however, that he sometimes used his authority forcefully (too forcefully for the taste of some). It was difficult to resist him.

His circular letters to the order took on the shine of real doctrinal encyclicals which would be completed by instructions or conferences given during the general chapter. "I have written a certain number of circular letters to the order," he told a friend who asked him about his writings. "Two a year for ten years, but that does not constitute a book."[17]

He was wrong in this, because the Monks of Bellefontaine made the book, *Les choses qui plaisent à Dieu,* out of them. His teaching was direct, concrete, intentionally elementary, but characterized by rare wisdom and profound knowledge of men. "Since I am a poor man, and I was afraid to teach my monks things I did not practice. . . . I made an inflexible rule for myself never to preach or prescribe for others anything that I did not do myself, or at least anything I had not decided to do. I have found that this works. That is the explanation for the fact that my circular letters and instructions during the general chapter are often so elementary and down-to-earth. I sometimes think of good things to say, but I do not say them, if they are not part of me. I think that otherwise I would have quickly fallen into hypocrisy and two-facedness, and that Jesus would have reproached me for my conduct from inside me."[18]

How did he proceed? When a subject was thrust upon him, because his knowledge of concrete situations had shown him the urgency of giving a teaching, he began by taking notes on the backs of envelopes. He wrote down the thoughts as they came to him. Afterwards the material was arranged, and he formed a plan. When the spade work was done he wrote rapidly with his small compressed handwriting, usually without erasures. Then he left it to jell. Later he returned to his dossier, looked it over, cut

[17] Letter to a priest, April 12, 1961.
[18] Letter to a nun, August 4, 1960.

things out, corrected and completed it. He usually had several persons criticize his work. He collected suggestions, developed certain aspects over again, modified his plan, took the best from what was told him. He often improved upon the suggestions made to him. He depended heavily upon someone else to illustrate his exposition with citations from the Cistercian Fathers or ancient monastic tradition. He had various collaborators. Most often he made use of those near him in the general's house, especially his secretary, the young Père de Bourmont. When the circular letter was ready, one could be certain that everything in it was really the expression of his own thought.

His circular letters seemed to many to be a kind of expression of his more or less admitted wish to substitute for the abbots in their teaching function. Dom Sortais certainly did not envisage them so, but being aware that something needed to be said, it was impossible for him to be silent. That would have done violence to his nature.[19]

He spoke incessantly of the greatness of the contemplative life. He knew perfectly well what its concrete demands were, and he could recall abbots and monks to their duties. He evoked the spirit of solitude and recollection, separation from the world and poverty at every opportunity. It was a kind of basic motif onto which the rest would be grafted like musical harmonies: "St. Bernard has defined our vocation," he said, "describing it in a beautiful formula: *Qui in claustro soli Deo vivunt, semper Deo adhaerent, ejus placitum considerantes.* It is men who live in cloisters and who only live there for God alone; they are united to God continually and try to please him; they are only there to please him, and it is as though they were on the lookout for what might give him pleasure."[20]

Dom Gabriel well knew that contemplation is a grace, an unearned gift granted by God to whomever he wishes, "but the

[19] "When I wrote these 20-odd circular letters, the possibility of collecting them someday in a kind of résumé of monastic spirituality never entered my mind. I quite simply told you what I thought needed to be said at the time when I wrote you, to put an end to a laxity or deviation I thought I had noticed, or to emphasize a particularly important aspect of our life." Circular Letter, July 16, 1961.

[20] Conference on the meaning of the monastic vocation, September 22, 1961.

Cistercian monk," he taught, "should do what he can to dispose himself to receive this grace, in order to urge God to grant it to him. Why? Because he has been called to share in an institute of contemplation, and because each one must try to achieve in himself the perfection of his state of life."[21]

Penance is the means par excellence by which the monk may prepare himself to receive the grace of contemplation: "We do not have to choose between two ways: contemplation and penance. There is only one way which is both contemplation and penance at the same time. They are two aspects of the spiritual life, which cannot be separated. There would be no contemplation without preliminary ascesis or penance, and he who receives graces of contemplation, far from neglecting penance, as though it were a stage he had passed, esteems it still more and willingly returns to it."[22]

But the contemplative life can take on many forms. The souls confided to him and for whom he would have to render an account as Abbot General, had been called by God to lead the contemplative life according to a definite ideal, that of Citeaux, which is essentially cenobitic. Dom Sortais rightly guessed that God rarely modified his first call. And so he was very circumspect regarding the movement favoring hermits in the order, which gathered momentum during the years 1955–60. He had had many opportunities to develop his thoughts on the subject, especially when speaking to the students at Monte Cistello: "These days we often hear the monks of our order asking if our way of life really corresponds to separation from the world. They are attracted by the eremitical life, and they think of it more than earlier generations of monks did. Of course God is free to lead the church and souls as he pleases and to call more souls to the eremitical life in the troubled world in which

[21] Conference on the obligation of a Cistercian to tend towards contemplation, September 23, 1961.

[22] Conference on contemplation and penance, September 25, 1961. "The illusion starts," he wrote, "from the moment when you flatter yourself on having made some meager progress (in the spiritual life) without paying the price. . . . There is no presumption on your part in wishing to advance to the intimacy of [mystical] union, but it would be a serious mistake to hope to get there in any other way than that of the deepest abnegation." Circular Letter, July 2, 1957.

we live. But after carefully studying the problem, I have noticed things which keep me from concluding that very many of our monks who think they are called to live as hermits are really called to such a life.

"I have noticed that these 'vocations' were clearly more numerous in the countries where life is more hectic, troubled and noisy. And I have also noticed in these same countries, that it was in the monasteries where there is less separation from the world and less respect for silence that the most aspirants for the eremitical life were found.

"I have noticed this so often—so constantly, I might say—that I think that in the majority of cases this desire for the eremitical life is nothing else but an aspiration for the eremitical aspects which should be part of our life, which the holy Rule prescribes."[23]

The decisive reason for his attitude in this matter was his sense of duty as abbot. Experience had shown him how easy it is, under the appearance of greater perfection, to go outside of the real will of God and escape the duties of one's state in life. Certain unstable temperaments are easily nourished on myths, and their example may be disastrous for monks who are not yet secure in their own vocation. Dom Sortais was capable in the discernment of illusions, and he did not beat about the bush when it came to saying what he thought, although he could be gentle about it, as this letter written to a monk belonging to an eremitical order shows; this monk was searching for a kind of life less "institutionalized":

"At the moment when you wish to leave X, in order to look for a more out-of-the-way place, you instinctively choose a place for your new residence, where young men with the same thoughts and aspirations as you will join you.

"And so, what you envisage spontaneously, without perhaps having a clear awareness of it, is nothing else but a new foundation, an enterprise which requires numerous contacts and much conversation, and which will end up getting you more tied up with the world than you would be in the monastery where you would have been willingly received.

[23] Conference for the students at Monte Cistello.

"However, if you decide to leave, could I recommend you to our houses? Very simply and truthfully I must tell you no.

"When the superior concerned consults me, which he will certainly do, I will advise him clearly not to receive you, not because I have any doubt that your life would edify the community, but rather because your life is really different from that of our religious, and we would run the risk of unsettling the vocations of the young who are still not secure enough.

"I believe that this vocation of our monks is a gift of God, and I think our duty as superior is to protect it as a sacred object which belongs to God at the same time and more than to us, which we have no right to dispose of as we please."[24]

With Dom Gabriel some sessions of the general chapter began to resemble meetings on formation. The Abbot General's conferences held an important place. He taught and gave information. He imparted all that he had to say on the union of the order, on mutual aid between monasteries, on the weaknesses of religious (such as infantilism, mediocrity and material activism), on the manner in which adaptations ought to be envisaged, on the advantages and the dangers of study and on the necessary ascesis of the intelligence.

His teaching on obedience is also worth recalling; he anticipated certain conciliar texts relative to this problem which is especially difficult for the younger generation. In his conferences on the abbatial charge, Dom Sortais gave a pertinent exposition full of wise psychology on "Obedience and Education of the Personality."

During the winter 1957–58, when he thought he was threatened with an early death, he proposed an urgent program: "I will spend the whole school year of 1958–59 at Rome, overseeing the construction of the general's house, in order that it may preserve the note of simplicity, and arranging the archives of the Abbot General for my successor. After all that is done, I will be ready to go, if God calls me. If he still delays it, I will start my trips again, although reducing their number and devoting more time to the order, editing some notes for the sake of the abbots who have a difficult task and need assistance. If the Lord still

[24] Letter to a monk, January 8, 1958.

delays, I will wait for him 'with my hands in my pockets' like Father Joachim after extreme unction."[25]

From this program thought up on a hospital bed, while a prey to the grimmest interior trials, came two series of instructions collected in brochures: ten conferences on the abbatial charge, given at the general chapters of 1958–59, and those on the regular visitation given in 1962. Many elements out of the first series found a place in *Les Choses qui plaisent à Dieu.*

The conferences on the abbatial charge originated from a previous set which he had given to abbesses. The principal source for these had been the conferences given to the superiors of the Maurist congregation by Dom Claude Martin, son of the great Ursuline mystic, Marie de l'Incarnation. These conferences had, in fact, been the object of a new edition,[26] and Dom Gabriel had read them, pen in hand. At this time he had prepared a plenary meeting of abbesses for the month of June in 1958, in which the mother superiors of the Japanese monasteries would participate. Finally, he modified the text, with reference to the needs of monasteries of men and relegated the references to nuns to footnotes.[27]

Dom Sortais' concept of the abbatial charge and all his experiences as abbot are set forth in 107 glowing pages and simple words about which he could have written what he told a young recently-elected superior, "I am going to entrust you with all that I have loved since the day I was elected abbot."

The collection on the regular visitation and the function of the visiting abbot is just as practical as the other: "It is a role," he said, "that is not one of the most agreeable."[28]

[25] Letter to a monk, January 28, 1958. Father Joachim was Count Joachim du Plessis de Grenedan, former dean of the law faculty at Angers, who had entered the abbey of Bellefontaine.

[26] Dom Claude Martin, *La perfection du chef, conférences aux supérieurs,* ed. Dom J.-R. Hesbert (Paris: Alsatia, 1952).

[27] He had, in fact, taken a different approach for the nuns. Thinking that they alone would be capable of understanding their own problems, he had asked and obtained permission at Rome to select abbesses to put into effect something analogous to the regular visitation in their monasteries, and he had gathered the superiors of the monasteries in a plenary meeting to study common problems.

[28] Letter to an abbess, September 10, 1953.

"The visitor," we read among other excellent pieces of advice, "should prepare himself for the scrutiny by prayer, telling the Lord that he wishes to see clearly and think correctly. He must make himself small in front of him who alone gives grace, for he knows that any man can be led to err or allow himself to be influenced by his prejudices or emotions and thus fail in his duty.

"Does the visitor admit his lack of experience? Then let him distrust himself, for he has a difficult task, and the function of a visitor cannot be extemporized. Does he think he has experience? Let him still distrust himself, for his experience might lead him astray by getting him to understand the problem which he encounters today in the same way as the one he succeeded in finding a solution for on another occasion, and cause him to make a mistake.

"It is bad luck for a superior to think he is prudent and experienced. The one who thinks he lacks nothing lacks everything. The best visitor is the one who knows his shortcomings, and because he is not infallible, asks God in the course of the scrutiny for the light and strength to listen and reply."[29]

Before his death Dom Sortais wanted to propose one more reform which cost him a great deal, but he felt that it was a case of the welfare of souls. The Abbot General was still abbot of Citeaux *ex officio.* Citeaux was his monastery and his community. He was consulted about the government of the abbey. He had to delegate someone to receive a novice for profession. Much inconvenience resulted from this. The abbey was deprived of the fundamental right of choosing its own abbot in conformity with the Rule of St. Benedict and common law; for the abbot of Citeaux was elected by the general chapter, and he himself then chose his auxiliary. In practice it was impossible for the Abbot General to take effective charge of the monastery. His functions absorbed all his attention; nevertheless, he was still the one responsible before the law.

And so Dom Gabriel put aside his reluctance at the general chapter of 1962 and proposed the adoption of a new statute. Citeaux would from then on have its own abbot like the other monasteries, elected by the community. The Abbot General would

[29] Conferences on the Regular Visitation (Westmalle, 1962) 12.

then content himself with the title of archabbot of Citeaux, and he would be the Father Immediate of that monastery. As for the Abbot of Citeaux, he would be the Father Immediate of the four monasteries: La Grande Trappe, Westmalle, Melleray and Port du Salut, the first four houses of the Reform of La Trappe.

In this way Dom Sortais thought he had found a solution for an abnormal situation. With the reform of the statute on the brothers, over which he pondered a long time (we will see more of this further on) the task which he had assigned himself was for all practical purposes achieved. He had influenced the development of the order in a very personal way, as none of his predecessors had done.

Chapter 21

THE COUNCIL

Immediately after the visit of Pope John XXIII to Monte Cistello and the dedication of the church by Cardinal Cento, Dom Gabriel flew to America. He visited the monasteries in Canada and New Brunswick, then went to those in the U.S., which he had not visited again in any thorough fashion since his vast circuit of 1952; then he went to South America, where the order had gained two new monasteries a short time before. "We now have 22 houses in the whole American continent," he wrote to a friend on February 14, 1961. "I ought to be flat on my back, but I am doing all right. I am almost always annoyed, but the Lord helps me to accept and bear these annoyances, and sometimes to solve the problems."[1]

His contact with Latin America surprised him. He heard people talk about the miserable poverty, which was greater than he had ever seen with his own eyes. All his letters of the period reflect it. He would have wished that the Cistercians who had brought the monastic life to these countries had had more humility and more real poverty in their buildings.

The trip was imprudent, because of all his accumulated fatigue. On June 25, six or seven weeks after his return to Rome, he was in the hands of his surgeons. "God willed that I be very sick. I have never suffered so much physically in my life. I was so weak that I could say nothing, could offer nothing, but Jesus knew he could take all. I was prostrate. I am still half-dead."[2]

[1] Letter to a monk, March 11, 1961.
[2] Letter to Mère Bernard, July 25, 1961.

Even after his recuperation from this new operation, his health was still precarious. "(The doctor) gave me two alternatives," he wrote to a counselor. "Either take at least a month's rest, or preferably a month and a half, during which I should be treated by hypodermic injections, or take the risk of a serious accident within a short time, from which I would have little chance of recovering. He spoke clearly and forcefully of the possibility of a uremic crisis or a crisis of angina in the chest."[3]

While continuing to prepare conferences on the abbatial charge and the regular visitation, Dom Sortais had two other projects on hand, which were of unequal importance. One was a circular letter which he would never finish on the middle-age crisis in the monastic life and the problems particular to monks who drew near the age of 40. In the U.S. the first wave of professed who entered after the war was very close to that age, and a good number of dispensations were already on the books.

The second project, already old, concerned the lay brothers. In the beginning of the order the institution of the lay brothers, who increased rapidly during the 12th century, formed as it were a second religious family at the side of the first. The lay brothers' life was different from that of the monks. Either the lay brothers stayed at the granges, or in the monastic building with their own special regular places. They celebrated their own Offices apart from the monks, and these were much shorter. They led a very simple life like country people, but although peasants, they were religious in the full sense of the term, and they followed a certain number of monastic practices. Many illiterate knights or even clerics preferred this simpler type of life, which was better adapted to certain temperaments and closer to nature.

This was one of the many forms that the monastic life had taken over the centuries, alongside the more complex or structured types. Beginning in the 13th century, the number of Cistercian lay brothers had decreased considerably. In the Trappist reform the institution of lay brothers had drawn closer to the life of the monks properly so-called, such that an outsider might think it was a lower form of monastic life, or a kind of inferior class within the community. In fact nothing could be farther

[3] Letter to a friend, October 10, 1961.

from the truth. However, important changes in social customs caused the regime adopted in the 19th century to be less attractive to the new lay brother novices called to the Cistercian life. A clear sign of this was the general decrease in numbers of the lay brothers. In certain monasteries, such as Port-du-Salut and Melleray, the lay brothers made up about two-thirds of the community in the mid-19th century. No such proportion was witnessed in any monastery around the year 1960.

Dom Gabriel did not think it was at all desirable to have the same way of life for all the members of the order. He took notice of the diversity of vocations and personal attractions, and he only sought the solution which would permit their satisfaction in the most judicious fashion and that most in line with the demands of contemporary life: "We must," he said, "be prudent, but we would be wise to adapt ourselves, if we wish to avoid being out of date and finding out some day that it is too late to act. It is true that every change includes some risk, but nothing is gained without risk, and without risk it is impossible to make any progress."[4]

He is completely recognizable in these lines. When he saw there was something to be done for the good of souls, it was impossible for him not to act. He did not like useless delays. He accepted the partial incertitude inherent in any solution. Ultraconservatism seemed imprudent to him. "To adapt consists in accomplishing an objective with the generosity and magnanimity of our holy founders who were real precursors in their own time, and that is what they would do if they lived in our time."[5] He took up a phrase of Cardinal Larraona here. Such was also the thought of Pius XII who returned to these ideas often.

It seemed impossible to Dom Gabriel to maintain a separation between choir monks and lay brothers, as though two communities were living under the same roof. Because of the more advanced scholastic formation and the higher level of general knowledge, the classic Trappist lay brother life seemed archaic and too austere to the young; besides, there was a general desire among them for greater participation in the liturgical life of the

[4] Second project for the statute on the brothers, rough draft.
[5] Letter written on December 9, 1957.

community and in the choral office: "If they willingly admit," he said, "that there are differences among the men on the level of functions, they reject everything that smacks of social classes."[6] Their community spirit is pained by the sole fact of a division inside a single monastery.

The problem evoked since 1953 had become more and more acute with the passing years. Blunders had been made in the order.

Cistercian legislation was tributary to a medieval notion which made full participation in the choral office a condition of the monastic state; therefore that legislation refused to see real monks in the Cistercian lay brothers. This was one of the most important problems, because this exclusion from the monastic state was painfully felt by many brothers. The constitutions spoke of "our brothers," and this seemed to imply that they did not belong; in fact, if a community could speak of "its brothers," it was because the brothers were not really part of it. Some of the best among the brothers stumbled against this sophism and could not break the circle in which it seemed to imprison them. For the abbot it was nonsense to refuse the quality of monk to the brothers.

However, Dom Sortais kept asking himself if adopting the statute of monks for the lay brothers would not involve *ipso facto* their obligation to participate in the whole Office like the choir monks, which seemed completely justifiably to run counter to their specific vocation in which work in silence and recollection concretely holds the first place: "Your soul is not formed by the liturgy as much as the choir religious," he wrote to them in the circular letter of December 8, 1954, "[but] it finds less difficulty than theirs, perhaps, in tending toward contemplation. You lead a very simple life which is more spontaneous and more direct, and in many ways it has more similarity to the workers' life led by the Holy Family for many years in the house at Nazareth."

The abbot was more attentive to the spiritual aspect of the problem than to the external appearances. He did not want the brothers' life to become a mere duplicate of the life of the choir monks. To his mind, reducing the part played by simplicity in

[6] Second project for the statute on the brothers, 3.

their way of life would result in making the lay brothers lose the more direct access to the graces of contemplation which they enjoyed.

He was even more convinced that it was the lay brothers' life which had led him to Bellefontaine, and that he himself had not had a particular desire for liturgical prayer and singing in choir. His prayer was most often nourished by other things. But he also thought there was less and less justification for the division of monasteries into two juxtaposed communities.

A first circular letter was sent to the capitular fathers on April 19, 1960, asking for suggestions and replies which he studied very carefully. A second letter written on June 13, 1962, discussed the replies he had received and asked for more precise comments.

On the occasion of the general chapter of September 1962 the new orientation was defined: "The capitular fathers decided that the order had taken a direction which could be described as follows: neither choir religious, nor lay brothers, but a single class of monks, all brothers and all equal, fulfilled, nevertheless, different functions in the monastery."[7]

The monastic vocation is fundamentally one, but all those who receive it do not live it in the same way, nor do they contact God in the same way. Taking temperaments as they are, Father Sortais thought it was necessary to create a kind of intermediate state out of the two already in existence on the level of the way of life: from the monks not involved in holy orders or in specific studies preparatory for them, and who either participated in the office sung in choir, or lent their aid more generally to manual labor, according to need. They would, then, be in choir or at work, according to the needs of the moment (and not according to their own caprice); when the needs of the group required it, they would lead a life of labor, either completely or partially, afterwards taking up again the partially choral life which they normally followed. A special formation for them would be assured, the extent of which would be determined for the order as a whole, with the possibility for each Abbot to decide the exact kind and to adapt.

[7] Ibid.

And so, in a unified community it would be possible to respect different vocations and to find the way of life best fitted to each one's abilities and aspirations. Similar arrangements were in preparation for the nuns.

The work of the council which opened on October 11, 1962, a month after the general chapter which had laid out the new orientation, would take up all the time of the Abbot General and delay the reform.

"Just think," he wrote on August 6, "I've received the first tome of schemas to be discussed at the council, 260 pages for seven schemas, and they are talking about 110! Imagine that! All in Latin to be sure, but woe is me! All in classical Latin. Expressions from Sallust and Tacitus. I have to atone in a few months for all my wasted years of high school, and especially the classes in Latin!"[8]

The routine of conciliar work was trying when the sessions opened: "I admit that I am tired. Every day, besides my usual work, I have on an average two meetings for the council, either at the Vatican or at Sant' Anselmo (monastic meeting) or at St.-Louis des Français (meetings of French bishops). Then there are special meetings with some bishop or other. . . . It will be the death of me, for it seems obvious that the council (if there are only going to be two sessions each year of two months each) will last several years. This is the prevailing opinion. There are 2,800 people who have the right to give their opinion, and a good number of them certainly have every intention to make it known to their colleagues!"[9] "If I make an intervention at the council, I will speak of this topic: *De accelerando Concilio,* and I will be assured of success. What a longing to talk! At least 160 interventions have been heard up to now on almost the same subject . . . we need to find a new method for the work. . . . But the slowness aside, much good work has been done! The bishops of one country go to the bishops of another, and they understand one another! Invitations to lunch! I 'receive' but very informally. The bishops march up to this place. It is very congenial."[10]

[8] Letter to a monk, August 6, 1962.
[9] Letter to a monk, October 20, 1962.
[10] Letter to a monk, November 4, 1962.

In fact, on the advice of John XXIII, Father Gabriel decided to multiply his contacts with the other council fathers and to form his own opinion by enlarging his supply of information. His difficulty in understanding spoken Latin and his elementary formation in theology kept him from following the debates in all their meanderings. But he wanted to mind his business as a "council father" at any price. It was a question of conscience. Therefore, he took part as far as possible in the exchanges outside of the *aula* of the council, in the theological conferences, and in the information meetings. He forced himself to do excessive work, and it would end in destroying his health. "I tell you openly that there are two councils: One of them is held almost every morning at St. Peter's; the other is held during the afternoons. It consists in meetings of the bishops of each country for understanding an exposition of a point of doctrine which will be discussed and voted on in the plenary sessions. A great theologian speaks, and it is very instructive. It is followed by an exchange of views. Then there are meetings where the bishops of the different countries get together to meet one another, and we understand one another better."[11]

"The afternoon is frequently occupied by private meetings or visits. These occupations make up what I would unabashedly call the afternoon council, unofficial, but just as important as the other, I really believe, and in any case intensely interesting for the new points of view and personal enrichment which these contacts with bishops from other countries or famous theologians bring."[12]

This work during the council, at its periphery so to speak, had, then, much importance for the abbot. Concretely these meetings held a larger place than the general meetings, because he could profit from them more. Does that mean that, after the fashion of journalists, he focused his attention on a kind of parallel council and enjoyed the backstage gossip? If he had been suspected of such, his reactions would probably have been extreme. He had such a sense of the church, such a sense of authority. His diplomacy was fashioned from his understanding

[11] Letter to a prioress, November 5, 1962.
[12] Letter to a missionary, November 2, 1962.

of people and tact, not cleverness and half-sincerity. He was as loyal as a soldier, without shortcuts.

On the other hand, the reactions of public opinion, provoked by journalists who relied on a superficial presentation of many problems, irritated him intensely. He was very sensitive to them, and sometimes he was overly alarmed at them. He was very touchy, as soon as he thought he detected an attack on his own authority as head of his order, and he was even more touchy, when it came to the authority of the pope. He could hardly understand, therefore, the positions of certain bishops. Msgr. Garrone who had his whole confidence, brought him gently to a less rigid conception of the obedience of bishops, and he helped him to form a more balanced view of the role of the fathers gathered by the pope to freely discuss the difficult questions of importance for the whole world.

"I am returning from the council in a very optimistic mood," he wrote after the first session was over. "What concrete results do we bring back from it? None yet. But does anyone find a place to ensconce himself in a building under construction, before it is finished? Does a field yield any good things before the harvest? But when it is time to gather it in, then we will see all that is due to the good seed of the autumn. The fathers sowed their seed at the council; next year will be the harvest."[13]

Dom Gabriel was not a man to get attached to shadows and imperfections. He had unfailing faith, and he knew that the Holy Spirit is always at work in the church. The council gave him the opportunity to discover the true dimensions of certain problems about which he had always had viewpoints that were too simple, simplistic in fact.

"I am sure . . . that the Holy Spirit is at work in the council. It is easy to see from the way in which each one tries to understand the ideas of others, in order to arrive all together at the discovery of truth."[14]

"I consider it a grace to have been called to take part in these meetings, to have heard excellent expositions on the greatness and the duty of the church, and her needs at the same time,

[13] Letter to a priest, December 23, 1962.

[14] Letter to a friend, October 27, 1962.

to have witnessed discussions that were always temperate and courteous, in the course of which prelates and famous theologians threw clear light on certain aspects of the same doctrine. Should we be surprised if all the speakers did not consider the material according to the same point of view? Will some see in that regrettable differences in thought and get worried about it? Would it not be better, on the contrary, to admire and rejoice at the riches of the deposit of our faith on this point? All the problems and even the most brilliant truths can be legitimately envisaged from one angle or another, and the unity of the church never seems more beautiful than when its beliefs are affirmed in various ways, and experienced afterwards in the liturgy, in a multiplicity of rites, whether splendid or impoverished."[15]

Eucharistic celebrations in all the church's rites, in the middle of the *aula,* before the general meeting was held, impressed him very much. He spoke of it afterwards, as of a lasting memory of the council. Among his monks he loved to reminisce about the appeal of good Pope John to contemplatives, thinking with him "that the prayers and sacrifices of contemplative souls would sustain in some way the deliberations of this vast assembly and assure its success on the supernatural level."[16]

John XXIII died on June 3, 1963. A few days previously Dom Gabriel was at the abbey of Melleray, near Nantes. When the newspapers announced a sudden worsening of the Holy Father's condition, he decided to return to Rome. Immediately he had himself taken to St. Peter's Square, and in the midst of the crowd that had gathered, he prayed under the pope's window. The death of good Pope John moved him greatly. On the feast of the Sacred Heart, June 21, Cardinal Montini was elected, and he took the name of Paul VI. The Council, closed *ipso facto* by the death of the Pope who had called it, was convoked anew, and the second session opened as planned in autumn 1963. Meanwhile Dom Gabriel had studied the schema on the church. He was surprised by an omission. The church did not appear

[15] Circular Letter, December 8, 1962.

[16] Allocution of John XXIII at the general chapter and to the community of Our Lady of the Blessed Sacrament at Frattochie, September 1, 1962, A.A.S. 54: 661ff.

in it in the aspect of the "Spouse of Christ *(Sponsa Christi).*" He wished, therefore, to prepare an intervention. His personal experience of human love and his personal life of union with God in contemplation had made him sensitive to this aspect of the dogma, which the schema did nothing to bring out.

The expression of his thought can also be found in a preface which he was asked to write for a book:

"Is the inseparable union," we read in this preface, "of the two fundamental functions of the church, spouse of Christ and mother of men, sufficiently brought out?

"The church is intimately united with the Word of God, who became flesh for the salvation of mankind, and it is precisely this union with the incarnate Son of God which is the source of her pastoral function. . . .

"It is by her union with Christ praying, teaching and suffering, that she transmits the benefits of the prayer, the word and the sacrifice of Jesus . . .

"In this perspective, completely centered around the incarnate Word, the church, mother of men, is not really distinguished from the church, spouse of Christ. She is both of these things at the same time; she is one, because she is the other: spouse because mother, but also mother, in order to become spouse still more, in order to be one day the perfect spouse, admitted to the wedding feast of the Lamb, with all the sons whom she has borne."[17]

Many of those who knew Dom Sortais believe that the extra effort imposed upon him by the council ended up ruining his health. He had undergone one last operation at the beginning of May in a Parisian clinic. It had been extremely painful. It would be in mid-activity that death would surprise him on the evening of the 66th general meeting. But before speaking of this, it is necessary to say a few words about his spiritual journey during his time as Abbot General.

[17] Dom A. Piel, *Les Moines dans l'eglise, textes des souverains pontifes* (Paris: Cerf, 1964), preface by Dom Gabriel Sortais, Abbot General of the Order of Cistercians of the Strict Observance (dated Pentecost 1963).

Chapter 22

SPIRITUAL CHILDHOOD

The heart-rending pain brought on by his nomination for the responsibility of Abbot General had forced Dom Gabriel to advance further on the path of renunciation. Did he perhaps still remain excessively attached to human friendships, to the joy of having a community, to the happiness of having sons? The paternal feeling was indeed strong in him on the bare human level. It is noticeable in these outbursts which do not deceive: "Oh, you don't know what it is to live day after day among famous people, without the happiness of feeling a tiny tot climb up on your knees and come to curl up on you, without receiving and returning kisses," he wrote to a young couple with whom he was friendly.[1]

The spiritual fatherhood with which he had been invested at Bellefontaine could have been unconsciously experienced after the manner of a compensation. In 1951 Dom Sortais simply agreed to give it up, but this does not mean he did not suffer. He trusted in God who required this new sacrifice from him: "When a soul is generous, I mean when it is loving, it cannot calculate and does not like to advance by stages. It sees what must be done, it grasps Jesus' desire, and it says, 'The sacrifice has been made.' It does not say, 'I will make this sacrifice.' It says, 'It has been made.' And in fact it has been made."[2]

No hesitation is possible! When God's will is clear, the soul finds its joy in conforming itself to it, even if it has to trample upon what it holds most dear: "You know, when you are with

[1] Letter to friends, September 30, 1945.
[2] Letter to a nun, February 12, 1957.

God, you will be all the happier for having said 'yes' to all that he wills."[3] His faith in God's wisdom was complete.

"Abandonment gives God greater glory than action. Abandonment is a true act of love, and a very intense one. It gives God glory for him to see weak creatures attach themselves to his will, and no longer desire anything else. The graces we receive will lead us to abandonment."[4]

Dom Gabriel was certain that every responsibility received without ambition is accompanied by the graces necessary to meet it. No suffering sent by God could exceed the strength of the soul: "The cross Jesus presents to us and places upon each one of us is never too heavy. If it seems so to us, it is because there is something in it that isn't right: Either we aggravate this cross by adding something to it, or we are not abandoned enough to God's will."[5]

And so he devoted himself resolutely to his task, even impetuously. Projects accumulated. He went out to meet the difficulties with his need to act, to create and to promote. So just a little over a year after taking charge, he was completely exhausted. It seemed to him that his life was going to end abruptly. In 1953, when he was operated on in Canada, he thought his time had come to leave the active life of the earth. After the peril was over, he showed his disappointment in a caprice: "Why," he asked the surgeon, "didn't you fail? By this time I would have seen God."

Since God still wanted him on earth for a few years, he put on his collar again. He was not without difficulties with the problem of the adaptations which raised strong resistance in the order. Instead of getting irritated over this, he saw it as an invitation to become a beginner all over again. He had always loved

[3] Letter to a nun, April 26, 1963. "A reasonable person reflects often before making a decision and again before acting. He does not want to get involved without a certitude of success, unless the action seems profitable to him. Such a person is unfit for contemplation. Love goes right to the end without reasoning, and contemplation presupposes this loving impulse which is evocative of the child, making him so lovable. . . . Contemplation moves on the plain of reciprocal generosity." Conference given at the abbey of Gethsemani, February 27, 1961.

[4] Letter to a nun, October 16, 1956.

[5] Letter to Mère Bernard, Palm Sunday, 1952.

St. Thérèse of Lisieux. The little saint's teaching had guided him along on his spiritual journey; he had assimilated it himself by teaching it to others. "God and the Blessed Virgin are the only ones I love more," he had said as far back as 1948.[6]

At the beginning of 1955 he again started to read the saint's works; the Carmelites had made him a gift of them for the library of the general's house. "In rereading the story of little Thérèse, I feel that I am going to relive the best time of my religious life, that in which I was only a young monk seeking God with all my heart. I was so happy, when I was a novice."[7]

With Dom Gabriel there was not much difference between "seeing" and "doing." This rereading of the works of St. Thérèse had decisive influence on his behavior: "[I had] thought of starting my novitiate over again, of doing what the Jesuits call a third year which is done ten years after the two years novitiate. In my case it would be 30 years after, but precisely for that reason, I have greater need of it. And Thérèse will be my novicemistress. I leave her completely free to take me in hand, to form me and to make me like herself for a year.

"I said 'a year' to avoid discouragement if she should ask too much of me, and also lest she be vexed with her new novice too quickly, if he does not please her.

"Don't think I'm joking. My third year has started, and I am quite serious about it. My happiness is very great. I go to my novicemistress for everything, and I admit to you that she reminds me of many things interiorly to which I would, no doubt, not have paid attention otherwise. I refuse her nothing, and my only wish is that she not hesitate to take advantage of it. I want to become what she wishes me to become, and at the end of the year, when I love God more, I will ask her to continue taking care of me. She does me so much good. The things I understand poorly with other saints seem very simple with her."[8]

These are not empty phrases. There is something decisive about this stage marked by special favors about which he wrote to several correspondents. The renewal of his relations with the

[6] Letter to Mère Agnès, October 6, 1948.

[7] Letter to Soeur Geneviève de la Sainte-Face, January 25, 1955.

[8] Ibid.

Lisieux Carmel begins a period of grace for him: "As far as my moral health is concerned, it is making rapid progress. I would need time to tell you about it. My interior life is much easier for me now. Little Thérèse has helped me very much. My conversation is often in heaven, as Paul recommended to the Philippians. But Little Thérèse also leaves me little rest: I must keep going, following her and doing her bidding. She asks many sacrifices, small sacrifices, all those that happen. This makes me very happy."[9]

A few months passed in this way, going deeper into the way of spiritual childhood. The abbot had certainly decided to enter it fully, without quibbling with God's demands: "God has filled me for several months," he wrote to a correspondent. "He has been using St. Thérèse of the Infant Jesus for this. It is difficult to express what I have learned through her. She helps me very much in my search for God. She has obtained for me the understanding of many things which were obscure or completely hidden. To tell the truth, she also asks a lot from me and lets nothing escape her. But it is so delightful to refuse God nothing, especially to have this filial trust in him that he expects us to have, which he cannot demand peremptorily, which belongs to those who truly love God. I understood what the suffering of the weak is, and of the little ones and of those who hope because of their weakness, who have rightly understood that lack of strength is the greatest strength in the world, when it is accompanied by simple confidence in the goodness of a Father, such as God is."[10]

Dom Gabriel was, in fact, following the road of abandonment to merciful love. He gave up asking himself questions, questioning himself at length in God's presence: "It is unnecessary to try to find out exactly where you are on the spiritual map," he said. "That does not mean much, and it does not please God. We must simply follow the path like children, without concern about anything, and especially without asking how high we are on the spiritual ladder."[11]

[9] Letter to a monk, February 18, 1955.
[10] Letter to an abbot, March 5, 1955.
[11] Letter to a nun, February 7, 1961.

Feeling poor meant nothing to him, being without any source of spiritual energy to face the "setbacks of fatigue and concerns."[12] He preferred to come back to God as to the source of all power a hundred times a day, like a beggar who gives away as quickly as he receives anything. "What do you want Jesus to do with a big man?"[13]

He was happy living in God's light, a light which fell plumb on his weakness and preserved him from hypocrisy and any thoughts of self-satisfaction: "It is so good to be and to feel that one is in truth in the presence of those one loves best. It brings us close to God before whom we are in truth. And he loves us all the same! It is unbelievable that he should love people like us!"[14]

Dom Gabriel never attained complete self-mastery. He would have infinite patience listening to meaningless complaints and tattlings of the convent. Then suddenly uncontrollable anger would break out, occasioned by an insignificant event. He would chance to make someone suffer, or terrorize someone, or awaken antipathy in someone. Excessive tiredness was usually to blame, but when he became aware of it, the damage had already been done. The abbot felt deep regret because of it, but he never despaired. It was an opportunity for him to come back to God just as often as a penitent full of confidence. He went so far as to write to a monk: "I would rather be a poor chap who wanders away from God from time to time through weakness, without ever losing his filial confidence in him, than be a man who commits no serious sin, but who does not have the soul of a child. What I want is to give my Father joy through my childlike attitude towards him. I like this better than having the personal joy of noticing and telling myself that I did not deviate from the straight path. Be sure you understand this, my son; the best would be to be faithful and keep your heart childlike; but if it is necessary to choose, I would rather be a prodigal son who remains the son of his Father, than be one of these faithful souls

[12] Undated letter to a nun. "When we remember what God is and what we are! . . . A mere nothing united to God . . . and that should be true all our lives. . . . Forget what kind of union; a deep union." Conference at the abbey of Igny, May 1963.

[13] Letter to a nun, June 2, 1947.

[14] Letter to Mère Bernard, June 13, 1961.

who seem to be without any love, who seem not to be faithful because of their filial love. The Pharisees were very faithful."[15]

To have the soul of a child! This is a leitmotif of his spiritual teaching, especially in his last years. In a project for a Circular Letter on the middle-age crisis in the monastic life we find this characteristic passage: "We reach the point where, in the distress which emphasizes our inability to pray, we finally send to God the filial cry which he has waited for so long to hear from us. Such a cry is worth all the prayers in the world. Who knows if our heavenly Father did not find it profitable to let us vegetate in powerlessness, in order to hear this cry and rejoice in its spontaneity and purity, determining in his fatherly love that this cry would become the basis of a real grace of union?"[16]

Dom Gabriel had stopped depending on his own love for God—he had found it too fragile, at the mercy of weakness after having clutched at it so long as though in despair: "Lord, you know everything; You know I love you (John 21:15-16)." He now abandoned himself to the certitude which was much more reassuring of God's love for him, despite all the doubts which might arise in his soul. St. Thérèse had helped him find this secret which is a pure object of faith: "Our confidence should not be based on whether we are good or bad. Before being a good child or a bad one, you are a child: that is your only right to grace. That is what our confidence must be based on, our right to be given grace and to depend on God's love. That is our support, not our fidelity, be it much or little."[17]

This filial sense became extremely acute at certain times. The abbot spoke confidentially of a grace he had received at the funeral of a little child whom he himself had baptized, Anne Richard of Cholet:

"Was it this child whom I baptized who obtained this grace for me, or your prayers? I do not know. What I do know is that

[15] Letter to a monk, March 7, 1956. "Let us look at the little children. They are our models so often! So many of them have a good time with anyone, they will not go to sleep, except on a heart which they know loves them. Confidence is the fruit of love, and its existence is only proven by abandonment." Circular Letter, December 8, 1953.

[16] Project for a Circular Letter on the Middle-Age Crisis (unpublished manuscript notes, written in 1961) part 3, 12.

[17] Conversation with some nuns on St. Thérèse of the Child Jesus.

God showed my unbelievable misery that he is unbelievably merciful. I spent some really sanctifying moments in which I understood how good God is, how his goodness had not been diminished by my misery and could never have been, even if I had been even more miserable than I was. I understood how much God loved me, and how it was as a Father that he loved me.

"My tears flowed abundantly, and it seemed to me that, without knowing whether or not I was responsible for all that was in me, I was united with my Father who is so good, and I loved him despite my profound misery.

"Oh! How the soul is invaded by humility, spiritual poverty and true charity in these moments of truth! If I could only think up one word to express what I felt was happening in me without my intervention, I would say that I felt 'filiated,' that I had become a son."[18]

What can you do then, except love God without reserve, well knowing that his heart is greater than ours?

"Be all God's, but seek him simply, like a child who knows that he is loved. You see, it is sometimes difficult to really love God, but it is not difficult to live like somebody who knows he is loved. This attitude makes God very happy, because it is already love, really pure love. Besides, does he ask much more than this?"[19]

Believe in love: that is Dom Gabriel's last word, and remain little before God like a child with its mother: "I think the tiny tots will not be judged, if they are very little, if they act as little ones, if they agree to be treated as tiny tots. The little ones stick close to their mommy, so close that they cannot be separated from her. The little one has no identity of his own. I know very well that this is my way, and it seems to me that I am much littler than when I was at Bellefontaine. The disproportion between my misery and incapacity and the important functions which I had the responsibility of fulfilling has made me small. This was the only way. But I did not become small by my own efforts. It was a grace of the good God."[20]

[18] Letter to Mère Bernard, August 6, 1951.
[19] Letter to a nun, November 18, 1955.
[20] Letter to a monk, February 18, 1956.

We have already seen how vehemently the Father General had stigmatized that caricature of the way of childhood which is called infantilism; it is interior instability, fragility in devotion to God, inability to make objective and reasonable judgments, obedience to the caprice of the feelings, no sense of responsibility and egocentricism. The lively sense of God's fatherhood and faith in the extraordinary mercy of God is something else entirely:

"God is our Father: this truth is deep and eternal. I cannot think of it without tears in my eyes and a desire in my heart to please God my Father. How pitiful and sad it is to let even one moment which we have at our disposal be lost, which could be used to love and praise God! . . . The extraordinary thing is that God has made us his sons, but then nothing is extraordinary in the abundance of his benefits. Quite the contrary, it is normal. Either he is a Father, or he is not. God is Father, and he acts like a Father, simply but completely."[21]

Such love can only be answered by an absolute love, by full use of the ability to love placed in us by grace: "The important thing, dear sons, even more important than the thing we ask for (in prayer), is the right use of the power to love placed by God in our hearts. That is the essential thing. To love as God wills, what he wills and as much as he wills."[22]

The surprising thing is that this filial sentiment is from the first addressed to God especially through the mediation of Our Lady. Dom Sortais had expressed his interior experience in formulas which would make some theologians flinch. But he had said the thing as he had felt it at the time, content to bear witness to his own consciousness, without trying to explain or justify it, except by images and symbols: "To tell the truth, I feel that being a son of God follows especially from being a son of the Blessed Virgin. It is she whom I find most easily, and in her I find God. You know how miserable I am. But I love Mary. It really seems to me that I love her more than myself. I am certainly capable of any kind of foolish act, but I am also capable of all kinds of fidelity. I love Mary more than myself, and I would willingly accept death and destruction, if thereby I could obtain the slightest increase of happiness for Mary. It seems to me that

[21] Letter to an abbot, June 6, 1953.

[22] Letter to a religious, September 25, 1958.

I would accept the prospect of never seeing her, if thereby I gave her one more joy."[23]

Let us not forget that his conversion as a student had begun with Our Lady's help. He had become her knight and servant, spontaneously adopting gestures of courtesy which expressed his love. Mary had led him straight to God. His spiritual life had been indelibly influenced by her: "I am too far from God because of my oft repeated miseries. I am closer to this maternal creature with whom I have very close ties, like a son with his mother. Of course God is my Father, but I am so little that I am like a king's son entrusted by his father to a woman's care in his infancy, who grows more attached to the woman than to his father, because he is so young. I know Mary is nothing compared to God, but I can only go to God through her. I am like a child who is only fed through his mother, living by her life, just like the king's son."[24]

He had had an absolute need for Our Lady a long time; she had been his only refuge in the long trial that had tormented him from his abbatial election until the beginning of 1958. He was convinced that a reciprocal relationship had been established between her and himself. He had entrusted himself completely to her. She could not abandon him.

"What would have become of me without the Blessed Virgin? I am afraid to think of it. But the Lord thinks of me and arranges things so that I feel a constant need for Mary my Mother. She, too, I think has something like a need for me. A woman needs her baby. She becomes sick, if someone takes him away from her. Mary needs to feel me close to her, for she knows very well, that if I am far away from her, I will be lost."[25]

He experienced her help in concrete—almost tangible—ways. He sensed her near him, present and ready to help: "The blessed Virgin? She is very good to me. She makes me climb up higher and then releases me, but since my weakness flinches at the slightest steepness, when she pushes me up at such times, she hardly ever leaves me."[26]

[23] Letter to a monk, November 9, 1958.

[24] Letter to Mère Bernard, August 10, 1957.

[25] Letter to Mère Bernard, January 26, 1959.

[26] Letter to Mère Bernard, September 19, 1956. "We will never love Mary enough, because Jesus' love for her was unlimited. Mary is involved in all the

In recent years, however, his devotion tended to become less preferential. After a very painful interior struggle in January 1958, God had returned the awareness of his love to him. He no longer felt himself as though pushed away by him whom he sought with all his heart. Because of this his devotion to Our Lady took on aspects that were closer to the place she occupied in the economy of redemption.

At the end of his life, in May 1963, he even made this surprising admission: "You see, I think I will not go to purgatory. I have suffered too much on earth. It seems to me that the good God would not be the good God, if, after all the suffering and trials he has sent me, he asked me to render an account. No, I have no fear of judgment. I do fear death. I am like everybody else. The moment of death has still something frightening about it. But after death I do not fear judgment."[27]

Many were the souls entrusted to him. He wrote them long letters of a very personal character, even though he was swamped at this time by an overwhelming correspondence: He was first 70, then 100 and finally 160 letters behind. He had the gift of understanding souls in trouble. He did not repulse them, for he did not wish to add anything to their sufferings, even if they were reprehensible. He gently tried to make himself understood, without giving reproaches.

On the other hand he was exacting toward those who he knew to be generous. His severity might seem excessive, but he inflicted no wounds, because immediately afterwards came tangible signs of affection. More than anything else he liked simplicity, humility and freedom from pretense. "I would like to see you get more and more simple, and I think the good God agrees with me. . . . Find the good God in the most simple occupations, as Mary did all her life."[28]

mysteries of Jesus' love" (undated). "Is it Jesus who will come to tell us that we love his mother too much? . . . Why should Jesus reproach us for using Mary too much in our interior life, He who wished to spend nine months with her alone, in her womb, forming one sole life with her, so to speak, one sole being, one sole blood." Circular Letter, December 8, 1951.

[27] Admission to a monk.

[28] Letter to a nun, September 11, 1959.

He did not encourage introspection, self-examination or inquisitorial research in the domain of conscience. "To my way of thinking, in the monastic life, many souls would find it advantageous after a certain period of time to do their examination of conscience in a perceptibly different way from that in which they did it at the beginning of their religious life. I find it abnormal and hardly profitable to spend time each day tracking down our failures, when by the grace of God these failures have become almost involuntary, and when in general no special time is set apart to think about the numberless gifts the Lord prodigally bestows upon us."[29]

For souls going through painful trials, he could find words of encouragement which were extremely precious and give welcome advice when it was most needed. His speech always bore the sign of his personal experience.

"Trials 'remarry' the soul to God, as Peguy wrote. It is very true. We sense more confidence, and we are more simple and true when we are crushed and reduced to nothing great, and when the future is closed to us. It is better that way. We become, almost by force, more dependent on God. From that point it is only a step to loving him more, with a purer love."[30]

"One of the most discouraging aspects of these difficult times is a kind of lassitude which follows the periods of trial. Careful analysis would reveal a kind of defiance of God, a kind of rancor against him. We would willingly say, 'From now on, do what you will.' This would not be filial abandonment, but the expression of ill humor, of an indifference coming ultimately from a certain disaffection towards an 'unfaithful' friend."[31]

"We should not be surprised, if we often remain powerless to praise God in work, when we are going through trials. It is almost impossible for us weak creatures. But words are not what count; what counts is attachment to God's will. This is always possible. We know that, even if it is done by constraint without any sensible joy, it is only more valuable in God's sight."[32]

[29] Undated letter to a nun.

[30] Letter to a nun, December 5, 1958.

[31] Letter to a nun, July 29, 1959.

[32] Letter to a nun, August 2, 1952.

The abbot's objective, finally, was quite unified. His governing of the order had the sole purpose of promoting the contemplative life, making it more accessible to the majority of monks. As a director of conscience he sought nothing other than to see that the souls he was responsible for became "a prayer" identified with their primary activity as their usual and only attitude: "Contemplatives ought to be fools for God. I think and am convinced that it is profoundly true. They must have a fixed idea of God; they must return to him as to their center, the source of their life, their end."[33]

The long temptation against hope that had tormented him since he first became abbot had forced him to deepen his awareness of the mystery of God's mercy. The exercise of his responsibility, so well-fitted to his deepest nature, had permitted him, on the other hand, to make more progress in his understanding of God's fatherhood. It was the spiritual teaching of St. Thérèse, many times recovered in the course of his life, that had helped him most to deepen his own spirituality. Instead of letting himself be discouraged by his weakness and the powerlessness he experienced when confronted with the awesome responsibility of his charge, he put his trust in God and Our Lady. He became more and more little and childlike, humble and abandoned, leaving to the Lord the need to solve the distressing problems presented by his own destiny and the future of his order.

His life ended in the peace of little children. After a renewed outbreak of suffering, interior battles and distress at the beginning of 1958, during his second stay in the hospital of Our Lady of Hope at Montreal, God had given him the certitude of his love, and the long temptation against hope had ended after more than 20 years.

At the end of the year 1961, forced to take three months of complete rest on the order of Father Paul Philippe, then secretary of the Sacred Congregation of Religious, who had learned of the exhausted state he had reached, Dom Gabriel went to find shelter at the nuns' monastery of Maubec. Aiguebelle was close by. He wished to take advantage of the community retreat to make his own with the monks, under the direction of the Carmelite Father

[33] Letter to a nun, October 7, 1962.

Lucien-Marie de Saint-Joseph. In his discretion he did not wish to ask the preacher for a special interview; his time belonged to the community; however, the father wanted to invite him one evening after Compline. The next day the abbot was radiant, and he confided that this conversation had been the source of exceptional graces of light for him.

Chapter 23

DEATH OF DOM GABRIEL

"You know the saying of Henry IV—it is perfectly historical, and that is why I allow myself to quote it in its realistic form: 'I don't want to die with my behind in feathers.'"[1]

Dom Gabriel had certainly resolved to go to the end of his powers, to die at his post. He was a fighter with his soul on fire, who confronted danger head on and never hesitated before a duty. Just a few minutes rest, when his weariness became too great, then he was off again. "Sometimes I tell the good God, that when I reach heaven, the first thing I will ask him will be that I may have a good long sleep in the Blessed Virgin's arms. That would be a good rest. How happy I would be!"[2]

He had longed for death during the war of 1939–40; later he had sensed its approach at the beginning of 1953. It had remained before his eyes afterwards, like a visitor who would return shortly. But he tried to curb his impatience by practicing himself what he had advised one of his directees to do: "Be a child of God, who does not bother about tomorrow, because he knows that tomorrow will be just as full of love as today. Oh yes, of course you will go to the Father, but wait for the time that he has set for your departure, and wait for it peacefully, for you know it has been chosen well."[3]

The perspective of an early death filled him with joy and extreme gratitude. He saw himself as a little child eagerly awaited at the Father's house, with his place set at the family table. "Our thoughts run ahead to find Jesus and Mary waiting

[1] Letter to a monk, November 1, 1938.

[2] Letter to a close friend, August 25, 1946.

[3] Letter to Mère Bernard, November 11, 1961.

for us, like parents waiting for children to return home at night. Jesus has gone to prepare a place for us. He was and is thinking of each one of us, of the happiness of each one. This fills me with emotion. I understand already that Jesus came to save us, to become incarnate and live among us. He was a lover. But after the reception he got from men, he has still gone ahead to prepare them a place, to prepare their happiness, to see how to make them happy, that is too much for me to understand. We will be with him for all eternity. He will never be without us again. Without you! Without me!"[4]

Among his beloved children he included the former abbess of Les Gardes, Mère Bernard, who had remained very much weakened after an accident and approached death in the midst of great suffering. Dom Sortais wrote to her often with affection, and in preparing her for death thought of his own which could not be long in coming. For him his spiritual daughter was a model which he proposed to imitate, but he was very careful not to let her suspect him of this: "The beautiful thing about her is her everlasting penchant for starting over, which shows that she has no self-assurance, she is nothing but frailty in herself, and her misery could add absolutely nothing to her filial confidence."[5]

This spiritual friendship has furnished us with some of Dom Gabriel's best letters and unrestrained self-disclosures, because he had a certain spontaneity which led him to open himself to those who asked his counsel. He incited them to confide in him by confiding and abandoning himself:

"My little daughter," he wrote one day. "If Jesus draws near you, don't be afraid. The one who is afraid to look at him shows he does not love him. Show him a smiling face. Tell him your door is open, that he can enter whenever he wants."[6]

Mère Bernard died on Saturday, March 10, 1962, at the abbey of N.-D. des Gardes in Anjou. "This Mother," he said, "was a great success for the Lord. I can only thank him for what he has done in my daughter."[7]

[4] Letter to Mère Bernard, May 25, 1960.

[5] Letter to a nun, January 31, 1957.

[6] Letter to Mère Bernard, October 13, 1957.

[7] Letter to a nun, March 11, 1962.

She had suffered very much. Dom Gabriel had helped her to bear her sufferings simply, without "make up," for there was nothing that he so abhorred, as those who played a role or acted a part. It seemed to him to be the very negation of the filial attitude and the way of spiritual childhood.

"Accept your sufferings; reconcile yourself to being very imperfect and to having a death similar to your life, a death that will need your Father's mercy, just like your life, and await your time to depart like a son or daughter."[8]

"We would like to suffer *well.* It would be so good to be told that our mediocre life had ended in a perfect death. I believe that for many reasons a death which seems mediocre to us is preferable to a *beautiful* death. It is more fitting for children who are glad to wait for everything and receive everything from their Father. To appear before God holding out your hand like a poor person who lacks everything is a better attitude than that of appearing before him with the support of a *good* life and counting on the merit of a *good* death. Abandonment is preferable to any other attitude, the abandonment of a child who relies on his Father's goodness for everything."[9]

This, then, was his ideal: to go at the time when God willed it, in the circumstances chosen by him, renouncing all his personal preferences.

Signs of forewarning were not scarce, but he was totally unaware of the "how." "I lingered at the clinic in Rome for the whole month of July and the beginning of August," he wrote in autumn 1961. "I had my prostate operated on, because the surgery I underwent in Paris and Canada turned out to be insufficient. I was very sick, and in much pain."[10]

The following year, in sending his photograph to the superioress of one of the Japanese houses (his monasteries of predilection), he described himself, "You will think I am old, and that is what I am. I was 60 on September 22, and I am going to finish my course. I think I am slowing up, like a plane about to land."[11]

[8] Letter to Mère Bernard, November 1, 1961.

[9] Letter to Mère Bernard, November 6, 1961.

[10] Letter to a female cousin who was a religious, September 14, 1961.

[11] Letter to a prioress, November 5, 1962.

This slowing up was very relative, because the council was about to open. In the eyes of those around him, Dom Gabriel continued with the same impetus, as though there were no slowing down. The force of his character created this illusion and hid the actual wearing down of his strength.

Between the first two sessions of the council he had visited several monasteries in France and been present in Oslo for the episcopal consecration of Father Willem Gran, a Norwegian monk of the abbey of Caldey in Great Britain; he had been cellarer at Monte Cistello for three years, and Dom Gabriel loved him tenderly. After this Dom Gabriel had gone to Belgium and Canada. The program for 1964 had been worked out in its main outlines: the abbot wanted to go to Bellefontaine first to make his retreat with that community. From January to April he intended to visit the African monasteries, and in July and August those of Great Britain and Ireland. He also had to prepare the plenary general chapter for September, as well as the third session of the council. Would it be possible perhaps to make the program lighter? Some had insisted to Father General that he should give up the African trip, because he had too much to do with the council, and his health was broken. Besides, wasn't it necessary to foresee another possible stay in the clinic?

On Wednesday, November 13, when the 66th general congregation of the council was adjourned, Father Sortais received at Monte Cistello Dom Prou, abbot of Solesmes, Dom Salmon, abbot of Saint-Jerôme, and Dom Dayez, abbot of Maredsous, with three Benedictine monks. He was his usual self: hospitable, affectionate, full of warmth and good humor. Then he went back to work: an unbelievable number of letters to answer and affairs to expedite. After dinner with the community, he accosted Father Master of the students in a passageway and spoke feelingly with him about a fault against the Rule, committed by many of the young monk-students.

Suddenly there was a cry: "Oh! The pain, pain in the back!" A chair was brought, but it was necessary to let him lie down. He was suffering too much to let him be moved to his cell. He felt like he was suffocating. The pain was unbearable. A doctor was urgently called, and he gave him an injection. It momentarily relieved the abbot who made a joke to reassure the monks who ran up to him in complete surprise. This remission allowed them to carry him to his bed. The moment he was lying down, he cried out a second time, "Oh! The pain!" His face was drained of color, and his eyes became fixed. He spoke again, "I am fainting." He had already lost consciousness. There was only time to anoint him rapidly. He had left his family forever. His doctor had warned him that overwork could bring on a crisis of uraemia or chest angina. That is, in fact, what had happened.

On the day of the funeral, a large procession of monks, abbots and bishops present for the council accompanied his body down the hill of Monte Cistello, taking the ancient Via Laurentina, which leads to the abbey of Eugene III. The coffin was laid in the church of Tre Fontane, before the body was buried in the small conventual cemetery full of cypress trees and the singing of birds, where three other Abbot Generals had already been laid to rest: Dom Wyart, Dom Ollitrault de Keryvallen and Dom Smets.

"Oh my sister," he had told an aged nun 87 years old, who had spoken to him about her haste to go to God. "Jesus desires it more than you do. He is counting the days." He had such beautiful words, such true discoveries of the heart! And he felt profoundly what he said.

And so Dom Sortais had held the seat of Abbot General for 12 years, stamping it with his personal style and giving the order an impetus which it had never before received from its leadership to such an extent, since the decree of Leo XIII, which had unified the various congregations which had come from the reform of La Trappe. Dom Gabriel was a great man of action, with powerful, bold conceptions, and he had an endless supply of original solutions. The tradition he wanted to be faithful to—it was a matter of temperament as well as choice—was not an inert, dead, intangible thing, a "maiden asleep in the woods" whom he had to avoid waking; it was a living reality, rich in hidden sources of strength, which each generation of monks received in turn, to promote and to adapt, before transmitting it to further generations without loss of its patrimony.

A man with prodigious dynamism, fervent, generous, irascible, prodigal with his time and with his heart: Such was Dom Gabriel. Frank, just, loyal and simple, incapable of dissimulation, having nothing artificial or studied: "To be true before

God, that is all that matters. . . . To be true: it is like a small link of a chain, nothing great, but it is all we could grasp," he said.

With his cutting judgments, he had caused fright by his powerful personality. He had hated meanness, cleverness and compromise.[12] He had been quick to disperse illusions in himself and in others.

"One says, 'I am frank' when he is harsh," he wrote, "'I am firm' when he is too rigorous, 'I am zealous' when he scolds without discretion, 'I am meek' when he is timid and weak, 'I am prudent' when he is only crafty, 'I am simple' when he pays attention to nothing, 'I do not calculate the consequences of my words' when he is really only silly, 'I am liberal' or 'I practice liberty of spirit' when he gives himself incredible license."

With him there was nothing mechanical, finished, or prejudged. He had extreme flexibility of mind; he was inventive, original and highly endowed with creative imagination.

His profound humility did not keep him from commanding vigorously and being firm, sometimes even to the point of obstinacy.

The abbot was a straightforward man who was never content with a few phrases. He possessed a healthy realism which permitted him to take the details of life into consideration.

But a man would not know him at all, if he did not remember his extreme sensibility and openness to others. It was much more than sociability, than the joy of communication with someone. He needed to unburden himself, to confide in someone, to give himself. His affectivity was highly developed. He was a lover, and his temperament inclined him to provoke affection. He used gestures which completely won over people's hearts. His soul was infinite. From the day on which his power to love was turned toward God, when that flame finally found unmeasured space before it, it was refined, in order to grow greater still:

"We radiate Jesus," he said, "when we are separated by our love from all that is not him, even those things that religious

[12] "The person who tends to measure his efforts and limit his gifts does not seem fitted to walk the path of contemplation, where God requires everything from the soul, before he gives the soul everything." Conference at the abbey of Gethsemani, February 27, 1961.

ordinarily keep—the nation, family and abbey—in order to take the blessings of the Cistercian spirit and observance to souls we do not know, but we know Christ loved them and ransomed them with his blood."[13]

His love for men who were his brothers had not diminished for all that, had not been lost, consumed or forgotten; quite the contrary. A new career was started for his limitless generosity. Dom Gabriel had had a passion for the good of souls, a solicitude that could not rest, until he felt that each one of them had been caught by God who was seeking for them.

"If God calls you, if God calls you, my child," Péguy has Madame Gervaise say, "When God gets after somebody, when God goes after a soul, works on a soul, there is much to do, we must go, we must walk. There is no escape. There is really no escape. God's hand is heavy. God's work, His secret operation is a consuming fire. How will our poor carcasses resist him?"[14]

Dom Gabriel happened to treat with partiality those whom he secretly preferred, but he also gave himself, even to those in whom he felt the least interest, without second thoughts, and he had infinite patience with them. He was a magnanimous person ready to forget meanness, even when he had been wounded, and he was often wounded!

The purely administrative side of his charge did not detain him. What he sought was human contact, contact with concrete human problems. He wanted to work with living material, because abstractions hardly moved him.

He was very present to God, to the other and to his everyday tasks. He tried to live every day in great light. His sense of duty took precedence over every other consideration. His passion was for devotion, poverty and sacrifice.

"Ask Our Lord for the grace and the strength to accept your cross," he advised a former prioress, "for the strength to offer up your sufferings and profit from them. You will be so happy when you appear before God, that you had not refused to walk the same difficult road that Jesus walked."[15]

[13] Circular Letter, July 2, 1956.

[14] Péguy, "Le mystère de la vocation de Jeanne d'Arc" in *Oeuvres Complètes*, éd. de La Pléiade (Paris: Galliard, 1967) 1210.

[15] Letter to a nun, July 7, 1960.

"It is charity which makes us hear the voice of the one we love in God's voice calling us to obedience. It is love which trembles with joy at this call, at the sound of this voice and rushes to fulfill the desire of the Beloved. This spontaneity is not the automatic switch of a will that has lost its legitimate self-control; it is the reflex of a loving heart which knows in whom it has put its trust."[16]

For him the secret of heroism lay in filial love: "I know only one way to reach perfect love in its simplest form: the love of a child for its father."[17]

Dom Sortais was a great pray-er. He constantly worked under God's watchful eye, convinced that he could only accomplish what he had to do by being united with God. He found there the strength to persevere at his task until the end. The life of prayer was absolutely fundamental for him: "Once you have close union," he said, "you have outgoing and true apostleship."[18] "Without close union with Jesus, there can be no question of radiation, of making others know and love him."[19]

He had immense esteem for the time of prayer, however urgent and important his occupations may have been: "The time of the great silence is the favored time of the day. You might be inclined to consider it a preparatory time, thinking the great silence prepares us for work time. I think the contrary is true. The hours of daylight should prepare us for the hours of the night, which belong to the union of our soul with God. The great silence . . . the observance should not be counted among those which mortify our nature . . . prayer, during which the soul is united with God, is saturated with God!"[20]

Among all others he loved the prayer at night, and he pictured the whole church in her role of nocturnal pray-er: "The supplication which ascends to the creator in the atmosphere of the silence of creation has penetrating force. Each evening an

[16] Circular Letter, June 21, 1963.

[17] *Notes sur la Règle,* commentary on ch. 4, 24th instrument of good works.

[18] Conference on the contemplative life, given at the abbey of Spencer, January 1, 1961.

[19] Conference on the contemplative life, at the Abbey of Mellerary.

[20] Conference given to the students at Monte Cistello for Recollection Sunday, on the silence at night.

immense vigil is organized from one end of the church to the other, which lasts until sunrise. Monks and nuns of different orders take their time at night watch. It is *laus perennis* which thus resounds all night long (by Carmelites, Dominicans, Capuchins, Carthusians, Cistercians and Benedictines); it is like a sacred torch which is passed from hand to hand by the religious families. It makes us think of the big fires lit in the desert by travelers to keep wild beasts away. The devil "goes about like a raging lion seeking someone to devour."[21]

But he also found God in the splendor of the created universe, the work of his hands: "Nature cries to God with a loud voice. All things repeat a teaching or a comparison: the sowing of seeds, the blooming of hay, the harvest, the large ears of wheat, the sheaves, the birds, the hens, the grapes . . . do away with the watertight compartments dividing prayer from work!"[22]

Dom Sortais' spiritual pilgrimage had been marked out by great graces, by bright periods followed by long years of suffering. Right after his temporary profession, the faith which he had so joyfully recovered, had been apparently withdrawn from him. He had been plunged into the night. After just a few years of respite, he had entered an interminable period in which hope in turn seemed to escape him. He had felt that he was on the rim of a nameless abyss. He who on the surface had seemed to be a man with certitude had been affected interiorly with dizziness before a pit of anxiety, and he had experienced anguish in a shoreless sea and pathless wilderness. His peace was the reward of heroic conquest. The only way out possible for him had been abandonment to the infinite mercy of God the Father and unlimited trust in the Virgin Mother.

But it had been impossible for him to lean his weight on his personal drama, to indulge in self-pity, in a sterile retreat upon himself. The apparent uselessness of his love for God had forced him to purify his love. Despite his limitations which he knew only too well, few men would have been able to utilize their ability to love as well as he.

[21] Tamquam leo rugiens, circuit quaerens quem devoret: 1 Pt 5:8, *Notes sur la Règle,* commentary on ch. 4, 37th instrument of good works.

[22] Ibid., commentary on ch. 50.

Rather than force, energy, determination or vitality, it is the power of love in the last analysis which best accounts for the soul of the Abbot General: love of God, love of his Cistercian brothers and love of all humanity.

"Sometimes overwhelmed by trials of health and spiritual trials, I surprised myself by telling God, 'Ah, if it had not been for You, Lord!' But I think it was my abbatial grace of state that led me to add, 'If it had not been for You, Lord, it would have been for them that I did it. I would have done the same.'"[23]

[23] *Notes sur la Règle,* commentary on ch. 64.

AFTERWORD

Four decades have already passed since the subject of the preceding pages, Dom Gabriel Sortais, died at the relatively early age of 61 after a life characterized by "the love of God and love of his Cistercian brethren and by a love of all men," to quote the author. This biography was providentially timed before most of Dom Sortais' contemporaries and collaborators mentioned in the foreword had themselves gone to God: Dom Vincent Hermans and Father Clément de Bourmont both died in 1993, Dom André Fracheboud in 1998, and Dom Ignace Gillet, Dom Gabriel's immediate successor as Abbot General, himself died in 1997. The author himself, Dom Guy Oury, O.S.B., died suddenly in November 2000.

Thus the one called upon to write this afterword to the English translation is the only *survivant* of Dom Gabriel's definitory council during the final years of his generalate. Hence it will be understood if this afterword, rather than an appreciation of Dom Gabriel, takes the form of a retrospective of the major changes that have come about in the order in the wake of Vatican II but, in reality, of the *aggiornamento* launched earlier still by Dom Gabriel himself. The fact that this writer had known him as abbot of Bellefontaine and had acted as his interpreter at several regular visitations later on, prior to becoming his close collaborator as American definitor in Rome until his death, will explain some of these rather intimate recollections which may flesh out some of the points mentioned in Dom Oury's biography.

Indeed, as soon as he became abbot of Bellefontaine in 1936 at 33, and a member of the general chapter, Dom Sortais made his strong personality felt. In fact, the first post-World War II Abbot General, Dom Dominique Nogues, confided to me in 1947 that he feared that the "young abbots" at the chapter would be activating for relaxation of the traditional austerity of the order. As Dom Oury points out, Dom Dominique "was a Trappist of the old school . . . intractable when there was question of the usages, each one of which he considered untouchable." And still he it was who arranged that this "young abbot" be the moderator [*promoteur* in French] of the chapter where he would dictate the agenda of each session and effectively "moderate" the discussions, the general himself being content simply to preside once he had given his opening talks.

Knowing that this young abbot was the heir-apparent—he had already been voted in as abbot-vicar—to rapidly aging Dom Dominique, it came as no surprise that once elected to succeed him in 1951 he continued not only to preside at the chapter but to be effectively its moderator which he did until his death. The actual moderator himself was reduced to simply announce the reading of each visitation card, maintaining an absolute silence for the remainder of each session.

The first major task Dom Gabriel felt obliged to assume was what I might call the initial *aggiornamento,* a much needed one, of the regular observances so dear to him as well as to his predecessor. But his attitude was and remained that, as he put it to the definitors, "if pluralism is allowed in a single monastery, all the others will soon be clamoring for it." Thus, the strict "uniform observance of the rules" insisted upon from the very beginning of the order and enshrined in the charter of charity, which the 1925 constitutions [Part II—Of Observances] stressed as "being required by the very nature of [the] order," came into play at the general chapter of 1953. It was at this chapter that votes were taken to petition the Holy See to allow additional sleep to both monks and nuns, to suppress the Little Office of the Blessed Virgin, and to diminish the frequency of the choral Office of the Dead. It had also been the general's intention to bring about the adaptation of the lay brothers' monastic status to contemporary needs and expectations, but the measures taken at that chapter were mainly liturgical ones, e.g., the ceremonies of profession, and these were very incidental to the overall question of the brothers becoming an integral part of the monastic community but with a special vocation, along with enjoying the rights reasonably flowing therefrom.

In retrospect, therefore, this initial *aggiornamento* was but an incipient one. The time had not arrived for either the Abbot General, the general chapter, or the Holy See for that matter, for the far-ranging "Statute on Unity and Pluralism" to be even conceived on the order level and as it was destined to be approved by the general chapter of 1969. In my opinion, had he lived to see that day Dom Gabriel would have felt that he had opened a Pandora's box and regretted it. And still, he was the one who had unwittingly initiated, in 1953, a healthy and entirely called-for process to ensure the organic growth of the order, now grown to international proportions and not only multilingual but, far more important, now embracing many different cultures that could no longer be that in which the order had been founded.

Precisely at this point must be brought up the fact that it was at the general chapter of 1960 that a tremendous improvement was introduced by Dom Gabriel in the actual workings of the chapter when in session: the use of simultaneous translation from French to English and vice versa. The number of capitulants who did not speak or even understand spoken French, the only language in which the chapter sessions had been conducted since the return of the Trappists to France from exile in 1815, had grown exponentially since the numerous English-speaking foundations from the late 1940s on. For non-French speakers, attendance at the annual chapters was a grueling and frustrating experience. It was no longer possible for the English-language definitor to convey the content of the interventions to more than two non-French language-speaking abbots on either side. By the very fact, none of these could venture to make an intervention except through this single interpreter which they seldom, if ever, did. Dom Gabriel realized this only too well, but he had no idea that the new system would result in "sowing the wind and reaping the whirlwind!" (Hos 8:7).

One of the earliest English-language interventions occurred when the proposed statute for the student-monks at the generalate came up for discussion. One of the "young abbots" voiced a criticism of the *modus agendi* of the students' Deans and said that they acted as policemen (translated into French as *agents de police*). To this the general took violent exception, saying that "there were no policemen at the generalate," to which the young abbot bravely replied: "But there are!"

From then on the ice had been broken and the abbots as a body became conscious at long last that when assembled at the chapter they were the ones who acted "as the supreme authority of the order" as stated plainly in the very opening sentence of the 1925 constitutions, and as such they have increasingly continued to act since the 1960 chapter. All the more that at subsequent chapters, with the proliferation of Spanish-speaking foundations in Central and South America, the need was felt to provide translations from Spanish into both French and English with consequently frequent interventions from Spanish-speaking capitulants, both monks and nuns.

Once again, in retrospect, the credit for this goes back to Dom Gabriel in having felt the need for simultaneous translations back in 1960, even if he did not then foresee that this meant finding translators; but that is another lacuna that need not be gone into here. Neither could he have foreseen that at the present time the same provision has had to be made for the Japanese-speaking capitulants, both monks and nuns.

The main topic which preoccupied Dom Gabriel in the final years of his life, however, was what he called "The lay brother problem." The fact that he spoke of a "problem" was a clear sign that he was thinking mostly of the European houses where the lay brothers had greatly diminished in number and their position on the social scale in their respective communities seemed glaringly that of second-class citizens; this situation is well-described by Dom Oury. But what Dom Gabriel missed, however, is that in most American monasteries there was no such problem, inasmuch as the vocations to the lay brothers at that time had continued to be on a par with those to the choir monks. To begin with, in some monasteries the number of lay brothers, both professed and those in formation, was roughly the same as among the choir monks. There were often as many college graduates among them as among the monks.

Naturally, many of the lay brother aspirants had had a technological education rather than a liberal arts one. There was never a question, however, of making previous education the norm, except perhaps having a knowledge of Latin and a reasonably good singing voice, for directing postulants to one class rather than to the other. In view of this, at least in certain monasteries including my own, competent lay brothers were chosen for all the posts that did not at the time require the priesthood. So there did not seem to be "the problem" that worried Dom Gabriel who had the very highest esteem for the lay brothers' vocation, one he would himself have chosen, he confessed, had the choice been his.

Dom Gabriel toiled for several years on this momentous question, realizing as he did that to effect a lasting improvement in the brothers' status a juridical one would be required involving a change, once again, in the constitutions and the possibility that such a change would involve their participation in the choral Divine Office in accordance with the holy Rule of Saint Benedict. Finally, on September 10, 1962, the general chapter voted that "All would be monks juridically speaking and in this respect all would be equal. The diversity of functions, however, that would be assigned to both the one and the other would safeguard the special characteristics of each vocation."

When the decree of unification (of the two classes) was finally granted on December 27, 1965, however, it contained the unfortunate division of the single class of monks into those who would be *"choro addicti"* and those who would be *"choro non addicti,"* thus creating once again two really distinct groups. Had he lived Dom Gabriel would surely have strongly objected and the decree would have been modified or set aside completely. What resulted when it was implemented as it was was that in many communities there was a marked impression, causing much pain, that the specific lay brother vocation had been suppressed at one fell swoop and replaced by two classes of monks with attendance at the Divine Office in choir being the mark of distinction.

From the very start, however, it was this writer's personal conviction that all that would have been needed to put the brothers on the same social footing as the choir monks would have been to grant them full voting rights and, if they preferred, the same monastic habit including the cowl. This is precisely what was done on June 11, 1965, when a Roman indult granted to all lay brothers and sisters voting rights in an abbatial election; and on June 16, 1965, the same habit as the choir monks and nuns. It was not until June 3, 1990, however, when the revised constitutions of the order were approved, that the divisions pointed out above were abrogated, by not being mentioned.

The updating of these constitutions can be said to have monopolized the time and energy of all the general chapters dating from that of 1967. This chapter declared itself to be the special one foreseen by the Holy See in its document *Ecclesiae Sanctae* for adapting and renewing the constitutions of all religious institutes according to the spirit and letter of Vatican Council II. The definitive text was not finalized, however, until the general chapter of 1987 and presented to the Holy See for approval. This in its turn did not occur until June 3, 1990, the solemnity of Pentecost. The long delay encountered in the presentation of the proposed text is another indication of the sea change that had occurred throughout the order after the death of Dom Gabriel Sortais, one that was the logical sequence of his own prudent and wise improvements in the order's chapter functioning although he could not possibly have anticipated it. To quote the historical introduction to the new constitutions: "To renew our constitutions according to the mind and spirit of the second Vatican Council, *consultation of the members of the Order had to be made* [emphasis ours] . . .This required many years with much work and energy but it was well spent as the elegant simplicity of the present document, so characteristic of the Cistercian charism, clearly attests."

With all due respect for Dom Gabriel's memory the present writer does not think that such repeated consultations of the grass roots of the order, the individual communities of both monks and nuns, would have occurred and even less the actual redaction of the final text by a single member of the order instead of the Abbot General and his council had Dom Gabriel been in charge of the project. But it would seem that he felt that such a thing was about to happen. On his way to a session of the council in 1963, he was quoted as saying to our Cistercian-Trappist bishop of Oslo, John Gran, that "he felt that he was losing his hold on the order." History had thus repeated itself since this statement had a family likeness to the prescient lament made in 1947 by Dom Dominique Nogues concerning "the young abbots," which was quoted above.

Mention was made earlier to the student-monks residing at the generalate. Dom Oury goes into detail about the plan that Dom Gabriel had in mind when he engineered the transfer of the general's house from the Aventine to a property ceded by the abbey of Tre Fontane at some distance from the center of Rome and which Dom Gabriel called "Monte Cistello." His plan was to combine the generalate with a studentate for monks coming to Rome to obtain the degrees now needed to teach the seminary courses in their monasteries, as required by the new *ratio studiorum*. But, as Dom Oury also points out, what the plan really called for was the setting up for both the definitors and the students of a monastery over which the Abbot General would function as did a local abbot. This was already the case for the council of definitors who were expected to follow a code of regulations made even more strict after the move to Tre Fontane. These councilors, then called definitors, were senior priests from different countries, speaking different languages. Under Dom Gabriel they could expect to be treated as subjects and being taken roundly to task when they did or said anything which the general did not happen to agree with.

As to the student-monks, Dom Gabriel wished to set up what Dom Oury called *"un monastère d'études,"* a monastic studentate, rather than a simple house of studies as in other orders. Once Monte Cistello received its first contingent of student-monks from all over the world in the fall of 1959, the general made it quite clear that he considered himself to be master of the house and everyone in residence to consider him as such. The students were expected to pay him their personal respects immediately upon arrival, whatever may be their confusion and bewilderment in their totally new surroundings, with a different horarium, food, and the lack of a common language except Latin. They already had had to make the acquaintance of the master of the students and within a very few days of their arrival had to begin attending classes entirely in Latin at the various universities *in urbe.* They were expected to combine trips by van to and from the universities twice daily with a full monastic schedule of choral Offices and other monastic observances. As a consequence, it must have been something of a let-down for the general to expect these monks, most of them were middle-aged priests who had held positions of trust and responsibility, to act in his regard as would the rank and file in a traditional monastery. What resulted is mentioned by the A. in somewhat veiled terms: a subtle tension between the two sides of the house, some of the students being actually afraid of the general who admittedly did his best to be available to them and solicitous for everything, including their health, that concerned them.

The A. does say that the general, already overburdened with the daily attendance at the sessions of Vatican II and "the solicitude for all the churches," that is, for each monastery of the new far-flung order, not to mention increasingly poor health, could be excused for reacting as he quite often did. The A. also mentions that he did feel sorry for his outbursts and apologized. This may have been true when he was abbot of Bellefontaine but I must candidly say that I never recall any such apology, at least to this definitor.

However, I must also say that I noticed that he invariably found some way of showing special regard *vis-à-vis* the one he had reproved and this by some act of consideration and kindness. I cannot now recall if it was an instance of this but less than a month before he died, knowing my love for classical music, both choral and instrumental, after my long years as choir director and organist, Dom Gabriel gave me his personal invitation as a council father to the concert given on October 19, 1963. This featured Bach's *Mass in B-flat* sung by the cathedral choir of Aachen accompanied by the orchestra of the Rome Opera, a splendid performance attended by Pope Paul VI.

And here we have touched upon one of the many traits of soul and of character that made Dom Gabriel truly great, not only in the sight of men but in the eyes of God. This personal regard, amounting to respect, for each person as an individual, came into play even more strikingly when someone proved troublesome in his or her community, which in turn considered it needful to submit the case to the general and his council. Without breaching the confidentiality surrounding the definitory's discussion of these cases, I can say I was always impressed and at times deeply moved at the care the general brought to bear to ensure not only justice but also equity, read charity, towards all concerned. Although in his travels throughout the order Dom

Gabriel had made a point of meeting practically each monk and nun of each community, these were by no means a *massa confusa*. At our council meetings, Dom Gabriel would pause and search his memory to identify the one concerned. In practically every instance he would suddenly say: "Oh yes, I remember him (or her) quite well." Then he would give some personal traits of the individual that would explain, or at least extenuate, what was faulty in the monk or nun's conduct. He would then advise a course of action stressing patience and Christian tolerance, at least for the time being, along with an earnest effort to understand why things were not going well. Never do I recall his advocating any harsh or negative reactions or measures. He was before all else a loving and understanding father to every member of the order, and especially towards the sick and aged and those experiencing a crisis of any kind.

I attribute this boundless compassion to Dom Gabriel's by now lifelong habit of "walking with God." As the A. spares no pains to bring out, the general's unwavering *memoria Dei,* his unceasing "remembrance of God," even in the midst of absorbing labors, struck all those he met in the course of each day. In an intimate conversation he was once asked if he sometimes found himself distracted from this attention to God. He replied: "Alas, yes! I may at times not think of God for all of five minutes." Thomas Merton once defined contemplation as *"simple openness to God at every moment* [emphasis ours], and deep peace, in which a person becomes fully and completely himself as he is intended to be, which is to say, a full and complete lover." This, I feel, was verified in Dom Gabriel.

The end came very suddenly but not unexpectedly, anticipated and even longed for as it was. The A. says that Dom Gabriel's last words were: *"Je m'évanouis"*—"I am fainting." But this is not perfectly accurate. What he did say, doing things with French panache as he always did, was: *"Je tombe en pamoison"*—"I am swooning."

It was my duty when he was placed in the coffin after lying in state to remove his abbatial ring and his pectoral cross, both of which were to be given to his successor at Bellefontaine. The first was replaced by a very inexpensive one. As to the pectoral cross, it occurred to me that he would have liked to be buried with a small pectoral cross made of teak given to him by our Japanese nuns and which I had located among his very few personal keepsakes. On the cross-bar, in gold Japanese characters, was the single word: glory. This seemed to me to sum up Dom Gabriel Sortais' whole life, as St. Paul puts it: "Christ in you, the hope of glory" (Col 1:27).

Father Laurence Bourget, ocso
Spencer, Paschaltide 2005

MANUSCRIPT AND PRINTED SOURCES

ABBEY OF BELLEFONTAINE

Dom Sortais' archives were gathered and classified by Father Emile Dixneuf as a special source; we will limit ourselves here to mentioning the general contents of each of the twenty dossiers:[1]

Dossier I: Writings on Dom Sortais

Dossier II: Various testimonies

Dossier III: Autobiographical documents
1. First notebook covering his novitiate and first years
2. Notebook containing prayers written down in 1913 by a relative
3–4. Letters concerning his entry
5. Personal notes on his ideal as abbot-elect
6. Farewell to Bellefontaine in 1952
11–14. Various written documents.
16. Travel journal, May 10–October 17, 1940
17. Letter on the role he played in the Resistance groups
18. Talk given in 1954 on his 30 years of religious life
20. Letter to the prefect of Maine-et-Loire (December 19, 1944) to defend himself when the communists of Cholet accused him of collaboration
21. Report of his taking the initiative to make himself a hostage at Nantes

Dossier IV: Writings of Dom Sortais
1. Circular letters, 1951–63
2. Prefaces for various books and articles
4. "Que fut l'epopée vendéen" in *Il y a cent ans la Vendée?*, Cholet: Vendée, 1943

[1] Editor's note: These sources, of course, do not exist in English.

5. Articles written for *Collectanea O.C.R.*
   "Sur les chemins que suivit saint Bernard" 15 (1953) 241–50
   "Le P. Camille Hontoir" 17 (1955) fasc. 1
   "Centenaire de Pierre le Vénérable" 18 (1956) 81ff.
   "Centenaire de Guerric d'Igny" 19 (1957) 201ff.
   "Hommage a Pie XII" 20 (1958) fasc. 4
   "Sa sainteté Jean XXIII" 25 (1963) 105–11
6. "Monachisme et témoignage" in *Citeaux in de Nederlanden* 1:1

Dossier V: The Order of Citeaux articles
1. Contemplative life at La Trappe
2. Government of the monasteries
3. The regular visitation
4. Admission and formation of subjects
5. Adaptation
6. Conversations on the monasteries of the order
7. Various publishing of the Cistercian Fathers, French translation of the Diurnale, etc.

Dossier VI: Monastic spirituality articles
1. Generalities
2. Ascesis
3. Contemplation
4. Contemplation and the apostolate
5. Priesthood and the monastic life
6. Various things

Dossier VII: Dom Sortais' correspondence

Dossiers VII–VIII: Letters sent to Dom Sortais

Dossier IX: Vatican Council II

Dossier X: Relations with the Carmel of Lisieux

Dossier XI: Relations with General Weygand

Dossier XII: Notes on spiritual reading

Dossier XIII: Retreats

Dossier XIV: War and captivity

Dossier XV: The Occupation, Marshal Pétain and the Resistance

Dossier XVI: The Liberation

Dossier XVII: Documents and notes

Dossier XVIII: Military identity documents and chronology

Dossier XIX: Documents on genealogy

Dossier XX: Sermons, short talks and conferences

MONTE CISTELLO

For this biography we have consulted the following dossiers in the archives of Dom Gabriel Sortais in the general's house in Rome:

Dossier II: Correspondence with religious and seculars (whatever does not directly concern the Cistercian order itself has been collected in this dossier)

Dossier IV: The Holy See articles
1. The sovereign pontiff
2. The law courts
3. The Congregation of Religious

Dossier V: Japanese accounts, the question of Laybrothers, the Spanish Congregations and Japanese chaplains and missionaries

PRINTED WORKS BY DOM GABRIEL SORTAIS

BROCHURES

Twenty-eight circular letters to the communities.

Besides these letters and some other documents, there is the collection published by the Abbey of Bellefontaine in 1967, entitled *Les Choses qui plaisent à Dieu.*

Conferences on the Abbatial Office. Westmalle: Trappist, 1960.[1]

The Function of Contemplative Orders in Mission Lands. Westmalle: Trappist, 1960.

The Implantation of the Monastic Life in Mission Lands. Westmalle: Trappist, 1960.

The Last Days of October 1960 at Monte Cistello. Westmalle: Trappist, 1960.

ARTICLES

Besides the articles in *Collectanea* already mentioned, there are some short articles in *L'Avenir de Cholet* and the *Revue du Souvenir vendéen.*

PREFACES

La Révérende Mère Cécile Chauvat, 1886–1943, Abbesse du monastère cistercien de Notre-Dame des Gardes. Siraudeau: Angers, 1950.

[1] Editor's note: Because these pamphlets may exist in English translation in various monasteries under a slightly different title, it seems best not to underline the title here.

L'Abbaye cistercienne de Bellefontaine. Bellefontaine, 1954.

Merton, Thomas. *L'exil s'achève dans la gloire. La vie de Mère Marie-Berchmans, trappistine missionnaire.* Paris-Bruges: Desclée de Brouwer, 1955.

Les moines dans l'Eglise. Textes des Souverains Pontifes. Paris: le Cerf, 1964.

Immediately after Dom Sortais' death a biographical study appeared among numerous death notices: "Le Révérend Père Dom Gabriel Sortais, Archabbé de Citeaux, 6e Abbé général des Cisterciens de la Stricte Observance." *Collectanea Ordinis Cisterciensis S.O.* 25 (1963) 325–42.

SELECTED BIBLIOGRAPHY

INFANCY AND YOUTH

Bazin, René. *Paysages et pays d'Anjou.* Angers: A. Bruel, 1926.

Bron, Ludovic. *Pierre L'Ermite,* préface de Mgr. Ruch. Colmar: Alsatia, 1938.

Catta, Tony. *La Vendée, la foi et la patrie.* Paris: Nouvelles Editions Latines, 1960.

Chastenet, Jacques. *La Troisième République,* t. V, VI, VII. Paris: Hachette, 1960–63.

Du Bourg, Dom A. *Du champ de bataille à la Trappe: le frère Gabriel,* préface du Comte Albert de Mun. Paris: Perrin, 1909.

Encyclopédie d'Architecture.

Encyclopédie du siècle, Exposition de Paris, 1900, 3 vol. in-fol. Paris: Mongredien, 1899–1900.

Gourdon, Pierre. "Esquisse vendéenne, Le Pays des Mauges." *Le Correspondant* 227 (1908) 366ff.

Héron de Villefosse, R. *Histoire de Paris.* Paris: Paris: Grasset, 1955.

l'Ermite, Pierre. *Je regarde ma vi.* Paris: Le Centurion, 1955.

Rilke, Rainer Maria. *Auguste Rodin,* trad. M. Betz. Paris: Emile-Paul, 1928.

Talmeyr, Maurice. "Un camelot du Roi, Maxime Réal del Sarte." In *L'Heroisme pendant la guerre, Portraits de belle-France.* Paris: Perrin, 1918.

Tirel, Marcelle. *Rodin intime ou L'envers d'une gloire, préface de A. Beuret.* Paris: Monde nouveau, 1923.

Weber, Eugen. *L'Action française,* trad. Michel Chrestien. Paris: Stock, 1954.

THE VENDÉEN WARS

Billaud, A. *La guerre de Vendée.* Fontenay-le-Comte: Lussaud, 1967.

Chassin, Ch.-L. *Etudes documentaires sur la Révolution française,* t. VIII–X, *Les pacifications de l'Ouest.*

Deniau, Abbé. *Histoire de la guerre de Vendée,* Angers, n.d.

Goudé, Abbé. "Les cimetières des martyrs d'Yzernay." *Revue du Souvenir vendéen,* 107 (juin–juillet 1974) 29–31.

Walter, Gérard. *La guerre de Vendée.* Paris: Plon, 1953.

BELLEFONTAINE AND CISTERCIAN LIFE

Anonyme. *Vie du R.P. Dom Urbain Guillet, fondateur de la Trappe de Bellefontaine,* par un religieux du monastère. La Chapelle-Montligeon, 1899.

Anonyme. *Odyssée monastique, Dom Augustin de Lestrange et les Trappistes pendant la Révolution.* La Grande-Trappe, 1898.

Anonyme. *L'Abbaye cistercienne de Bellefontaine.* Bellefontaine, 1954.

Chautard, Dom Jean-Baptiste. *Les cisterciens trappistes.* Conférences de la D.R.A.C., 1931.

Coubard, Dr. Charles. "Dom Jean-Marie Chouteau, Abbé de Bellefontaine et des Gardes, 1841–1929." In *Bull. de la Soc. des Sc., Lettres et Beaux-Arts de Cholet,* 1931, no du Cinquantenaire, Luçon, 1931.

Dimier, A. *La sombre Trappe.* Saint-Wandrille, 1946.

Estienne, Yvonne. *Les Trappistines.* Paris: B. Grasset, 1937.

Grolleau, Ch. and G. Chastel. *L'Ordre de Citeaux, La Trappe,* coll. *Les grands Ordres monastiques.* Paris: B. Grasset, 1932.

Le Bail, Dom Anselme. *L'Ordre de Citeaux, la Trappe, Les Ordres religieux.* Paris, 1924.

Maire, Elie. *Trappes et trappistes.* Paris: Lethielleux, 1921.

Merton, Thomas. *Aux sources du silence,* trad. Jean Stiénon du Pré. Paris: Desclée de Brouwer, 1952.

Tricoire, Abbé L. *Notre-Dame des Gardes.* Angers: Siraudeau, 1942.

Rancé, Abbé de. *De la sainteté et des devoirs de la vie monastique, réédition.* Paris, 1846.

Uzureau, Chanoine. "Les religieux feuillants de l'abbaye de Bellefontaine, 1642–1791." *L'Anjou historique* 13 (1913) 471–86.

"Le deuxième Abbé de Bellefontaine." *Revue de Bretagne* 51 (1914) 125–32.

Vérité, Hippolyte. *Citeaux, la Trappe et Bellefontaine.* Paris: Haton, 1883.

MONASTIC LIFE AND THE ABBOT BEFORE 1940

Anonyme. *La Révérende Mère Cécile Chauvat, 1886–1943, Abbesse du monastère cistercien de Notre-Dame des Gardes.* Angers: Siraudeau, 1950.

Anonyme. "Le Révérend Père Abbé Général, Dom Hermann-Joseph Smets." *Collectanea Ord. Cist. Reform.* 7 (1940–45) 3–11.

Brard, Bruno. *Dom Vital Lehodey, abbé de Notre-Dame de Grâce de Bricquebec (Manche), 1857–1948.* Paris: Lecoffre-Gabalda, 1973.

Chaigne, Louis. *Témoin de la vérité vivante, Mgr. Gabriel Martin, 1873–1949.* Paris: B. Grasset, 1961.

Charrier, Henri. *Dom Jean-Baptiste Ollitraut de Keryvallan, Abbé de Citeaux, 3e Abbé Général des Cisterciens de la stricte observance, 1862–1929.* Westmalle, 1930.

Dansette, Adrien. *Histoire religieuse de la France sous la IIIe République,* t. II, 1879–1939. Paris: Flammarion, 1951.

Delperrié de Bayac. *Histoire du Front populaire.* Paris: A. Fayard, 1972.

Lehodey, Dom Vital. *Directoire spirituel des cisterciens réformés, éd. révisée.* Bricquebec, 1910.

———. *Les voies de l'oraison mentale.* Paris, 1908.

———. *Le saint abandon.* Paris, 1929.

Maire, Elie. *Images de Dom Chautard, Abbé de Sept-Fons.* Paris: Flammarion, 1938.

Martelet, Bernard. *Itinéraire spirituel de Dom Chautard,* éd. Saint-Paul. Paris-Fribourg, 1967.

Misserey, E. *Du doute à la contemplation: Soeur Claire de Jésus, religieuse bénédictine, 1894–1923.* Maresous: Coll. Pax, 1928.

Synéty, Robert de. *Psychopathologie et direction.* Paris: Beauchesne, 1934.

Tonquédec, Joseph de. *Les maladies nerveuses et les manifestations diaboliques, préface du Cardinal Verdier.* Paris: Beauchesne, 1938.

Vallery-Radot, Irénée. *La mission de Dom Vital Lehodey.* Paris: Le Cerf, 1956.

THE WAR

Anonyme. *Livre d'or des Congrégations françaises, 1939–1945,* préface de Mgr. Théas. Paris: D.R.A.C., 1948.

Aron, Robert. *Histoire de Vichy, 1940–1944.* Paris: A. Fayard, 1955.

———. *Histoire de la libération de la France, juin 1944–mai 1945.* Paris: A. Fayard, 1959.

Auphan, Amiral. *Histoire élémentaire de Vichy.* Paris: France-Empire, 1971.

Baumont, Maurice. *Les origines de la seconde guerre mondiale.* Paris: Payot, 1969.

Benoist-Méchin. *Soixante jours qui ébranlèrent l'Occident,* 3 vol. Paris: Albin Michel, 1956–57.

Chapman, Guy. *Why France Collapsed.* London: Cassel, 1968.

Cras, Hervé. *Dunkerque.* Paris: France-Empire, 1960.

Etat-Major de l'armée, Service historique. A*tlas des situations quotidiennes des armées alliées, Campagne 1939–1940.* Paris: Ateliers de l'impression de l'Armée, 1967.

Evrard, Jacques. *La déportation des travailleurs français dans le IIIe Reich, Les grandes études contemporaines.* Paris: A. Fayard, 1972.

Flament, Abbé Pierre. *La vie à l'oflag II D–II B, 1940–1945,* préface de R. Ikor. Paris: Amicale de l'oflag II D–II B, 1957.

Michel, Henri. *La drôle de guerre.* Paris: Hachette, 1971.

Molinié, Général. *La 25e D.I.M. dans la bataille,* s.l.n.d.

Roy, Bernard. *Les grandes Heures de Nantes et Saint-Nazaire,* préface de l'Amiral Decoux, avant-propos du duc de Rohan. Paris: Ozanne, 1951.

Weygand, Général. *Le général Frère, un chef, un héros, un martyr.* Paris: Flammarion, 1949.

Weygand, Jacques. *Weygand, mon père.* Paris: Flammarion, 1970.

VICAR GENERAL OF THE ORDER

Anonyme. "Le Révérend Père Abbé Général, Dom Dominique Nogues." *Collectanea O.C.R.* 8 (1946) 1–2.

Anonyme. "La démission du Révérend Père Abbé Général, Dom Dominique Nogues." Ibid. 14 (1952) 2–3.

Anonyme. "Images du Révérend Père Dom Dominique Nogues." Ibid. 20 (1958) 72–80.

Deroo, André. *L'épiscopat français dans la mêlée de son temps, 1930–1954,* préface du cardinal Liénart. Paris: Bonne Presse, 1955.

Marteaux, Jacques. *L'Eglise de France devant la Révolution marxiste,* 2 vol. Paris: La Table ronde, 1958–59.

ABBOT GENERAL

Anonyme. "Notre-Dame de la Consolation, Yangkiap'ing." *Collectanea O.C.R.,* 8 (1946) 302–04.

Anonyme. Ibid. 10 (1948) 57–59 and 225–26.

Anonyme. "Notre-Dame de Liesse, Cheng-Ting-Fu, pendant la guerre." Ibid. 8 (1946) 116–18.

Anonyme. "La situation de nos monastères au Japon." Ibid. 8 (1946) 304–06.

Anonyme. *Notre-Dame de Bellefontaine, Fête de saint Benoît, 1952, Bénédiction abbatial de Dom Emmanuel Coutant,* éd. Avenir de Cholet et Courrier de l'Ouest, 1952.

Anonyme. "Bénédiction de la première pierre de Monte-Cistello, et la nouvelle maison généralice." *Collectanea O.C.R.* 20 (1958) 271–73.

Dubois, Dom Jacques. "L'institution des convers au XIIe s., forme de vie monastique propre aux laics." In *I laici nella societas christiana dei secoli XI e XII, Settimana Internazionale di Studio,* Mendola, agosto 1965.

Fesquet, Henri. *Le Journal du Concile.* Forcalquier: Robert Morel, 1966.

Fracheboud, André. "Un moine de Caldey élevé à la dignité épiscopale, Son Excellence Mgr. Willem Gran, évêque-coadjuteur d'Oslo." *Collectanea O.C.R.* 25 (1963) 112–15.

———. "Les évenements de 'Monte Cistello.'" Ibid. 22 (1960) 393–98.

Laurentin, René. *L'enjeu du concile, Bilan de la 1re Session.* Paris: Le Seuil, 1963.

———. *L'enjeu du concile, Bilan de la 2e Session*, 1964.

Moakler, N. "The Consecration of the Church of Our Lady of Monte Cistello, October 27th, 1960." *Collectanea O.C.R.* 22 (1960) 398–401.

Pean, Bernard. *Les convers à Citeaux, Essai juridico-historique.* Melleray (mimeographed copy in the Solesmes library).

Serrou, Robert, and Pierre Vals. *La Trappe, lieu de silence, de prière et de paix*, préface du Cardinal Tisserant, éd. Pierre Horay. Paris, 1956.

Wenger, Antoine. *Vatican II, 1re Session.* Paris: Le Centurion, 1963.

———. *Vatican II, Chonique de la 2e Session.* Paris: Le Centurion, 1964.

INDEX

CISTERCIAN PUBLICATIONS

Texts and Studies in the Monastic Tradition

Texts in English translation:

- Monastic insights from the desert, and from christian monks and nuns East and West
- Cistercian homilies and treatises from the formative twelfth and thirteenth centuries

Studies of the monastic tradition:

- Its history, customs, architecture, liturgy, and influence, from desert beginnings through the Middle Ages and into the present day
- Reflections on prayer and the christian vocation by contemporary contemplatives
- Audio and video resources on monasticism as well as books published abroad and not readily available in North America

All books are available singly or by series standing order. Standing order customers automatically receive new titles as they appear at a 25% discount from the list price

Series:

- Cistercian Fathers
- Cistercian Studies
- Monastic Wisdom
- Cistercian Liturgy

Editorial Offices

Cistercian Publications • WMU Station
1903 West Michigan Avenue • Kalamazoo, MI 49008-5415 USA
tel 269 387 8920 fax 269 387 8390
e-mail cistpub@wmich.edu

Customer Service—North America: USA and Canada

Cistercian Publications at Liturgical Press
Saint John's Abbey • Collegeville, MN 56321-7500 USA
tel 800 436 8431 fax 320 363 3299
e-mail sales@litpress.org

Customer Service—Europe: UK, Ireland, and Europe

Cistercian Publications at Columba Book Service
55A Spruce Avenue • Stillorgan Industrial Park
Blackrock, Co. Dublin, Ireland
tel 353 1 294 2560 fax 353 1 294 2564
e-mail sales@columba.ie

To explore the range of titles offered by Cistercian Publications, please request our free complete catalogue from one of the customer service offices or visit our website at **www.cistercianpublications.org**